Against the Workshop:

Provocations, Polemics, Controversies

Against the Workshop:

Provocations, Polemics, Controversies

Anis Shivani

Tom Denworth
Dann Spiotta
Alexander Memon
Moshon Mumby

Texas Review Press
Huntsville, Texas

FIRST EDITION, 2011
Requests for permission to reproduce material from this work should be sent to:

Permissions
Texas Review Press
English Department
Sam Houston State University
Huntsville, TX 77341-2146

Cover design by Nancy Parsons/Graphic Design Group

Library of Congress Cataloging-in-Publication Data

Shivani, Anis.
  Against the workshop : provocations, polemics, controversies / Anis
Shivani. -- 1st ed.
      p. cm.
  Includes bibliographical references.
  ISBN 978-1-933896-72-4 (pbk. : alk. paper)
  1. Fiction--Authorship--Study and teaching (Higher)--United
States--History. 2. Poetry--Authorship--Study and teaching
(Higher)--United States--History. 3. American fiction--21st century-
-History and criticism. 4. Creative writing (Higher education)--
United States. I. Title.
  PN187.S45 2011
  808'.042071173--dc23
                              2011025247

For Mehnaaz

My Best Critic

Contents

Acknowledgments

Many people took a chance on me early in my career and allowed and encouraged me to express my unfashionable views. Among them I must single out Eric Miles Williamson for publishing me as frequently and in as many places as possible, as he once promised me early on; without him, this book would never have come together. I must also give a special thanks to Richard Burgin, who also encouraged me every step of the way, and took a risk by publishing many of these provocations in *Boulevard* over the years. I would also like to thank editors Marc Watkins, Kevin Prufer, Robert S. Fogarty, Michael Tyrell, Alfredo de Palchi, Dan Latimer, Wayne Chapman, Charlie Alcorn, Stephanie G'Schwind, Christina Thompson, Laurence Goldstein, Jonathan Freedman, Robert Lewis, Robert Stewart, James Engelhardt, Hilda Raz, James Schick, Richard Mullen, Richard Gooder, Sebastian Barker, Stephen McCarty, Willard Spiegelman, Stephen Corey, Brad Tyer, Chris Tomlinson, Michael E. May, Nicole Lamy, John McMurtrie, Colette Bancroft, Steve Paul, Bob Hoover, Steve Bennett, Craig Jarvis, and Jody Seaborn for supporting my work. An especially strong note of thanks to Amy Hertz of the Huffington Post for her courage in standing behind me and for her exceptionally democratic vision of books and their readership. Thanks also to Jessie Kunhardt of the Huffington Post, as well as Sammy Perlmutter. Many thanks to Rigoberto Gonzalez, Steven G. Kellman, H. L. Hix, Jay Parini, Clayton Eshleman, Kelly Cherry, and John McNally for their support. Above all, my thanks to Paul Ruffin for taking on this book and believing in this project. Malcolm Cowley, Edmund Wilson, George Orwell, Cyril Connolly, Dwight Macdonald, and John Aldridge always peer over my shoulders, spurring me on. Every word here was read, critiqued, and often prompted into being by my wife, Mehnaaz, whose impeccable judgment I never cease to admire.

The essays and reviews were originally published as follows:

The Adirondack Review: "Reckoning Globalization's Discontents"

American Book Review: "How Competence Has Killed the American Short Story"

Antioch Review: "The New Biography of Pathology"

Austin American-Statesman: "Two Poets of Southwestern Alienation"

Boulevard: "The Agent's Letter," "The Creative Writing/MFA System is a Closed, Undemocratic Medieval Guild System that Represses Good Writing," "Is Postmodernism in Decline?" "The Young Do Not Write Novels Anymore," and "Writers in Universities"

Cambridge Quarterly: "American Poetry in an Age of Constriction"

Chelsea: "The Best American Poetry Gets Better" and "Honest Clarity"

Colorado Review: "Reflections on the Conversant Buddha Soul" and "The Poet as Anti-Narcissist"

Contemporary Review (Oxford): "Decadence, American-Style"

Cream City Review: "India Abroad: How Not to Alienate the Western Reader When Writing About the Indian Diaspora"

Harvard Review: "Midwestern Pastoral at its Best" and "Interim India"

The Huffington Post: "America's Most Prominent Emerging Poets Respond to the Obama Administration," "Announcing the Death of the Post-9/11 Novel," "Voice in Fiction: An MFA/Creative Writing Shibboleth," and "Why the New *Best American Poetry* Sucks Even More Than Its Twenty-One Predecessors"

The Midwest Quarterly: "Is This the Best American Poetry?"

New Letters: "Rehabilitating the Working Man from the Clutches of False Realism"

North Dakota Quarterly: "Publisher's Reader's Notes on Recent Submission"

Pleiades: "Why Is American Fiction In Its Current Dismal State?"

Prairie Schooner: "Don't Be Cruel" and "Feminist Poetry the Way It Used to Be"

St. Petersburg Times: "The New Ecopoetry"

San Francisco Chronicle: "License to Kill: The Biographer's Deadly Art"

South Carolina Review: "White American Male Playing It Safe: The Growing Phenomenon of the 'Kirby Poet'"

Southern Humanities Review: "Can Writing Be Taught? The Systems-Theory Rationalizations of an Insider"

Texas Review: "New Rules for Writing Fiction" and "Why Is It So Difficult to Write about the Working Class?"

I also wish to think Bill Henderson for reprinting "The MFA/Creative Writing System Is a Closed, Undemocratic Medieval Guild System that Represses Good Writing" in The *Pushcart Prize XXXVI*.

X

Preface

I wrote these essays and reviews over the better part of the last decade, so it's natural for my views to have evolved during this period of time. I would go easier on Dave Eggers and Bob Hicok, for example. I have a greater appreciation for the pure play of language poetry and similar experiments than I showed in my early years, although I wouldn't walk back from my criticism of language poetry and other experimental writing having assumed a rather self-satisfied posture. The biggest shift has been the more complicated way in which I view realism now.

Yet, for the overwhelming part, I find myself resoundingly agreeing with the ideas presented here from the earliest stages of my critical consciousness. If anything, I believe in the fundamental principles I began articulating about a decade ago with more ferocity and zest than ever. The political turmoil of the last decade, upon retrospect, does not seem to have provided a lasting impetus for a more public fiction or poetry—or at least, writing that reaches beyond select audiences. And as we likely head into a period of long national decline, the prospects for pure imagination seem even bleaker. I began to be worried about the ascendancy of memoir over fiction a while ago, and today I would hammer at the displacement with even more zeal. Ten years ago, it seemed possible that criticism might get a boost from the democratic potential of the emerging technologies; for the most part, these hopes of mine have not yet been realized. The Internet remains mostly a barren, cliquish, superficial landscape of rote opinions and dumbed-down values. Reviewing is in a truly sordid state today, much worse than I could have anticipated ten years ago, and this affects the general climate for literature. Poetry, as an obscure art left alone by cultural monitors, ought to have risen to the occasion more than fiction, but mostly it has failed to do so.

My worries now would have less to do with the failings of establishment poets like Billy Collins or Jorie Graham, and more to do with the constrained social environment for the newer generation of poets—the intellectual landscape as a whole seems less conducive during the perpetual "war on terror" than in the aftermath of the cold war for any kind of meaningful poetics. Moreover, the MFA system, as I articulated early on and continue to do so, has helped freeze organic literary development, so that we've been deprived of whatever movement(s) ought to have developed after the fires of 1970s avant-garde literature died down.

I find two recent books emblematic of the crisis in American literature: Mark McGurl's *The Program Era*, which validates the creative writing infrastructure in functionalist terms, and David Shields's *Reality Hunger*, which gives up on imagination altogether. These two lines of thought seem to me a culmination of some of the most pernicious ways in which literature was affected by the platitudinous multiculturalism of the preceding two decades. For a serious critic today, it's like working at Mount Everest with a tiny pickaxe—the ice is frozen, the intellectual construction solid and immoveable. The sleek hype-machines seem to take it all in stride.

All hell broke loose in the summer of 2010, however, when I wrote a piece for the Huffington Post on overrated writers in America—a firestorm ensued in the blogosphere, and passions were uncontrollable on both sides of the divide. Similar, though lesser, reactions occurred when I put my criticism of the MFA system online. The whole thing was positively medieval, as the blasphemer was secretly admired and publicly assaulted at the same time.

The overblown reaction suggests to me that all is not well under the tranquil surface, and that the reading public is hungry for criticism from outside the system's boundaries. I wish the Heather McHugh piece in this book—composed in her voice—was the kind of rebel yell with more of a chance of registering. But the short manifesto on global fiction has been a pleasant surprise. Soon after writing it, I read V. S. Naipaul's *Half a Life*, which seemed to me to perfectly illustrate the presumption of an unprecedented global audience expressed in my "new rules"; Rana Dasgupta's *Solo* would be another ideal example of the new global novel I talk about in that manifesto.

So there are developments to be cheerful about, although I think that most of the positive signs are coming from other literary cultures, whereas American literary culture seems to become more, rather than less, insular, despite advances in global communications. I don't know how to explain this—the debate about tired old major publishing houses versus innovative independent presses seems somewhat beside the point, a tactical explanation at best, that leaves much unanswered. At least the gatekeepers everywhere are visibly biting the dust, and that's all to the good; had this been the case a decade earlier, my worry about poetry being bottled up in safe confessionalism would have been less marked.

With the passage of time, I've assumed a more explicit cosmopolitan posture, which lets me put even negative developments in American literary culture in a more tolerant perspective; I don't yet know how this affects my future criticism. If the decadence I talk about in one essay on the short story seems less noticeable now, at least to me, is it because the culture has deteriorated to make lower denominators unremarkable, or have I simply given up on the possibility of reform from within? Refusal of a strong readership on the part of American writers is a key note that runs through a number of these essays; I now think that strong writers will refuse to bend to this ultimately humiliating posture, and assume the strongest of readerships. In the latter part of the book, and in the work I've been doing recently, my greatest inclination has been to search out underappreciated writers who presume just such a strong audience.

Criticism, as I learned from my article on overrated writers, is dangerous business—but also its only justification. As a self-taught writer and critic, not bound to institutional prerogatives, I've had less than normal fear about which minefields to tread, and have sometimes naively, sometimes willfully, chosen the most dangerous ones. Criticism excites me, and prompts me to be a better writer—it is an addiction of sorts, perhaps the most positive one a writer can have, rewardingly self-serving in how it feeds one's own inner fires. I hope I won't suffer the charge that my delirium has eased over time.

— Anis Shivani
Houston, January 2011

Introduction

by Jay Parini

I've been reading these critical essays by Anis Shivani for a few weeks now, reading and rereading them. Some I had seen before, and some were new to me. I'm quite convinced that Shivani is among the sanest voices in criticism today. His eye rarely wavers, and he has a keen vision and a cruel wit. His writing is often mordantly funny, and quite often his essays and reviews pose a challenge.

The status quo bothers Shivani, as it should bother anyone who believes that good writing is essential for the health and prosperity of the culture at large. He sees the world of "creative writing," as fostered by the M.F.A. programs and promoted in various journals and supported by American publishers as lacking in direction and freshness, unwilling to meet the society at its most elemental level. Again and again, he asks the hard question: Does the emperor really wear no clothes?

He looks at a variety of emperors here: highly funded novelists and poets, teachers of creative writing, and so forth. Needless to say, he finds problems wherever he looks, and he isn't afraid to call a pothole a pothole.

For example, in his essay on the state of American fiction, he begins: "Contemporary American fiction has become cheap counseling to the bereaved bourgeois." He goes on to suggest that the scope of American writing is way too restricted, being focused on the domestic sphere. The audience that these writers aim for, as he says, is severely limited. The lack of moral energy in contemporary writing upsets him. He looks at past writers he admires, from Kafka and Musil to Waugh and Greene, and he finds these writers anemic.

As Shivani says, there is hardly any serious criticism in the United States nowadays. That is, there is a paucity of writing about writing that looks with any genuine skepticism at what is being produced, which is often prose and poetry with a high gloss of technique but lacking depth and originality.

There is something to consider in his notion that the decline of American fiction "is a sign of the decline of elite liberal consensus." There may well be a vacuum that is being filled by an "anti-politics" that stresses personality and charisma over content, over genuine debate. One cannot imagine a figure such as Mark Twain, for instance, having such a dominant role as Twain once had.

Shivani directs his animus at M.F.A. programs, which in his view "are killing writing in this country." Of course a lot of interesting writers have emerged from these programs over the years, and it must be admitted that universities do support writers in a way the broader public does not. But I give Shivani a lot of credit for his willingness to interrogate the matter, to question what goes on within the walls of the academy. Easy answers will never be found in response to many of his questions, but that is as it should be. The questions must be asked.

That so much good American writing is marginalized, unread, even unwelcome by the public at large, is troubling, and at a time when reading itself seems threatened at every turn, we need critics like Shivani to challenge us, to scrutinize the scene, to toss ideas into the ring for debate.

In his wide-eyed, close reading of so many writers, Shivani often makes me sit up, argue with him, think hard about what he has said with such conviction. "A consistent characteristic of contemporary American poetry is the flattening of history in the individual's private agony," he writes, for instance. Is this true? He makes a good case, and it's a fascinating thought: that the subjectivity of so much contemporary poetry has to a degree helped to sideline the art itself. Poetry must indeed be a response to history, to the pressures of life, to the moral difficulties of living fairly in an unfair world.

This is spiky, often whimsical, intelligent, and quarrelsome writing. Yet it's the sort of criticism that is sorely needed today. Agree or disagree with what Anis Shivani proposes, these essays on a wide range of topics will get you thinking, will make you question your own stances and rethink cherished positions. Reading him, I thought of H. L. Mencken, that great curmudgeon: the critic-as-porcupine. One needs such creatures in our overly pleasant world of American letters, where the arguments are often too tame, and where prejudices lie so deep they cannot be seen for what they are: constructs themselves, conditioned by the environment.

Against the Workshop:

Provocations, Polemics, Controversies

Ayesha Pande
Lyons & Pande International, LLC
55 West 116th Street, Suite 314
New York, New York 10026

December 25, 2005

Preeta Samarasan
c/o MFA in Creative Writing Program
University of Michigan
3187 Angell Hall
Ann Arbor, Michigan 48109-1003

Dear Preeta:

What a pleasure it was to hang out with you at Madras
Masala that cold December day in Ann Arbor. It sure got the
sinuses flowing! Over the years I've met some of my most
brilliant prospects at the Michigan MFA program, and let
me say up front, none more promising than you.

Let's get right down to it. I've had a chance to finally
read your manuscript last weekend (I was in bed with a
horrible cold). It's a winner! — with substantial revisions, and
a new approach to some of the characters and plot angles.
If you're willing to take my advice, I even have an editor
in mind — Anjali Singh, moving soon to Houghton Mifflin —
for whom your book would be a perfect fit. But let's not get
too far ahead of ourselves.

Evening is the Whole Day is a wonderful title, for a novel
set in postcolonial Malaysia, evoking, for me at least, the
heat and humidity of the tropics, those bright endless days
when nothing moves and yet everything shifts. I know you

said the title came to you first, when you thought of the novel nine years ago. Your manuscript incorporates the best of Rushdie and Roy, with elements of a novel about to be released, Kiran Desai's *The Inheritance of Loss*. It's remarkable *Evening* would so strongly parallel *Inheritance*—a Booker candidate if ever I saw one.

I suppose the frameworks of national history and family secrets are integrally connected. To unfold the one is to expose the other. You already have that down. Your language is sensual, all-encompassing, adventurous, comic and tragic at the same time, lush—yes, that's the word, lush—without putting me off. Once I accept your sweeping lyrical eye, I'm willing to let you take me anywhere you want. I don't know anything about Malaysia—but because of your inclusive language, especially as you faithfully translate Indian-Malaysian dialect, I *trust* you to show me the class and race and gender conflicts of modern Malaysia. You instigate authority with your unique voice. *The voice is all.*

It's important to begin with the Big House—so much symbolism here for the reader (never forget, we're addressing an audience that doesn't know Malaysia) to latch on to. Rushdie starts off with the big house in *Midnight's Children*, as I remember. You can never go wrong taking his cues. The Big House. Can it include everyone? I love the blue-peacock façade you have Tata, the patriarch of the family, cover the house in. It conveys so much. The false brightness. The relentless sordidness inside, the abuse and mistreatment of women, Chellam the servantgirl, Uma the bright teenager headed for Columbia University, Paati the worn-out matriarch, even Amma, the lower-middle-class girl the toplawyer Appa marries as his personal contribution to nation-building. The Big House which actually is smaller than its surrounding humbler abodes. Perfect.

So we have Appa, the Oxford-educated lawyer, married to Amma, the frigid neighbor beneath his social class he courted during the time of nationalist hope; three children, Uma, the genius eighteen-year-old girl, Suresh, the imperturbable eleven-year-old boy, and Asha, the imaginative six-year-old girl; Paati, getting older by the minute; and the periodically visiting Uncle Ballroom from Europe, the proverbial prodigal son, Appa's brother and instigator of unnecessary strife in the family. The ghostliness of the house is positively Faulknerian (as an aside, I'm not a great Faulkner fan, can hardly read more than a couple of pages of him at a time, but I speak of the connotation of the label in the popular mind, which is our concern anyway). You have all the elements. You only need to ratchet the tension a bit, enhance the already suspenseful structure.

First, what I already like. The dreamy fluidity of language, its saturating impact on the environment. How Asha's "last *please* quivers, turns to liquid, and seeps into the damp soil, suffusing the roots of the tamarind tree in its desperate grief," or how Amma "smiled to herself, and the wan light of her smile seeped out through the shutter slats and pooled in a patient, watery circle on the top of Appa's Brylcreemed head," or "All around the table there was a unanimous sucking in of breath so deep the house turned for three seconds into a vacuum, still and voracious, and a sparrow flying past an open window was pulled against the mosquito netting and held fast for those three long seconds." You can't do this often enough. Readers want to know that in this world the slightest gestures have *meaning*.

When you capitalize concepts, like "punished Chellam (for Leading Us On, for Pretending to Love Us like siblings...)," or "though In The Beginning she sat in it only to relax after lunch...one day she made an official announcement that she was Old and Tired," it evokes Roy, of course, and I want you to use this technique whenever you can.

When Mr. McDougall, the Scottish owner of the house, sells it to Tata after the imperial jig is up, you write that "King George VI had relinquished the cherished jewel of his crown...he'd dropped it as if it were a hot potato, towards the outstretched hands of a little brown man in a loin-cloth and granny glasses; a taller, hook-nosed chap in a still-unnamed jacket; and three hundred and fifty million anonymous Natives who'd fiercely stayed up until, by midnight, they'd been watery-eyed, delirious with exhaustion, and willing to see nearly anything as a precious gift from His Majesty." Very Rushdiesque.

Also Rushdiesque, and you've got this down pat, is the dialogue: "Amma threw away your bowl already, what to do? Eat faster-faster, don't tell anybody....Nice or not, Paati?...Bondas hot-hot....So long didn't eat, is it?" Or, "Chhi!...There also you must put your hands, is it? Cannot keep quiet ah?...Whatta-whatta grand place this Station Hotel used to be in the British days, you know or not?... Since they took over they've kept it like their face only." Or, "Putting your mouth nose all where people put their backside...get sick only then you know." Or, "Don't simply-simply waste it on magazines and kacang puteh." Or, "*Tsk*, no ifsandorbuts....What is all this answering back? For a small thing like this also too shy or what?" Or, "Action-action only Uma and Chellam, don't want to talk to us means why should we care?" Or, "Nowadays people doing all type funny-funny thing." Or, "Aiya boy-boy, stop it...people not joking-joking here...Faster-faster go home." *Simply-simply, only, itself,* these become integral rhymes.

Do Malay Indians really speak like that? The point is, it's what's authentic. The reader accepts it, and so is more willing to trust your story. Your *images* are true to the place: "Heat rises from the road in shimmering waves, as in a TV dream."

Sudden transformations, precise to the moment: "And at that moment, just as the minute hand on the hall clock touched the six, Aasha ceased to be a baby. The dimples in her knees smoothed themselves out. The creases in her thighs sizzled and melted. Her knuckles turned bony. Her forehead flattened." Little girl turning decrepit in a precise second. This is the kind of thing I know editors like Anjali passionately fall in love with.

I could go on. The way you make lists, enumerate things a, b, c, d, or 1, 2, 3, 4, is also integral to the Indian novel by now. It adds to the atmosphere of so much stuff being crammed into short lives, impossible to contain. You cannot *ever* have an overstuffed novel, is my primary advice to aspiring novelists; understuffed, yes, overstuffed, never! This is why you need the sensual, Nabokovian, Faulknerian language, to hold the enormous stuffing. Minimalist, cautious, restrained language would get in the way, if you see what I mean, would be utterly insufficient to the task. I like how Asha communicates with ghosts, with Mr. McDougall's six-year-old drowned daughter, and with Paati's ghost. It makes me think of Isabel Allende. It can only be good that reading your manuscript evokes the best of so many excellent writers. The reader quickly connects to the paradigm.

Now let's talk about what we can do to make it even better. Incest works as a complete metaphor in your novel. The ultimate perversion of the most beautiful human instinct, sexuality turned on its head, to yield a monstrous inward turning instead of turning outward. But rather than incest with Uncle Ballroom—the reader expects it all along, especially after the late-night dancing scenes—make Appa, the father, commit incest with Uma. That would make the trauma, the utter paralysis and breakdown of communication that takes up the first nine-tenths of the novel, more convincing. An uncle you can almost excuse. A father, never.

I would also get rid of Appa's political activism in the early years. It creates an imbalance. Any kind of politics in the novel—any novel—must really earn its place. Ask yourself, Is this indispensable? Can I make the point another way, without burdening the reader with historical details he may not care about? A suggestion: make Appa a leading criminal prosecutor, taking up the cases of brutal killers. I can't think of a better way to bring issues of race and class and gender into focus. The cases can be illustrative of national conflicts, far more intriguing than politics. You already have the kernel of it in the violence you describe (so integral to our concept of tropical climates): "three of the neighbors died violent deaths (a man run over by a burger van in the building's car park; a woman slashed, strangled, and dumped at a nearby pig farm; a second man decapitated, skinned like a goat, and hung from a hook in the bicycle shed)." Simply make this part of Appa's caseload.

Don't worry about critics' allegations of too much happening, too fast, in what they allege is deviation from mundane realism. I know, MFA students are only too exposed to the inner critical voice—or the external voice, like James Wood's domineering one, for example—but it's better to silence the critic while you write. The grandmother, Paati, for instance, why couldn't her decline, after her refusal to acknowledge the incest, take place before our eyes—rapid almost beyond belief? In the tropics, people grow up too fast, but by the same token, they also die too fast.

You have Appa having a brief dalliance with a poor Indian servant on Kingfisher Lane. It sounds too tentative, loses impact for me as a reader. Give him a Chinese mistress—why not a char kuay teow noodle stall owner in the downtown market?—give him three little "Chindians" with that woman, have Appa send off this plump, ugly Chinese woman to package tours in Singapore, Hong Kong, and Australia, have the no-good Chinese husband return to Malaysia to almost knock off Appa's head with a cleaver after he finds his wife in bed with him. Trust me, this will only make the overall story more plausible. There are no extremes in love and lust.

Like Desai's novel—I'll send you the galleys, I know you'll be passionate about it—stuff in everything, so we can reel in every kind of reader. Always err on the side of appealing too broadly, not too narrowly. The girl who burns herself alive the day Uma leaves for America, the epileptic boy who turns into a babbling prophet once a year, the collapse of the nearby limestone caves which kills one of the Big House servant's eight children and husband at once, none of it is too much to put in. Your language will carry it all.

Some more substantive criticisms. Cut out the entire section on the 1969 race riots. I don't think readers will be interested in that kind of detail. I would have Amma give birth to Suresh in the middle of the riots, but use the riots as background only. Likewise with the sections about Uma having already moved to America to study at Columbia. These parts, frankly, did not ring true to me. It may be that you need distance from your American experience to write realistically about this milieu; you may have to leave the country for a while before you're able to pull it off. In time, it'll come. For now, I'd stick strictly to Malaysia. Don't let the reader get distracted, question your grasp of any culture.

It's great that you show so much empathy for Chellam *servantgirl*, as she's derided by Asha and Suresh. How Uncle Ballroom gives her a few ringgit here and there for her Spectacle Account, which, of course, she'll never fund. You have the correct idea in conveying from the beginning the undefined mystery about her: what exactly has she done to earn expulsion from the Big House? It carries the story forward, invested as we are in such an empathetic character. However—and this is a big caveat—Chellam must always remain secondary to Uma as the novel's center of interest. I can't tell you exactly why, but it just feels right. Empathy is one thing. Identification is another. I don't necessarily want to read a three-hundred-page novel about how a poor servant girl is exploited. That her plight has been exposed is enough for the caring reader.

You have slowed down Paati's death scene in the bathroom to an excruciating degree, and I like that! It's so evocative of Ian McEwan, Briony's perceptions in *Atonement*. Readers will pick up on that instantly, even moviegoers. Who pushed Paati? Make it even more ambiguous. In a declining family, everyone shares the blame, isn't it?

Your formula is impeccable. The postcolonial disillusionment combined with the prominent family's unraveling is an equation with demonstrated payoffs. In later novels you can build on the formula—so leave room for growth in future work, don't feel you have to conclude everything in *Evening*. So many stellar writers evoked— Rushdie + Roy + Desai + Allende + McEwan + Zadie Smith—

how can we go wrong? The Big House, the Big National Letdown.

You have sequenced the novel chronologically in reverse, so that we start with the stasis and agony, not finding out until almost the last pages the precipitating event—incest—that caused the downfall. I would change nothing about this structure, except to perhaps consider ending with a scene of Uma finally departing for America. This would give the reader just enough hope to balance the novel.

I like nothing better than to pick up writers early on and stay loyal to them over the course of their careers, so I'm always looking to the next book, and the one after that. Preeta, a standard agency contract is enclosed. Should you feel interested in taking my advice and revising the manuscript to produce a novel which I can then passionately take to editors, I would be honored to have you as my client. About the time you graduate from Michigan, in a year and a half's time, would be ideal for you to finish the revision; that's when your marketing potential would be at its greatest.

I'm in Paris for the New Year, but back in New York soon after, so let's talk then.

Sincerely,

Ayesha Pande

PUBLISHER'S READER'S NOTES ON RECENT SUBMISSION

JANE EYRE, BY CHARLOTTE BRONTE

I don't for a minute buy Jane Eyre's character. Is she saint or mortal? Decide. That business about splitting up her fortune four ways? Implausible. And the forgiveness business—her dead aunt, anyone who crosses her, sooner or later Jane must forgive. So tiresome. How does it square with her stand-up-for-myself persona? Basic inconsistency here. What does this book remind you of, another book that's done it all, with *soooo* much greater conviction—and far less verbiage about gloomy British moors and insufferable madwomen? *The Nanny Diaries*! Now, there's a pair of writers Ms. Bronte might learn some lessons in craft from. If only Ms. Bronte had a tenth of that kind of ability to draw the reader in, by making the heroine more sympathetic, someone we could fully identify with! I got sick of that Master stuff long before the end. Rochester is a villain, who plays on little Jane's sympathies, exploits her plainness. And is it necessary to make plainness such a virtue? *Puh-lease.* I like to get an expensive haircut once in a while, and an unnecessary facial—Ms. Bronte would have me trembling with guilt every time I spend money except for a noble purpose. I won't even get into the persistent racism, the objectification of numerous Others, the vilification of the mentally challenged and the colonized peoples—there's enough of that to keep us busy with lawsuits and vitriol, should we ever publish such a book. And it's too long by at least a third. The entire middle part could go. The book gets easier to read once Jane is on the streets, begging, starving, destitute, but then St. John Rivers's tiresome character enters to spoil our identification with Jane. Another impossibly romantic, unworldly, abstract type. Has the writer heard of characters with flesh-and-blood interests? Do any of these characters play sports? Do they like to hunt and fish? And why can't we see them have sex? One can be discreet and yet descriptive. My basic problem with this maddening book is that I just couldn't get totally interested in Jane's fate. I didn't really care. Perhaps if the writer had made Jane prettier. Why is the writer so hung up over plainness? *Both* the hero and heroine ugly? How do we propose selling that to our marketing people? Where would Barnes and Noble place that on their shelves? The anti-self-help manual for those proud of their immunity to plastic surgery? But I suspect even making Jane more attractive wouldn't have helped. The book is in the end unsalvageable because of Jane's fussy, fusty, finicky character. Every moral issue has to be split a hundred ways. We're told we're privy to what goes on in her mind and heart, but this reader at least could never fully enter that world. I thought there was an incalculable distance keeping me away from Jane's inner core, whatever that is, because of the supremely high esteem Ms. Bronte shows for the character of Jane Eyre. Maybe the writer struggled too much with the semi-autobiographical aspect when she introduced fantastical elements along with the harsh realism. The madwoman in the attic, the last-minute revelation of Rochester's existing marriage, Jane popping up at her cousins' doorstep, of all the places in England—these are all clumsy plot manipulations not worthy of a writer otherwise as promising as Ms. Bronte. For there is real talent here, some genuine ability to be sympathetic to the working class, the travails of orphaned girls at charity schools, and so on— but the ornate dialogue, the inability to decide between realism and fantasy, the noble construction of Jane Eyre's character, the inherent masochism implied in attraction to Rochester's manipulations, these would all have to go. The writer needs to know: the publishing industry is not in the business of constructing ideal (read, impossible) characters, great role models, if you will. Leave that to our new Christian, evangelical sections. Simply to paint the world as it is is enough.

Decision: Pass, with nice note to writer, encouraging future submissions.

WHY IS AMERICAN FICTION
IN ITS CURRENT DISMAL STATE?

1.

Contemporary American fiction has become cheap counseling to the bereaved bourgeois. Its scope is restricted too much to the trivial domestic sphere. It promotes grief, paralysis, inaction: a determinism for the post-politics society, where ideology has no place. Mired in appreciation of beautiful (or rather prettified) language for its own sake, without connection to ideology—although that is an ideology of its own, and perhaps the most corrosive and debilitating ideology of all—serious fiction writing today has lost any connection with a wide, appreciative readership. There are no more writer-oracles in America, nor even writer-visionaries or writer-sages. There is only small writing, with small concerns and small ambitions. Very little fiction today aims for a universal audience: the market segmentation of specific niches of writing forces writers to address discrete audiences, those who already read their particular brand of writing, while great possibilities of disrupting the fixed manners of reading go ignored.

The conventions of literary fiction are that the bourgeois hero (more likely the heroine) be vulnerable, prone to shame and guilt, unable to fit the pieces of the larger puzzle together, and on the same banal moral plane as the "average reader": *sympathetic*, in other words, someone we can "identify" with, who reflects our own incomprehension of the world, our helplessness and inability to effect change. Then there must be full accounting of motives and intentions, causes and effects, actions and consequences, in a step-by-step, gradually unfolding manner, all in the aim of achieving psychological credibility—as if humans were predictable voting machines, as if all that happens lies within the boundaries of explicability; and the result is not explanation, but unintended mystification, not psychological profundity but sheer tiresome exposure, unwanted nakedness. The culture of confession—exposé in the interest of integrity—rescues the bewildered fiction writer; time after time, the hope triumphs that there is something in the muck of memory that might after all salvage the writer from his struggles with telling a good, full-blooded story packed with real people and real events.

The generation of writers now coming up is frightening in its moral austerity. Can one imagine an O'Connor or Yates or Cheever among them? Can one imagine them grappling with the paradoxes of civilization: Why is there a repetitive decline into desperate fascism? Why are enlightenment principles so frail? How does evil defeat good more often than not? Where does evil come from, if we all claim to be good? If there are any hints of connection in contemporary fiction with the marked trends of the day—fascism, globalization, corporatization, surveillance, dehumanization—they tend to come from older writers, those who didn't come up through the current establishment process for breeding writers, or from writers rooted in East European or South Asian or East Asian or Latin American cultures, those not yet fully assimilated into the seamless fiction writing matrices of postindustrial America. Can one see a Schnitzler or Kafka, a Musil or Broch, a Bely or Bulgakov, a Waugh or Greene, among all of today's puny, humorless writer-souls?

The younger fiction writers today, Mr. K.'s all, are themselves entirely self-constructed as bourgeois citizens, playing by the rules of the publishing game, pursuing their grants and promotions and accolades from wherever they might come, hungry for any scrap of attention from the limited sources each niche is likely to offer them. Writers today are polite, sociable, inoffensive, wanting to spark no controversy, staying clear of any dangerous, big, meaningful ideas, even at the cost of their own increased commercial viability. To win the game by making a large statement, and thus causing discomfort within one's established social zone, is not worth winning the game at all.

Obscurity, in this sense, is self-earned, self-desired—not an entirely unhappy outcome for the cowed writer. There is not a rebel amongst this homogenous crowd. They mean to antagonize no one, let alone the powerful state in its many tentacular manifestations, or the men and women who make the rules of the social game. Watch them at readings and conferences, making eye contact, acting like team players, uttering only banalities, and creating an atmosphere of good feeling, routines with which they've had great success since grade school onwards. If it weren't for their pleasing personalities—the ultimately "sympathetic" characters?—one wonders if they'd ever have succeeded in the publishing business.

There is no magic in contemporary literary fiction. And the players go on celebrating their own death.

2.

The critical and review establishment is enslaved to the dominant modes of fiction writing. There is hardly any *criticism*—if we mean by the word skeptical investigation of the quality of writing—in America today. Different branches of established criticism each have their hobbyhorses to ride on, but on the whole the tendency is to go along with what's already out there, rather than think of alternatives. The sacred cows are extremely untouchable; lucrative careers are at stake, after all, and one must be ever so careful these days.

The establishment liberal organs dutifully endorse the heavy hitters, offering only the mildest of critiques of the latest Tyler, Munro, Hoffman. The preference is for strict realism, neither too carried away by language nor too intimidated by it, produced in formulaic manners by various mass-producing factories (when a writer becomes big enough, he becomes a factory of his own). The quality and gloss of finish, apparent mastery of so-called "technique" and "craft," and conformity to the rules and regulations of realistic fiction are always to be preferred over boldness, risk-taking, flouting of rules toward principled objectives, or the glimmer of a challenging metaphysical orientation on the part of the struggling, surfacing writer.

An acerbic—self-hating?—reviewer like Michiko Kakutani is the prototypical gatekeeper. The slayer of many a frightening, aggressive, precocious fictional dragon, she is the Alan Greenspan of the literary establishment: the very hint of inflation is to be fought off at all costs, including the risk of inducing a self-fulfilling recession; critical policy must be conservative in the extreme, favoring the account balances of the already well-heeled; and the markets must be soothed at the first signs of genuine rebellion among the have-nots, distracting the conversation toward productivity and growth increases.

European fiction, because it accepts politics and ideology as inescapable, is typically scorned for being "polemical," as is any fiction that has any point to make (the supply chain must be validated, the leading American houses must always be accorded prime status as incomparable producers, even if the situation in fiction might be akin to the clunky American gas-guzzlers of the seventies, out of tune with the realities of means and resources). The piling up of irrelevant details for their own sake is appreciated as indispensable grounding in reality (for the liberal critical establishment, the postmodern revolution in epistemology has not yet occurred; they're still going by the rules of Locke and Hume). Mediocre new writers, whose only talent seems to be to have understood the rules of the marketing game, are lauded week after week as brilliant. Old favorites mired in repetitive self-imitation are still offered as awesome masters.

Liberal guilt disallows critical appraisal of the many

forms of victim fiction produced today. American grown South Asian writers can today do no wrong, just as East Asians were the hottest thing a few years ago. Of course, they must not be overtly political, must not have any detectable ambition, or they'd be violating the stereotype of the grateful minority. But as long as they act obedient and obsequious, their fiction gets the liberal seal of approval.

The reviewing establishment has little trouble with the blurring of lines among memoir, autobiography, and fiction. The rise of the memoir as a popular form is coincident with the decline of the novel: both suggest a failure of imagination. Boldly imaginative works, not rooted in memoir, are increasingly disappearing from the marketplace, to no establishment reviewer's consternation.

The little magazines have their own constituencies to serve. The writing teachers who produce most of the fiction the literary journals cover are almost never subjected to criticism. The quality of the reviews in most journals is embarrassingly thin; the idea is to use the flash and glint of erudite language to puff up the writer, who may some day turn out to be the granter of favors in return. With a handful of exceptions, the journals are engaged only in the mutual flattery business.

The few deviants among the reviewing establishment, those who seem to work from a critical apparatus that might have existed before the populism of the sixties put paid to objective standards, are the crusty, white, "elitist" old fogies, who lament the end of print culture and the associated disappearance of heroism of any sort. This outnumbered species will soon pass on.

3.

In an ideal world, the specialized production of fiction writing in an academic setting wouldn't dominate. The connection between the writer and the culture would be reestablished. This was more or less the model until the late twentieth century, and it worked well. But today fiction writers are really academics, in thrall to heavy teaching workloads, enamored of conferences and colonies, committed to correcting grammar in composition classes and putting up with undergraduate writing, in love with distractions, domesticity, family values, self-restraint, and linearity. They are university employees who happen to have a slight talent for writing. Tens of thousands of well-meaning middle-class individuals believe they can be writers; while India and China produce software engineers and material physicists, this is our venue of creativity.

There is too much writing, so overwhelming in volume that the most committed reader can't keep up. The little good writing gets drowned out. The response is that this flood will get sifted out in due course anyway—perhaps a hundred years' time—so why worry? In the meantime, let everyone do their thing (everyone has to make a living, and since we don't have the aptitude to be computer programmers…). But we can already tell who the very good writers of the age are. Why do we need the rest? Accepting the existence of bad writing, being casual about its profusion, dulls the critical sense. Writing is now an industry, with precisely the economics informing any industry, like microprocessors or automobiles. Supply creates its own demand (obscure literary journals that even graduate writing students don't read, but use as credits to land jobs teaching other illiterates how to become writing teachers), brand identification is promoted, market slots get increasingly more arbitrary and narrowed, and there are legions of publicity and advertising executives (the award-givers honoring their own students, or people who could have been their students) to legitimize the whole venture.

No amount of thinking about alternative solutions can alter anything. Fiction writing is the way it is because America has turned it into the last great Fordist model of production. Can one imagine, in this age of fascistization, a loosening of the monopoly of the gigantic media corporations, which have absorbed nearly all of publishing? Can one imagine a situation in which aimless college graduates, who twenty years ago would have prolonged their removal from the skunk hour by enrolling in law school, suddenly acquiring a civic consciousness, or an appreciation for the life lived outside the academic spotlight? No, they're used to monitoring and being monitored, inhabiting a world where health insurance is a given and a steady paycheck expected, and where indices of measurement of success proliferate.

Without much experience of the real world—other than family matters, like divorce or abandonment, or personal incidentals like menstruation, abortion, or mental illness—fiction writers publish stories often from the child's point of view, itself a highly suggestive fact. Open up any current leading journal, and the typical story starts off with these phrasal bits: "My mother...my father...I was in the sixth grade...my friend Ellie...in the backseat of my parents' car..." There is no plot, no bildungsroman (pointless little epiphanies don't count), no larger purpose to the minor childhood incident being recounted (this easily turns into the memoir form). These writers haven't progressed to the adult stage enough to write from the adult's sensibility.

Romanticism, existentialism, stoicism, nihilism, all are forbidden modes of perception; only a constricted bourgeois realism, steeped in paralysis and grief, is accepted. If writers lived in proximity with real people— even when they live in exciting places like New York, they thrive in self-enclosed circles—they might produce a different kind of fiction: adult fiction for adult minds, who have moved beyond paralyzed disbelief at the big, bad world's intolerable cruelty.

The romantic notion was of a genius, who sprouts spontaneously, and produces great works and does heroic things (dying early helps too); now we have the peculiar American notion of health-conscious, sexually abstemious, profoundly earnest writers teaching other writers "craft" in workshops over many years. At the leading conferences, drunkenness and ribaldry have been banished; now the presentable, charming, well-behaved writers get together to plot their next career moves (in a parallel universe, their brothers and sisters are acting similarly at sales conferences in Wichita and Omaha). No great writer of the past is conceivable in this model.

4.

The decline of American fiction is a sign of the decline of elite liberal consensus. The vacuum in political ideology is being filled today by an anti-politics, of personality and charisma, leading to gradual submission to authoritarianism among all potential sources of resistance. Without a vibrant class politics, without a political ideology arousing passions, there is no vibrant fiction. This doesn't mean that the writer must have a political agenda of his own, and must use his fiction to promote that agenda. But try to imagine a Twain or Dreiser or Baldwin coming out of today's pacifying video culture, beholden to no great minds of the past, attached to no inspiring tradition, unmoored and free-floating in a world with only bits and pieces of political (il)logic: no coherent narrative is possible in such circumstances, except the narrative of the private self, cut off from external nourishment.

The MFA programs are killing writing in this country. It is not so much that new media are sapping the appeal of the novel, reducing our attention spans, leading to forms of perception that can only be fragmented and disjunctive. Dos Passos rose above the challenge of movies, integrated the new perceptual apparatus into fiction, enlivened literature with his relish for the increase in methods of processing reality. It is not that there are now too many competing media to take in reality, but that reality itself has vanished into the ether of too much reality. Fiction writers, bred through the democratic process, are told that their every insight is valid (no, it's not); that there can be no judgment banishing them to the ghetto of the failed and uninspired (yes, there must). Expectations are set so low that to meet them all one has to do is dig into the finitude of the self and crown oneself king or queen for the day.

The greatest concern is that the astute reader of fiction will disappear altogether—again, not because movies or the Internet or cable television are working in a zero-sum game, but because writers are too small-minded to understand that with every acceleration in the profusion and vitality of media comes a reduction in the word-for-word quality of production, which is the gap the writer must rush to fill in. Each addition to media is potentially life-giving to written narrative. There is no replacement for the use of print to tell a convincing story. But today's writers, so humble in their self-presentation, don't believe this. They grew up drawing nourishment from other media; at bottom they think that perhaps Steven Spielberg can work magic of a kind denied them. They underestimate the reader, they underestimate reading itself. By persisting in this mistaken belief, they make the prophecy self-fulfilling. Why doesn't Richard Powers have the same popular following as Neal Stephenson? Why can there not be a Hemingway or Highsmith to take advantage of the narrative possibilities offered by new media? Dave Eggers is the best we have? He is the embodiment of a director's lifetime banishments on the cutting room floor.

Competing with new media on their terms— by reorganizing the structure of narrative to meet the requirements of the presumed illiterate reader—diminishes writing. The very notion of competition suggests defensiveness. Defensiveness means a lost game.

The individual fiction writer would have to be strong enough to take the moral offensive against writing that deludes the reader into thinking that his private ignominies are worth celebration and memorialization. He must buck the trend by going against the monopoly on career rewards currently held by the writing industry (which for all intents and purposes blacklists and boycotts real outsiders, although of course the terms of the game can't be framed so bluntly), and by fighting the herd mentality of publishers whose interest it no longer is to discover great fiction and build writers' careers, but who only want to replicate the last great sensation.

How many individual fiction writers are that stubborn, Promethean, Nietzschean? The current setup works fine for the bottom line of the publishing industry. No one has any self-interest in elevating the quality of fiction. The future is a world only of chick lit (this genre is the epitome of all fiction today; it is where serious fiction draws its motivation from). To come to writing from a strong moral position, some belief in universal values that makes one sleepless and distraught, will be like a fat, bald, ugly man crashing in on a slumber party of blonde supermodels.

5.

Contemporary literary fiction has chosen to marginalize itself from mainstream culture. It has its own niche, like specialized Foucauldian sociology or Derridean philosophy, catering to the sensibilities of other experts in the field. The writer adopts a politics-neutral stance, excluding any sense that characters' lives are influenced by politics. The fear is of being branded politicized, in which case no serious reviewer will want to deal with the writer anymore, and of being called preachy or moralistic or sermonizing by the reviewing community.

The typical fiction writer tends to be vaguely liberal about women's or gays' or minorities' rights. He is ultra-sensitive about not writing anything offensive to any constituency, and mortally fearful of painting with broad brushstrokes. He takes care to mark down any budding writer who might want to speak truthfully about minority or majority groups (it's open season, however, on white males, in the teacher's own writing). Beyond that, he doesn't have a grasp of politics.

Interact with him and you sense someone permanently in fug, a brown haze of depression and worry perpetually hovering over him, reducing him to a man politic and deferential in the extreme. He dare not take on the cruel monsters who threaten to take away social security and biometrically identify us at every point. Oh, most are against Christian theocracy, but who wouldn't be? It's a safe gesture, and it never intrudes in the fiction anyway. As long as one writes about blameless (flawed but lovable) characters in "beautiful" language, one's aesthetic position is secure.

Has any of them—with the possible exception of older writers like Roth—had to say anything about our traditional liberties being suspended? Has any of them written substantially about this dark night of the nation? (Just now, Susan Choi and Neil Gordon and Russell Banks are beginning to turn to early seventies radicalism, the safely removed Weather Underground being a favorite theme.) Then what is fiction for? To write one more time about the sister who suffered abuse at the hands of the father, the mother who goes not gently into the night of Alzheimer's, the husband who philanders and the wife who refuses emotion? One more time, in the same toneless, placid, paternalizing style, dotted with little points of light that threaten to emerge as dire epiphanies?

The Vonnegut lovers aren't going to go near these domestic tales of patient grief. They want plot, action, resolution, character, while the workshop trend is to write plotless stories, where nothing happens (to have characters in interaction with the outside world, leading to actual events, would be to be as bad as those terrible genre writers, wouldn't it?), where the reader isn't granted the intelligence to pick up the characters' situation from our common, universal fate as human beings, and where the language is uniformly unimpressive, without flourish, decoration, fancy, imaginative leap, unpredictable flow, as if the same writer were behind every single novel and story in America.

The denial of language's possibilities is the most significant political statement by the contemporary fiction writer. In workshop, the process is of subtraction (just as in focus groups run by dumb politicians appealing to the dumbest among the electorate): let's take away everything that can't be agreed on as ruffling no feathers, daring into no unpredictable verbal territory. Let's reduce the fiction down to its barest minimum (all American fiction is minimalist in a sense—there is no European or Asian or Latin American-style maximalist pursuit of the indefinable). What about David Foster Wallace? Who can actually read Wallace, or at a lesser level Moody or Antrim? The possibilities of the English language these days seem to be available mostly to writers not homegrown, while those who take the pledge of allegiance pledge also to hunt down every last adjective from their prose, every last embellishment of language that might take us deeper into the heart of darkness.

This sunny American fiction is politically conservative, because it reduces language to silly putty, shaped and reshaped at the will of the writing instructor, or his ghost hovering over the writer (is today's American fiction writer ever in love with solitude? It appears not; one imagines him writing at a noisy Barnes and Noble, not in an ancient, noble library). All the politically charged events of the day are left to the genre writers to manipulate for their ends; the serious writer is trained to look down on politically aware fiction: that's just journalism. There are no AWP awards there.

BOULEVARD SYMPOSIUM: WRITERS IN UNIVERSITIES

University teaching has the following overlapping, deleterious effects on writing: a) shrinkage of the writer's audience to likeminded academics; b) disinterest in fiction and poetry of public import; c) inability to redraw the given boundaries of the chosen genre; d) lack of risk-taking and subversion, because of the shrunken reconceptualization of the writer's status; e) infinitesimal subdivisioning of writing, rather than branching out to encompass competing genres — a typical academic malady; f) focus on immediate reward rather than continuance of the literary tradition; g) withdrawal from public engagement, to the fatal detriment of literature's timeless values; and h) reorientation toward the lowest common denominator, dumbing down writing.

These tendencies reinforce each other. Academics fall into the habit of writing for peers, removed from the insecurities of the market; true, university writers may sometimes sell plenty of books, or land $50,000 or $100,000 awards, but these are contingent on their good standing in the academy; to preserve their status, they must always write to please their peers, not the common reader. Academia makes a lot of show of being in touch with the times, but as its utter inability to respond to the last several years of fascism suggests, reality of an intractable kind cannot be allowed to penetrate the temples (they're still taking back the night, instead of taking back the country). Queer scholarship, ethnic studies, cultural studies, now these academia can handle. The writer in the academy may write of generalized grief and pain, but may not locate their sources in political ruin.

The first two tendencies lead to the next three, the writer no longer expected to be the tribune of the people, but rather a tribune of the academy, and hence doing everything he can to consolidate a secure little niche for himself, where his specialization can continue to garner publication and awards. One can argue that removal to academia's safe precincts could just as well spur risk-taking and innovation, since the writer doesn't have to depend on the next check to feed himself and family. In fact, academic competition, if anything, is more venal than that of the pure marketplace, the distinctions increasingly trivial, all work being commentary on the established contemporary canon, in our medieval scholastic cloisters.

A related tendency is not only to shun writing of a political nature, but to reimagine the writer as fundamentally apolitical, in a postmodern version of "art for art's sake." The last tendency might seem the most counterintuitive: doesn't the academy provide the space and time to reach for a higher literary denominator, isn't that the whole point of joining it? But a quick check of the facts shows that it is the marketplace's pressures that lead to true innovation, not the quasi-communistic imperium of academia.

These are unavoidable occupational hazards of academia, regardless of the discipline being taught and learned. They apply with equal force to the discipline of creative writing, with powerful effects for our literary culture. There is nothing new in pointing out these obvious disadvantages; Cowley, Kazin, and Aldridge often did so over the course of the twentieth century. But as the assimilation of all intellectual ventures strictly within academic precincts proceeds full-speed ahead, ruthlessly stamping out offending competitors, its consequences are more blatant than ever to see. Simply speaking, writing has become academic, with all the reductions this implies.

Writing becomes subject to academic fashions. The creation of multiple brands of ethnic literature has occurred alongside the rise of ethnic departments. More students in Latin American and Asian American studies, more teachers required, more books needed to cater to the lowest-common-denominator taste of undergraduates and to churn out graduate theses. Writers in the university supply particular groups of critics with targeted fodder. A large part of writing today, almost wholly in memoir and poetry, is grief-oriented, very much in tune with the academy's overall shunning of liberal optimism. Diversity politics makes up much of the rest. Academia's "publish or perish" motto correlates with steady cumulative output, which no one, however, reads. Honors and awards are a staple of academic self-enrichment—they now absurdly proliferate in writing too: Poet X being recognized for lifetime achievement with a massive financial award, so that he may return the favor to his selectors a few years later.

Without the oversupply of writing produced in academia (350 writing programs, and counting), and the resultant degradation of the work in monetary terms, independent writers not affiliated with academia might still be able to live by writing alone, as they used to, if they have the skills to write for the reading public. (The repression of independent writers is extreme, extending even to ensuring increasingly minimal or no access to university research libraries, not to mention the definite bias against them in both publication and competitions.) So not only do writers in academia degrade the quality of writing, they make it almost impossible for unaffiliated writers to reach their highest potential, because opportunities have been curtailed.

Writers stop moving back and forth between their primary interest and other fields of media, as used to be the case, thus failing to enrich journalistic writing—and vice versa. We see the extinction of the writer-critic (Eliot, Pound, Wilson, Updike, Vidal), leading to a severe diminishment of both imaginative writing and criticism. Instead of informed writer-critics, practitioners deploying both skills simultaneously, we only have popular reviewers (whose paradigm is the one-note Michiko Kakutani, willfully unknowing of the twentieth-century literary canon), scholarly critics (deconstructionists who have demolished the traditional function of criticism in their arcane race/class/gender academia-as-battleground linguistic pursuits), and the few actual writers who review reluctantly and occasionally, only to praise the distinctly modest work of their peers.

Revealingly, the defense of writers teaching in universities is always about convenience, protection of the writer from commercial forces, patronage, quantity — never about quality. Who is the patron? What does he want? The liberal humanist university today doesn't wish to stir any waves, doesn't ask any tough questions about the tendencies in the population engendering a permanent fascistic revolution (only assumes pseudo-emphatic culture war stances, to feed the elite's shame and guilt). Writing is a solitary, not a communal, act; oppositional, not social; best done amid physical constraints, not comfort; a vocation, not a job. What about the deadening effect of the routines of academic life, added to family and other bourgeois obligations?

University writers teach simplistic rules. The writers' own writing then begins to reflect it. In fiction, it is all voguish impressionism, without the necessary essayistic component; they only show, don't tell. So-called didactic, preachy, judgmental attitudes are banned. There can only be likeable characters, no omniscient third-person narration, no satire. The same reductions apply in poetry: only free verse, disengaged from its own tradition. To feel like real teachers, writers have to make their work correlate with the rules they're teaching: how can it be otherwise, if the sense of authenticity is not to be lost altogether? At some point, compartmentalization from the stupidity of freshmen being taught basic English becomes impossible, and the mind rots.

How can young mercenaries, relentless résumé-padding seekers of Yaddo-MacDowell-Bread Loaf-NEA, fellowships (given by one's friends), and awards (within particular niches), write anything politically risky? It's one thing to teach when you are already an established writer (like Frost, Auden, Yates, Cheever, Berryman, or Ashbery), or at least have formed your basic mold (as was true in the past), but another thing altogether to start from day one, learn the writing trade from inside the university. If you never have to rely on writing to support you, what kind of writing does that breed? More significantly, what kind of writer does that screen out? Too early an attachment to the academy leads to a tremendous impoverishment of experience. Accountability demands a direct link between the quality of writing (as judged by readers) and one's compensation.

Today, almost no one who's not a corporate-type (i.e., too individualist, in the narrow materialist sense) can be a successful writer in the first place, because you can't get through the university credentialing system, dutifully respecting the literary icons of the moment (the Denis Johnsons and Aimee Benders), as though nothing else of substance had ever been written. Young writers in the academy are profoundly underread, have very limited models.

Another sign of the deleterious effects of writers gaining their livelihoods from the university is that there have been no new movements since modernism (so-called postmodernism being only a late derivative)— America should have been the country where the next major movement arose, since we're the leaders of western civilization, for better or worse. But literary culture seems to have frozen still, in very large part because of its integration into the academy.

Just as our government has become sclerotic to the last degree, doesn't and can't respond to real needs, so is writing completely immersed in its own internal compulsions. Moreover, government doesn't want to reform, since to do so would be to bring in the disaffected population which it serves the elite's interests to exclude; similarly, writing doesn't want to reform (in the sense of getting more readers), since it would mean the end of the bubble. A hysterical proposition: book publishers *want* to lose money (to maintain a phony aggrieved posture), don't want new readers, just as the political system doesn't want new (more demanding, younger, browner/blacker/ yellower, poorer) voters. The influx of a new audience (like voters) would cause unbearable stress on the system, and it, in its academic frozenness, must be preserved at all costs.

Yet another effect of the writer's assimilation in the university is the degradation of the literary journal. These no longer review books by independent authors (shunning the mainstream press as though it were leprous), devoting the increasingly diminishing critical space to effusive praise from student writers of their present and future masters. There is no general aesthetic or political commentary. Criticism per se has been all but banned, only fiction, poetry, and the personal essay can grace the pages of the formerly august quarterlies (only a few honorable holdouts, like *Antioch*, *Michigan Quarterly*, and *Georgia*, remain, the rest having succumbed to popular fashions). The fires of New Criticism cooled down long ago, and deconstructive jargon would have been jarring in their pages, so the literary quarterlies abandoned criticism.

Writing has become a subset of mass culture, popular culture's influence not only pervasive but idealized. This is one way to ensure writing's perpetuation as a harmless artifact that won't interfere with the steady procurement of a livelihood. Everything must be done to eliminate the independent writer, in ways subtle and not-so-subtle, like Wal-Mart crushing mom-and-pop stores, and one way (like Chinese products sold at below-market prices) is to establish a degraded popular-culture-saturated product, access to whose sensibilities is an effective screen against the outsider.

To the extent that a readable fiction exists (even if it isn't necessarily pathbreaking), it is typically produced these days by the few remaining writers outside the university: for instance, Tom Perrotta, Dana Spiotta, Aleksander Hemon, or Mohsin Hamid, who acquire loyal audiences. You can make your own list of independent writers, and compare them to the university writers. Typically, the independents, after striking success, soon get assimilated in the academy. What would T. C. Boyle—as good as he is—have become had he not been part of the academy? One wonders. The pressure against resisting a secure livelihood is immense, and with family and other obligations, often not possible. That should tell us everything: what type of writer prefers security over independence? What kind of writing then ensues?

With assimilation into academia, the usual principles of ranking (academia is obsessive about grading) come into play. Writing programs like Stanford like to take young and inexperienced writers, then mold them according to the rules. Invariably, it's the Iowa Writers' Workshop graduate's mediocre, if not outright pathetic, first book of stories or poetry that gets the contract, via the semi-literate visiting agent's link with the New York publisher, while more talented writers, not affiliated with the writing programs, keep slaving away in the anonymity of the little magazines.

The false argument is that the university removes the obligation to work at unproductive tasks, hence freeing up time to write. Then why do writers in the academy typically suffer from such low productivity? The university writer tends to produce a novel every five to seven years, if not longer. University writers adopt one style early on, their marketable niche, and slowly and cautiously repeat it until retirement. You know exactly what you're getting with each of them, once the specialty has been established, never have to worry about surprises. Antonya Nelson is not going to start writing about Eastern European exiles in the 1930s. Donald Hall will always be Donald Hall.

Drudgery of one kind has merely been replaced with another kind. How is the writer, in our hypercapitalist culture, to survive, the question will be asked. Marry a rich (or at least a self-sufficient) woman; it's a time-honored custom. Steal, cheat, borrow, lie, move to rural Vermont and live in a shack and grow your own food, do anything but sell your soul to the academy. Then stake all your bets on success in the marketplace (of course, that idealized marketplace of ideas doesn't exist, but one must act as though it does): a radically different model than getting assistantships and fellowships, then muting individuality to seek tenure.

I offer Nam Le of *The Boat*, twenty-nine-year-old Vietnamese-Australian (fellowships from the Iowa Writers' Workshop, Fine Arts Work Center, Phillips Exeter Academy), as the paradigmatic case: earnestly sensationalistic ethnic fiction (daringly ethnic, roaming beyond his Vietnamese ethnicity, latching on to the dominant clichés of various cultures) both literature departments and newspaper reviewers can easily lap up; oversized accolades from university writers (Mary Gaitskill, Charles D'Ambrosio, Adam Haslett) that veteran writers of decades-long experience can only dream of; star power he can bank on as long as he offends no teacher or publisher with anything the least bit original or disturbing; utter lack of rhythm and sensitivity and music and harmony and pleasure (surely, he finds writing laborious, painful, debilitating in the extreme), and his own supernatural confidence that he possesses all of these qualities. Soon he should be getting the Hodder and the Guggenheim and the NEA and the PEN/Faulkner and perhaps (if the Jhumpa Lahiri gods smile on him) the Pulitzer, for his joyless work. The cumulative thrust of 350 writing programs has finally managed to produce this angerless coda to minority writing, a fake book by every measure.

The July/August 2008 *Poets & Writers* profiles five young writers, who have achieved early success following the same model: Rivka Galchen (MFA, Columbia), Nam Le again, Leni Zumas (MFA, U Mass, teacher Hunter College), Salvatore Scibona (Iowa, administrator at Fine Arts Work Center), and Preeta Samarasan (MFA, Michigan), the last of whom is asked how her novel came to be published by Houghton Mifflin: "My agent [Ayesha Pande] came to visit the MFA program while I was still in my first year. I signed with her that summer and finished a draft of the novel by the end of my second year. She sent it out immediately, but only to three or four editors…Happily, two of those editors made offers within weeks." Typically, these writers began the book eventually published in their early twenties. Often, these are one-hit wonders, having exhausted and marketed their little experience in their first book, before settling down to academic routines. Their books, I don't doubt, will sound exactly alike, as though the same person wrote them: the same terse, visual, pseudo-cinematic, present-oriented, contextless, superficial, earnest style, without a sense of tragedy.

A relative of my wife's called out of the blue recently, wanting her daughter to make contact with me "writer-to-writer." This young Bangladeshi girl has plotted her career with consummate skill: Prison Education Program Director at Suffolk Correctional Institute; Hoopes Prize-winning thesis: a novel about "a young Chechnyan freedom fighter who becomes a suicide bomber, from the girl's own perspective" under Jamaica Kincaid at Harvard (young Ivy-Leaguers have taken to feverish portrayals of distant wars and genocides, often from the point of view of children, to great acclaim), which earned a double summa from Peter Sacks and Lan Samantha Chang; résumé-building stints at *Details*, *GQ*, *Slate.com*, and for heft, *The New Republic*; story collection in progress at Iowa under Marylinne Robinson's tutelage (hello, Ayesha Pande!); Stanley International Research Fellowship for research support for novel, including travel to Paris, and research at Yale's Beinecke Library. This is the high-end version of Kaavya Viswanathan, the young Harvard author recently exposed as a plagiarist; it is all so programmed, so determinedly credentialing, yet she is assuredly the next sensation-of-the-moment.

Step back jarringly and think of Dreiser, Anderson, Dos Passos, Lewis, Hemingway, Faulkner, Steinbeck, Updike, Salinger, and Vidal, and among the poets, Pound, Eliot, Moore, Williams, Stevens, Bishop, Lowell, and Plath, all independent of the university. Mere coincidence that no one competes with such quality today? Or structural inevitability?

AMERICAN POETRY IN AN AGE OF CONSTRICTION

1.

There is a narrowness to American poetry among its best-known practitioners that defies easy explanation. The contemporary American poet inhabits a perpetual comfort zone, choosing to restrict himself to articulating private sorrows and occasional joys in language that does not inspire, in metaphors that do not invigorate the life beyond the page, and in rhetoric that suggests a closing in, a shutting down of means and ends, rather than an opening up to the excitements and thrills that might be beyond the immediate ken of the hemmed-in poet.

Confessional poets confess with the expectation of bleeding death on the premodern operating table. Those who play tricks with language, as intriguing as the effects sometimes might be, eviscerate any notion of a meaning beyond the performative capability of language, thus reducing both language and its consequences to manageable levels. Poets have forsaken keen knowledge of public figures, public events, and public history, so that even when forced on occasion to confront a large-scale tragedy (usually it's this which obligates them to pen a few lines to "deal with" the crisis, rather than a Whitmanesque exposition that embraces the good and the bad, before calamity strikes), they approach it through the screen of private experience.

Imagine the alternative of approaching private experience through the prism of public experience, which may be said to have been the aesthetic of some of the leading modernists, and certainly many poets preceding them. One can chart a decline even in confessional poetry, from the vast historical ambition of Lowell, to the institution of the lachrymose self as the central (ahistorical) figure in Plath, to the display of mere histrionics in Sexton. The ideal today is poetry that barely reaches the level of passable prose, and seeks to underwhelm and underimpress. With few exceptions, humor, and its more refined cousin wit, are nearly extinct in American poetry. The occasional bursts of humor in some poets known for this quality buttress the helplessness of the private protagonist, rather than channel energy back and forth between the individual and his culture, to enliven both. Satire, the stooped uncle with wilts on his back, has been utterly homeless for some time.

The work of iconic American poets embodies their self-perception as individuals of very small means (both in terms of life choices and language choices), satisfied with cheap fireworks for a childish age of theft and gloom and self-doubt. The rule of self-censorship is faithfully observed, lest the poet's language and emotion become threats to anyone but the narrow academic audience. Poets seem to broach the capacity to make connections that might shed light on divergent worlds of experience, only to withdraw in favor of rigid compartmentalization of perception and sensibility. If a poet's mother suffers from breast cancer or her father is institutionalized for Alzheimer's, that is all the experience means, the nuts-and-bolts and nitty-gritty of the story itself, nothing beyond it. The reigning aesthetic is to blank out implication and responsibility from the individual's minute cloister of a view to the world.

2.

Perhaps the leading poet of the age who aspires more than anyone else to trigger no sensation whatever—watch her back off the moment she comes close to generating emotion of any sort—is Jorie Graham. She is the mistress of the line gone haywire, the sentence lost in clouds of pseudo-philosophical confusion, and the occasional half-hearted concrete image (her detested "thing") buried under mounds of unvisualizable, tissueless, off-putting verbal façades. Graham makes it impossible for the reader to get a grip on whatever she's after (she, in her prolonged academic tiff, might say this is precisely what she wants): in her poetry, opacity functions as a mutual wink between reader and poet that this is after all meaningless work, at best a distraction. Graham wears us down by refusing language its independent, historical, contextual place. She is the poetry world's answer to American academics fascinated by outdated French deconstructionists, equal purveyors of false difficulty.

Graham commits violence against language of so many sorts and with so much gluttony that one is tempted to give up on poetry as an ethical project; and one suspects this may not be far from what her endlessly looping, excessively remonstrating, and yet simplistic and backboneless verbal tirades seek to accomplish. Graham wants to remind us, in every poem, that verbal acquisition leads nowhere.

In her first collection, *Hybrids of Plants and of Ghosts* (1980), image still tenuously threads casual metaphors and philosophical declaratives. But Graham's self-consciousness of the futility of the concrete as root and adhesive is evident in her misapprehending "A Feather for Voltaire":

A man full of words

is a garden of weeds,
and when the weeds grow,
a garden of snow,
a necklace of tracks: it was here, my snow owl perhaps.
Who scared it away?
I, said the sparrow,

with my need, its arrow. And so here I belong,
    trespassing, alone,
in this nation of turns

not meant to be taken
I've taken.

Graham has recruited Voltaire as soulmate in her projection of poet as lonely sparrow, taking wrong turns to no effect, flying over words that sprout as weeds. Voltaire—standing in for the enlightenment—once was, and now is no more. All is insubstantiality, so predicts Graham, self-fulfillingly.

In the opening poems of her second collection, *Erosion* (1983), Graham is much farther along in her ambition to reduce the vastness and meaning of the public sphere to the random emptiness of her private world. In these poems, Graham proceeds to sever the connection between object and reflection, thing and word, the impulsion toward pragmatism. Like the deconstructionists, she echoes, in "Wood Wasps in the Spanish Willow," that "the dream of reason / produces / monsters." This dictum is placed within quotes, to distance the poet from accountability, but we know this is where her heart lies. There is no such ambiguity in the title poem:

> I would not want, I think, a higher intelligence, one
> simultaneous, cut clean
> of sequence. No,
> it is our slowness I love, growing slower,
> tapping the paintbrush against the visible,
> tapping the mind.
> We are, ourselves, a mannerism now,
> having fallen
> out of the chain
> of evolution.
> So we grow fat with unqualified life.

Slowness is the aesthetic attitude to aspire to. Indeed, her future verbal wanderings are the paradigmatic accumulation of fat, like the American nation getting obese over the last two decades. Mannerism takes the least effort; Graham's later work seems to make a fetish of the appearance of effortlessness. We grow old, we grow fat, we grow rich: and history can't waylay us anymore.

After the first two collections, where history can still be a menacing presence at times, and not all cataclysms can be reduced to the rubble of the cut-off self, Graham becomes an established poet, and abandons all restraint, entering the region of pure excess. The common reader would be at a loss to understand whence comes her fussy, precious, ornately ignorant attitude toward history.

Hannah Arendt has famously talked about the banality of evil, the individual taking refuge in the collective will to avoid personal responsibility. When Graham evokes public memory—in "From the New World," this happens to be the pursuit of alleged Nazi criminal Ivan Demjanjuk (never hesitate to use the Holocaust as your trump card, your quick password to emotional authenticity)—it is to file it away harmlessly, in a thicket of proof-free words, expanding in all directions, returning nowhere. The irrepressible poetics, impossible to conceive of as trespassing any rules, suggest a pervasive unaccountability, of the poet toward history, of history toward the poet, of all toward all.

"The Hiding Place," which locates itself in the cataclysmic events of 1968 Paris, is that sought by the fluent self, a free-floating internally propelled speech-machine immunizing the poet from taking in any unmediated experience that might, heaven forbid, alter her. As in other poems typical of her middle period, Graham shuns the opportunity to make meaning of history and hides instead behind the responsibility-freeing scrim of simulacra: is it a "photograph" or a "news account," rather than direct perception of history, that sways us? Now we can see that Graham's true project is to strip language of all significance, all resonance, step-by-step, methodically, like a butcher feeding his starved family: not a shred of meat must remain on the bones. Her shield of denial is summed up in "Detail from the Creation" as: "Things are like other things." In her subsequent work, Graham will deconstruct the vestiges of narrative poetry, by introducing narrative fragments with some slight connection to reality, only to bury them in proliferating abstractions. From here on, all of Graham's poetry is inclined to prove that the choice of detail to illustrate an argument is purely arbitrary. In a region where all is likeness, even metapoetry is part of a world where nothing, therefore metapoetry itself, exists independently, as in "Picnic": "And why should I tell this to you, / and why should *telling* matter still, the bringing to life of / listening, the party going on down there, grasses, / voices?"

"Chaos (Eve)" is an example of a perfectly nonsensical poem, with no narrative center. The arbitrary details of Christian mythology in much of *Region of Unlikeness* only prove that all things equal all other things, and that therefore, as in "Detail from the Creation of Man": "There's this story / where we continue, continue, fleshy and verbal over the globe, / talk talk, wondering what have we done—" In "The Phase After History," Graham again sums up her credo (the post-metapoetry poet must always keep summing up her project, as the only semi-worthwhile subject): "The house like a head with nothing inside. / The voice says: come in. /The voice always whispering *come in, come.* / Stuck on its one track." The bothersome (schizophrenic?) voices will, in Graham's future poetry, assume overwhelming importance: they are everywhere, instructing her to look at one thing or another, the voices knowing that there is only "wilderness / of materialized / meaning." The commandments will finally "make detail withdraw its hot hand, / its competing naturalness" so that there remains "absolutely no / story" even if there is an arbitrary sound to be made and there is "its cupful of wind that could / transmit meaning." The elite, academic poet goes on waiting, as commanded by the voices; meanwhile, the world burns around us.

Materialism is shunned as delusion in Graham's unironically titled *Materialism* (1993), which argues for giving up the idea of a conclusive reality of the self. In "Steering Wheel," the poet says, "there are, there really are, / things in the world, you must believe me," clearly suggesting, however, that there aren't. "In the Hotel" begins "1) start in the middle and 2) be self- / effacing said the voice." How else to spurn "The day unfolding its stern *materialism*"? How else to declare "The author gone"? Three poems called "Notes on the Reality of the Self" suggest the unreality of the self. The reader wonders: Has the poet ever worked a day in her life? Materialism contains gratuitous insertions of excerpts from real philosophical treatises, as though to reduce philosophy to rubble—Derrida would love this— by placing it in the ruins to which Graham has brought language. A rude interpretation of the later Wittgenstein permeates much of this brand of poetry, which demeans the consciousness of futility by seeking over and over to rephrase it in calming terms.

In her last two books, beginning with *Swarm* (2000), the poetry becomes more and more image-stripped, the abstractions so abstruse as to defeat the will of the most persistent reader. The manifesto, in *"from The Reformation Journal (2),"* now reads: "The path of thought also now too bright / So that its edges cut / So that I'm writing this in the cold / keeping the parts from finding the whole again / page after page, unstitched, speaking for sand." *Never* (2002) culminates in Graham's great yearning for a unified field of infinitely parenthetical utterances, taking in everything: prayer, empire, freedom, into a cage assembled as a hole, with nothing outside its boundaries. There is no possibility of evolution, no trace of honor of any kind, no more temptation to say "things," only "endless erasure," the credo now summarized in "Covenant" (between reader and poet?) as: "This is an age in which imagination / is no longer all-powerful." The merest hint of narrative possibility degenerates into drivel. True to form, her newest book, *Overlord* (2005), is her most unreadable work to date.

3.

Sharon Olds's poetry is an excuse to exemplify extreme biological determinism, of a sort that has no patience for humanist ideals of any sort. The circumscribed world of breast, nipple, cunt, and penis is meant to draw the reader in, at the explicit cost of shunning connections between the mind and the body: this is a bleak, repressive, bewitched world where the modern interaction of mind and body has not yet made an appearance. The body speaks for itself, as its own self-contained, vulturous, enervating, troublesome entity, and must be replenished with the essence of spirit, leaving the fragile vehicle—the poor human being—with nothing but exhaustion to mark her days. Olds succeeds in reducing various radials of corporeal experience to a singular point of focus: the death of man, man as subject, man as author of will. The poets got there first; they were the first to reach the mountaintop of the nipple, the mound of the belly, to persuade chary prose writers: shame is a quality of humanness; adopt it and risk snickers from the world-weary.

Typical of her contemporaries, Olds remains shamelessly loyal to the same brand of form and content throughout her oeuvre: over a quarter century, the stylistic variation is non-existent, suggesting the penetration of determinism in the very interpretation of unvarying experience (each leading American poet is a guild of one). Compare a 1978 Olds poem with one from 2006, and despite the many rites of passage that must have occurred in the meantime, the poet signals absolute disinterest in the evolution of the individual and collective mind.

When the body's functions are elevated to the level of cosmic event, the body is actually cheapened. In "That Year," from her first collection *Satan Says* (1980), menarche is compared to the first rumblings of Auschwitz in Social Studies class. The poet realizes that she is a Jew, and so "a survivor"—but twinning this consciousness with that of menstruation deletes the guiding emotion behind the poem, if there is any: is one as much of a survivor for having a period as for being a Jew? "Night Terrors" assure her that "there is no / chance of survival," and yet survive she does, to write poems that were they written by a man would have been censored for their latent hatred toward the assemblage of flesh that is woman: "she's a hole in space," as Olds says in "Tricks." In a typical Olds poem, there is gratuitous piling on, to achieve an effect familiar to spectators of the new media: a numbing of senses, a bothersome questioning by the heart: Is this really going on? Can she really be saying this? Where is her shame? Am I, the reader, tough enough to get into a psyche so reduced to anatomy?

In these early poems, the characteristic Olds turn at the end—a nugget of wisdom, unobjectionable from even a rebellious teenager's point of view—already appears frequently, as if to deny the poem's preceding sense of pointlessness. In "Feared Drowned," the concluding piece of faux wisdom is: "Once you lose someone it is never exactly / the same person who comes back." Here, as in her unvarying disruptive enjambments—always end the line at the verb, the adjective, the preposition, if you can—she is seizing attention for herself as the poetess, the princess of survivorship, who at every turn refuses the taste of what used to pass in earlier decades as revolt: as in "Late," where the poet is "tired," Friedan-like, of "the women doing dishes" and of women wanting to feel men's "hard cocks" against themselves, but where she concludes, "We are sealed in. The only way out is through / fire, and I do not want a single / hair of a single head singed." Well, we imagine escaping unscathed to that extent is an impossibility, so the poet shall remain sealed in.

In her earlier poems like "The Housewives Watching Morning TV," "The Love Object," "Young Mothers I," "Encounter," and "Fishing off Nova Scotia," there is at least some consciousness of existential dread, which lends the poems some interest, but which the poet later in her career abandons for the self-sufficiency of prurience turned inward. Olds's poems becomes less and less interested in inviting readers to a feeling of universal significance: the poet's experience is hers only, and it can be related, but expect nothing of a connection, let alone understanding. Striving for universalism, after all, is the great bugaboo of the academic establishment. An early indication of the

extremes to which Olds will carry the relentless exclusion of
the reader from participating in some universal absorption
is evident in "Fish Story," where the mother "eyeballing the
slick girl," her "firm / slit a noncommittal fish mouth / smiling
neither way," is observed as not having any aspiration to
commonness. The boys and girls and husbands and fathers
are possessed in extremity by the poet, so exclusively and
intimately that the reader's perception is made irrelevant
from the outset.

The last poem in *Satan Says*, "Prayer," sets the stage
for Olds's dominant obsession in all the rest of her work,
the expulsion of the child through the vagina: "let me not
forget: / each action, each word / taking its beginning from
these." It is significant that it is the infant's "gleaming sex"
emerging from her own contracting sex that immobilizes the
poet into a lifetime of mystification by way of exploration
limited to the body.

In "The Issues (Rhodesia, 1978)," from *The Dead and
the Living* (1984), Olds declares her independence from
cold objectivity, beginning with "Just don't tell me about
the issues," and concluding with "Don't speak to me about
/ politics. I've got eyes, man." The eyes can only take you
so far, as Olds demonstrates in poem after poem, her
perception lingering on her father's penis as he sits on the
toilet, her son's cock at different stages of growth, and her
daughter's evolving mound as she develops through the
years, all providing opportunities for the daughter/wife/
mother to insinuate prurience as the only aesthetic around.

There is never a real presence of the outside world:
when Olds is not observing body parts, she seems at a
loss. When she takes a dispirited stab at including the
outside world, as in the opening poems of the *Gold Cell*
(1987), she can only come up with sensationalistic carnage
stolen from eighties television, including "The Abandoned
Newborn" and "Outside the Operating Room of the Sex-
Change Doctor,' lame attempts she soon gives up to return
to building fantasies of having been tortured herself in
"The Chute"; constructing the evil father as the displaced

arena of all politics, as in "The Blue Dress"; giving voice to the attention-starved baby-boomer adopting the forgiving posture in "After 37 Years My Mother Apologizes for My Childhood"; and drilling our senses with her heavy-handed biological determinism in "This" (the female's breasts and cunt are all; the men process through these apparatus in quick order, helpless as her). This is when she's not indulging in paranoia that describes all of the external order as a series of threats compiled to hurt her daughter, a search for the ubiquitous "evil / in the human heart" that has made her generation complicit in giving us the modern surveillance state: in "The Quest," when she passes by buildings, she can only sense inside them "...rope, / ironing-boards, sash, wire,/iron-cords," that can exploit her daughter as "a raw target."

The claim is often made in pop psychology that men are good at compartmentalization; in the new anti-feminist poetry produced by female poets, compartmentalization is carried to its limits. Unable to talk about the rest of her own life apart from the quadrangle of nipple, cunt, breast, and penis, Olds thinks that meditations on death are no more than regurgitations of scenes of death seen on television or in books of photography. Once this digression into memorialized death is quickly over, the poet can return to her biological understanding of life. "The Family" portion of *The Dead and the Living* includes the emergence of her older sister's breasts clearing the way for the poet's own and thus protecting her, and "The Children" portion includes watching her son as "he shakes himself dry, cock tossing like a / horse's white neck" in "Six-Year-Old Boy" and noticing "the precise / stem-mark" of her growing daughter's sex in "Pajamas."

When it's not the outside world encroaching on her family fortress, the poet toys with the idea of self-originating predation in all its forms. Constructing the most vampirish fantasy in recent poetry in *The Father* (1992), Olds wallows in every bodily extremity imaginable, in the drawn-out death of the father figure. The book consists of one episode after another of what the poet thinks such a death might be like, in all its minute details; it is one of the most inauthentic literary deaths, because its only intent is to show off the poet's prowess in violating every rule of good taste, decency, privacy.

What can be the end result of such obsessive haunting of bodily parts—removed from their spiritual context—but the infantilization of the self, a circular possessiveness? This is precisely what happens in Olds's later work, like *The Wellspring* (1996) and *Blood, Tin, Straw* (1999). The heavenly fantasy for the poet, in "My First Weeks," from *The Wellspring*, now becomes imagining herself being extruded through her mother's womb. With the slight glimmerings of existential dread gone, in "For My Mother" the poet wonders: "Where does it come from, the love of babies—." But the question is not addressed to the mother, it is the poet's conception of herself at seven, thinking of her mother as her "first child, really."

The same possessiveness is evident in "Parents' Day," where the child sees the arriving mother as "mine." Now as this child comes of age in "Necking," making out is seamlessly interrupted by images of the "rape / and murder of our classmate," without so much as a pause. As soon as her "vagina opened, / slowly, from within, from the top," in "First Birth," the poet knows she "was nothing, no one, I was everything to her, I was hers," her baby's toy. We have now entered the mode of infinite regression. In "Physics," the poet tells us she has "not grown up / yet, I have lived as my daughter's mother / the way I had lived as my mother's daughter, / inside her life."

As soon as the child is born, the genitals signal mutual, circular possession, as do all bodily elements. In "The Hand," the boy's contentment is presaged by his moment of arrival in the world, when "His eyes seemed even then to focus, / as if he knew this place, or had not / expected to know it." With the introduction of pervasive gratification at the mere fact of physical existence, the payoffs at the end of the poems get smaller and smaller, as in "The Cast," where the visitors in the hospital waiting room "smiled, the way we smile / at a wedding, when we see the two who have been joined." Or in "The Siblings," when the older brother goes down the elevator to get his coughing little sister "*a treat,*" which suggests that "he will accompany her down into life." In "The Transformed Boy" and "My Son the Man," the poet calmly equates her son's growing into adulthood as enslavement to the body's limitations.

As though Olds were on the same page as her fellow emotional survivors of a political world that keeps breaking in with bad news, "May 1968" is reflective of a great many poems of our era where global public experiences are reduced to subjective, private perception. Olds possesses public events in the same blind manner she possesses her father's cock and her daughter's vagina: gracious flourishes to the shape and means of her own corporeal existence. In tune with the mood of the times, "His Father's Cadaver" can only be described as poetry for the Howard Stern shock-jock age, where the body is the sum of all knowledge, and there is nothing beyond it. No sensation is being aspired for, as in the lower realms of television. Her last collection, *The Unswept Room* (2003), represents a room so thoroughly swept up that the poet's integrity has entirely disappeared in the cleaning-out process. Apologies have become apologetics.

4.

Like Graham and Olds, Louise Glück is a poet of modest talents reaching for more than what she is capable of, and eventually taking herself too seriously until she sputters out in pseudo-profundity. Her first collection, *Firstborn* (1968), engaged well with the outer world, keeping the narcissism of the perplexed self at a respectful distance. Her stylistic influence then seemed to be a clean-cut Williams, her interest in the steady, yielding image consistent, and her thematics a sort of Plath for the moderately depressed.

The poems here are hard-earned, tight, and enigmatic;

the reader struggles along with her (the sense of effort on her part is also palpable, generating some endearment or even sympathy from the reader) and participates in constructing a slightly off-kilter, demented, disturbing reality. The tautness of the lines makes the Plath derivation more striking, for we wonder about the pervasive feminine self-destructiveness in a psyche apparently as healthy (because outward-oriented) as Glück's. The ambition, when the poet interacts with the hard artifacts of nature, is not to reduce them to playthings for the poet's demented soul, but to preserve their external otherness. If there are hints that the poet is about to appropriate "things" to ease the sickness of her being, they are only muted, as in "Phenomenal Survivals of Death in Nantucket," where she says, "I see the water as extension of my mind, / the troubled part."

From here on out, Glück could have taken any number of paths—or could she have?— perhaps going deeper into her mental resources to write a more urgent poetry. But by the time she gets to *The Triumph of Achilles* (1985), her interest in taking herself seriously as an important poet, steeped in mythological sources, becomes the defining thing about her. She now seems to write poetry for the sake of writing poetry; one wonders if the newfound plain language isn't a cover for thinness of ideas (if one looked hard enough under the poems in *Firstborn*, there was always a danger that the ideas might collapse, but then those early poems didn't thrive on rigorous scrutiny—the superficial verbal surprises sufficed). The regression from a cultured language to a more demotic one is typical of the other poets discussed here; although the writers claim that a plain-spoken style was always their preferred mode, such was definitely not the case in their early work. As the individual self bloats up to displace the arena of tradition, the language becomes weaker and weaker, the poetry more ephemeral.

Between *Firstborn* and *The Triumph of Achilles*, there is a gap of seventeen years, broken only by the slim, unimpressive *The House on Marshland* (1975), a crisis of prolonged silence that suggests Glück's early impulse to write poetry was exhausted. In the intervening volume's "To Autumn," the poet looks back at "having / flowered earlier" and "the long / decaying days of autumn when I shall begin / the great poems of my middle period." It would take seventeen years of effort for Glück to raise the finicky self to mythopoeic status. The poetic energy of the sixties, drawing on the exuberance of that decade, vanishes entirely. The new self that emerges is both inflatedly mythologized and unheroically quiet. In keeping with the dominant self-presentation of today's professional poet as drawn not irresistibly to her calling, but essentially a teacher lucky enough to write some, in between blocks, Glück has written of herself in essays as an insecure disciple grateful to have ended up as a poet.

The Triumph of Achilles reveals the poet having duly run out of steam, after the early imitative feminism inspired by Plath and other hard-edged poets of the late fifties and early sixties. The poet has settled into domesticity, and with any exigency gone, she is content, in "Summer," to be "artists again," with her husband, and to "resume the journey" toward happiness, that comes in the maturing phase of "deep isolation" of the "absence of regret." The inward turn of the seventies permeates this twisted gesture, consisting of fake happiness following fake unhappiness, which nevertheless satisfies the poet at some deep level. Humorlessness is characteristic of the victim mentality; it's the tenor of protest literature that has replaced the bite of sixties rebellion; go no farther than "The End of the World" to be attacked by Glück's new humorlessness. In "Legend," the artificer of parables, seeking quick fixes in her Jewish identity, anticipates the onset of adult grief, and begins uttering her earliest platitudes.

The political overlay of the sixties gone, the poet as Sisyphus—"the life of art is a life / of endless labor," she informs us in "The Mountain"—must now dig deep into her childhood, to discover phony vulnerabilities: "there's no action, no development of character," she tells us in "A Novel," from *Ararat* (1990). She starts exploiting her sister to envelope us in a fog of nonexistent risk and danger (true to the false anxieties propagated by insecure intellectuals in the decades following the sixties): "A child all alone / can disappear, get lost, maybe forever," as Glück tells us in "Children Coming Home From School"—and this is only a child to be met at the bus stop. There is nothing poetic about Glück's work here, as when she says, "My son and I, we're the living / experts in silence," a sentiment an administrator of family relationships might well have uttered.

If we compare "Labor Day" from *Firstborn* to the poem of the same name in Ararat, we realize that the verbal complexity, the tightness of meaning (even if on a less ambitious scale than Plath), the emotions, are gone; Glück has accommodated herself to the intellectually flabby eighties. The impulse now is to present adults as perennially grief-stricken: in the new "Labor Day" (notice the privatization of the most class-informed holiday), the father has died, and the mythos of the grieving adult finds appropriate expression in a sort of irrational, pre-enlightenment, religious poetry, denying material necessity; do we ever hear what *work* the closed circle of Penelope and Odysseus and Telemachus do? The closed-off family becomes the only realm of celestial music.

The poet's persona is now of a woman leery of confession even as all she does is confess. Perhaps this reticence to accept the overflowing of preliteral emotion explains the recurrence of the small, unearned bit of payoff at poems' ends (the favorite Olds tic) that now leaks into Glück's work: "that's what you want, that's the object: in / the end, the one who has nothing wins," as in "Widows," or "Because a wound to the heart / is also a wound to the mind," in "The Untrustworthy Speaker," or "this, this, is the meaning of / 'a fortunate life': it means / to exist in the present," in "Lament," all from *Ararat*. Endless such profundities recur, until in the last phase of Glück's work, entire poems are strung together with such words of wisdom—this is essentially what her newest collection, *Averno* (2006) amounts to. A favorite motif of the poets assayed here is the trivialization of death;

again and again, we're told that death doesn't matter (a Plath carryover), or doesn't matter as much as death in life, caused by perpetual grief. In "Lullaby," Glück tells us, "The dying are like tops, like gyroscopes— / they spin so rapidly they seem to be still." All this discounting of the finality of death—what political purpose does this serve?

Glück's tactic in *The Wild Iris* (1992) is to recall some of the verbal complexity from her earliest work, but to redeploy it toward an unvaryingly horizontal emotional scale. In the Zen-like calm prevailing in this collection, there is no excitement to the language: the poet as leader of her civilization is someone who accepts with equanimity whatever happens. In "Love in Moonlight," the attitude about the soul is that it is "filled with fear that is moonlight really, taken / from another source..." Aiming for a Grahamian universal reconstitution of a plane emotional field, including all known existing things stripped of their thingness, in poem after poem Glück tells us of paralysis after emotional death. The flowers given voice hint that the poet is aware of her stance: "why / disdain the expansive / field," in "Field Flowers," and "The great thing / is not having / a mind," in "The Red Poppy." In another parallel with the other poets here, trivial, causeless uncertainty—not epistemological dread, or existential anxiety— pervades the mood in "The Silver Lily."

Meadowlands (1996) is Glück's insertion of the Odysseus myth in the sad-making machine that is her family. The result of this academic exercise is to reduce the significance of the original myth, with such banal assertions as: "Nothing / is always the answer; the answer / depends on the story," in "Moonless Night." Odysseus—Glück's husband—appears as insensitive Neanderthal male shrew, right out of a demented seventies sitcom. Telemachus— Glück's son—is the naïf who rings false at every step; his confessions are aimed to butter up his mother's grief. Penelope—Glück herself—is her own best counselor: the couple encounters emergencies "to test / love and to demand / fresh articulation of its complex terms," in "Parable of the

Swans" (Glück engineers an awful lot of parables in her late phase). When Penelope-Glück says that "it came to light that the male and female / flew under different banners," we think of contemporary male-female differentiators like Deborah Tannen, John Gray, or Carol Gilligan. One of these pop counselors might well have declared, "Trust me: no one's going to be hurt again," as in "Heart's Desire."

All of *Vita Nova* (1999) is a string of banalities, for which Glück is a glutton. Reflecting so much of contemporary American literature, in "Aubade" Glück talks about a "grief I thought I couldn't survive." In the post-feminist phase, Glück admits to her "two desires: desire / to be safe and desire to feel." Her poetry now becomes abstract, image-free, spineless, like Graham's. Consider this stanza, in "Roman Study":

> And then it occurred to him
> to examine these responses
> in which, finally, he recognized
> a new species of thought entirely,
> more worldly, more ambitious
> and politic, in what we now call
> human terms.

"The New Life," also strongly evocative of Graham's pointlessness, leads us on a wild-goose chase. In the poems in *Vita Nova*, names and places function as codes, without context. Glück strives desperately for wisdom, only to utter such banalities as: "I thrived. I lived / not completely alone, alone / but not completely, strangers / surging around me," in "Formaggio," or "also the courage I will have acquired by then / to meet my suffering alone / but with heightened fortitude," in "Evening Prayers." "Timor Mortis," "Lute Song," "Earthly Love," and others consist of unremarkable strings of statements, held together without images, concluding only as in "Lute Song" that the "wish to survive" must be tuned into. The poet is healed in "Condo," as "deep serenity flooded through me, / such as you feel when the world can't touch you." The alternative to reason is blind hope, and the solution is to appreciate "Abstraction," in a poem called "The Winged Horse," that might well be an ode to Graham: "Come, Abstraction, / by Will out of Demonic Ambition: / carry me lightly into the regions of the immortal." Glück is "weary" of her "other mount, / ...Instinct out of Reality," and calls on Abstraction to take her "far from here, to the void, the star pasture" — or shall we say *unified field*? The attitude evoked is one we know from contemporary spoiled celebrities, who create a big fuss of their various misfortunes, making their emotional addictions pay off. Glück faithfully follows in her art the trajectory of her own life, as it dictates her moods and rhythms and choices; never is there a hint that there could be an artistic life removed from real-world emotional pressures. There is no sign of an aesthetic filter, only eternal self-counseling. We suspect — as with the attention-grabbing celebrities — that there is a kind of pleasure in elevating mild suffering to the summum bonum of human existence.

Having done with husband and children, Glück returns to the theme of childhood in her last collection, *The Seven Ages* (2001). She sounds more and more like Graham, Glück's poetry by now abstract to the point that a single typical poem, "Civilization," can contain as many abstract words as "perception of beauty," "desire for knowledge," "obsession," "human passion," "conceded," "offended," "enslavement," "isolated," "without pattern," "summoned," "resurrected," "communicate," "substance," "magnitude," "serene," "glorious," "chaos," "relationship," "apprehended," "mastered," and more. Self-presentation as machine is in full thrust in "The Sensual World," a Grahamian refutation of the reality of objects, things, the material world, where we get the idea that Glück has finally run out of "things" to talk about. As we will see Levine doing, in "Mother and Child" Glück tells us that "Some machine made us; machine of the world," or "Machine of the family," or "Machine of the mother." Infantilization — along with mechanization — proceeds to the point where "veiled," dark genetic cells now become "pivotal," the master document. Poems like "Birthday" are unreadable compendiums of abstract unpoetic statements such as:

> I remember that age. Riddled with self-doubt, self-loathing, and at the same time suffused
> with contempt for the communal, the ordinary; forever consigned to solitude, the bleak solace of perception, to a future completely dominated by the tragic, with no use for the
> immense will
> but to fend it off—

Or this in "The Empty Glass":

> Well, it all makes for interesting conjecture.
> And it occurs to me that what is crucial is to believe
> in effort, to believe some good will come of simply *trying*,
> a good completely untainted by the corrupt initiating
> impulse
> to persuade or seduce—

She seems to claim this, in "From a Journal," to be an entirely new form that she has invented, when in fact her powers have vaporized. The ideas now ascribed to children, her sister particularly, do not seem to belong to children; rather, they are of censoring parents. Her actual manifesto now, as in "Rain in Summer," might well be: "It was all going on much too long: / childhood, summer. But we were safe; / we lived in a closed form." Rejecting the sensual world of things, rejecting all reality, finally there is safety in "fixed conditions." The shrewish husband is gone even, and in stasis is nirvana. At least, Glück knows, in "Ripe Peach," the "terror of the physical world" forcing her contemporaries to return to intellectual childhood. The adult sentiments of the reading public are pushed aside by the poet's pathetic weakness, her fear of death. Finally, virtue can be made out of weakness, as in "Summer Night":

And the art always in some danger of growing repetitious.

Why not? Why not? Why should my poems not imitate
  my life?
Whose lesson is not the apotheosis but the pattern, whose
  meaning
is not in the gesture but in the inertia, the reverie.

The poet, in reality, is apprentice to no intellectual tradition, but to the exhausted subject of her own once half-alive emotions.

5.

Philip Levine, who professes a working-class background and disattachment to academia, has a different problem. Unlike Graham, Olds, and Glück, poets of maximized mediocre talent, Levine's undeniable wit is evident in a handful of early poems. But it is difficult to be Whitmanesque in ambition and scope when you are constrained to limit your argument to the sensible and pragmatic, rather than being boundlessly optimistic like the master.

What has made Levine, a poet of such promising initial talent, become a showcase today for his own self-imitative mannerisms (a problem he seems aware of, guarding against it preemptively, as if to immunize himself from the inevitable criticism)? Why did Levine write from a minimally self-conscious stance only for a brief period in his middle years? How does a man sprouting into a giant return to pygmy, comfortable among other pygmies? What happened to the fiendish imagination?

On the Edge (1963), *Not This Pig* (1968), and *Red Dust* (1971) are early efforts with little of the confessional. Here, Levine attempts to overcome the limitations imposed by establishment culture on the working person's perceptual means. Levine begins by being attuned to emotional exchange between the animate and inanimate worlds. His early political anarchism makes him not take the recondite self too seriously; he's after a state of mind beyond the daily ups-and-downs of work, family, politics. But as he tries on stylistic variation, struggles to reach for profundity, we can already detect that this poet's métier is soon to be compromised in the cultural environment within which he functions, that he will soon be called upon to reach beyond himself or delve deeper. And he falls right into the trap, trying the first route first, beginning with *Pili's Wall* (1971), the worse *They Feed They Lion* (1972), and the disastrous turn in *1933* (1974). Instead, the cannibalism of his private life would last him indefinitely.

Levine, while capable of the early occasional gem, is more comfortable when he adopts his almost unvarying style and tone, beginning with *One for the Rose* (1981) and extending through *Sweet Will* (1985), *A Walk With Tom Jefferson* (1988), *What Work Is* (1991), *The Simple Truth* (1994), *Mercy* (1999), and *Breath* (2004). He has settled into making a revelation of non-revelatory moments, shunning his youthful anarchism, what used to be his pleasure in trying to make whatever he could of correspondences between apparently arbitrarily related phenomena. The exuberant language of *They Feed They Lion*'s "Salami" and the title poem itself are less suited over the long haul to Levine's sensibility than the plain style of "New Season," from *The Names of the Lost* (1976). In late middle and old age, Levine, the self-declared progressive, conforms to the right-wing principle of each according to his station and place (the bottom-feeder worker grateful to be allowed to live, the urban and suburban upper-middle-class person sniggering at the worker's search for contentment). After his ruinous flirtation with overt sympathy for fighters in the Spanish Civil War or the American civil rights movement—in such over-sentimentalized poems as "To P.L., 1916-1937," "They Feed They Lion," or "On the Murder of Lieutenant Jose del Castillo by the Falangist Bravo Martinez, July 12, 1936"—Levine resigns himself to the Reagan-Bush era return to medieval attitudes toward destiny and mobility.

The movement back and forth between philosophical outlooks is given up entirely, in favor of settled harmonics, where the working man is essentialist working man; and surely, no other proposition was going to be politically acceptable during the conservative relapse. The more that practical political options—even verbal playfulness with anarchism—seem to become circumscribed for real people, the more determinedly poets must make mythopoeical constructs out of what little material there is when one doesn't undergo evolution of any kind: hence the uncomplaining Detroit motor worker, the transmission fall guy, the assembly-line poet who takes the blows as they come, a sight to warm the heart of any Republican country clubber. Levine has moved with the times, entrapping himself in an art that seems to evolve from, but is actually a refutation of, his early aesthetic.

The humor of an early poem like "To a Child Trapped in a Barbershop," from *Not This Pig*, which contains a hidden challenge to the deities in its address to the restless child, becomes transformed over time into a humorless plea for the poet to be heard by the powers-that-be. Compare Levine's self-questioning interviews in *Don't Ask* (1981), an early compilation of conversations where he plays the amateur answering amateurs, to the poet basking in the settled myth of Levine, the daunted working-class poet vary of experimentation with styles and voices, in the more recent collection of interviews, *So Ask* (2002). In "Hear Me" and "The Last Step," from *Seven Years From Somewhere* (1979), Levine's direction is still a refusal to identify the worker as the sum of his work, of his waiting and longing. The urge to overexplain, make what should be implicit explicit, to reach almost toward bathos of self-whispering, becomes visible in "Lost and Found" in *Ashes* (1980). The conservative temperament since that turning point of the late seventies and early eighties—for Levine as for the country—has meant not leaving anything unsaid; American culture feels most comfortable in the territory of the said and the sayable. Levine has foundered in this swamp for a quarter-century, obsessively negating all tentative affirmations, presumably to the satisfaction of the über-conservative internal cultural censor.

Thus, in *One for the Rose* (1981), the poet is dressed up as a do-nothing, know-nothing schlemiel—perpetually wavering, uncertain, self-degrading and morose—of the Woody Allen or Jerry Seinfeld kind. The characteristic mode, as in "The Poem of Flight," is uncertain flight that aborts into abstract cancellation, at the first flap of the wing:

> I suppose I must square my shoulders,
> lean back, and say something else,
> something false, something that even I
> won't understand about why some of us
> must soar or how we've advanced beyond
> the birds or that not having wings
> is an illusion that a man with my money
> refuses to see. It is hard to face
> the truth, this truth or any other,
> that climbing exhausts me, and the more
> I climb, the higher I get, the less I
> want to go on, and the noise is terrible,
> I thought the thing would come apart,
> and finally there was nothing there.

"The Myth" now is of the poet as "stubborn, truculent, stupid," a jarring postmodern presence that seems somehow appropriately placed in the mythology of Levine's hardworking, gritty urban America. In the same collection, the reader is struck by the suspicion that Levine is determined to root out all beauty—by way of imagination, rather than abstract negation—from his future poetry. In "Get Up," the desperate, unearned attempt to elicit pathos on the poet's behalf is disappointing:

> ...If I

were serious I would say I
take my stand on the edge
of the future tense and offer
my life, but in fact I stand
before a smudged bathroom mirror
toothbrush in hand and smile
at the puffed face smiling
back out of habit.

In other poems in *One for the Rose,* such as "My Name," the poet in his middle period of fame can't seem to get beyond "a heaven of meaningless words." In "Roofs" the poet tells us that even as a child he recognized that the "clouds passing over… / were only clouds, / not faces, animals, or portents." The poet is entering the region of literalness that unexcitingly marvels at the mundane, accepting only the trivial as subject matter. In "I Wanted You to Know," we pick up hints of Levine struggling to imbue the trivial facts of his childhood and early adulthood with false significance, a project he will pull off to complete success in later work. "Never Before" is the anti-poem, of negation following negation, evoking more pathos toward the poet. "The Conductor of Nothing"—here meaning the train, but it could just as well refer to the poet himself—is Levine's exclusive persona from here on out.

In "One for the Rose," each of his mistaken turns early on smells to him now "like an overblown rose, / yellow, American, beautiful, and true," making us yearn in the last line for negations of all the terms, for they are not overblown roses but underfed ones. "The Radio" represents an aesthetic that borrows from censored movies and books, Levine's manly code providing for a reticence that precludes him from writing about sex, matters of the flesh. The suggestion that nothing ever actually happens or is ever actually recorded makes us almost yearn for Olds's specificity of nipple and cunt. In "Depot Bay," Levine comes off as Olds minus sex, flab unrescued by the sensationalism of sex. But like Olds and Graham, he is not beyond randomly appropriating the borrowed pathos of the Holocaust, as in "To Cipriana, in the Wind," to try to draw us into his unexciting negations. "Rain Downriver" makes us realize that Eliot's aesthetic of wavering paralysis came out of an age sick to death of authentic heroism, whereas Levine's comes out of an age already steeped in anti-heroism, so that the battling non-heroisms create a really flat effect. Eliot, when his narrators spoke of their own absurdity, made us think of the heroic unabsurd in the collective miasma; Levine is on his own with his professed ridiculousness.

Levine approaches Olds's lack of constraint in the transitional *Sweet Will* (1985), particularly in "A Poem With No Ending," which makes us crave for an ending, in "Late Night," where place-names hide place-negations, and in "Last Words," which promises that survivalism is the last resort of an exhausted aesthetic. The succeeding collection, *A Walk With Tom Jefferson* (1988), has brief moments of genuine wit, as in "The Whole Soul," "For the Country," "I Sing the Body Electric," and the title poem, perhaps a last breath of life, before Levine assumes, in *What Work Is* (1991), the fixed character of the poet set on denying every last trace of heroism to gestures that give the appearance of heroism: to be banished is the myth of rugged individualism of an earlier America, where mobility might conceivably lead to success, where a man might reinvent himself over and over, where risks might sometimes pay off in blustering rewards, and where even the opposite sex might be charmed. This is Levine domesticated—the ideas in the American founding documents, the legendary apparatus of the pursuit of happiness that has until now sustained us, purged and expunged—so that the men only seek escape in fruitless meditation away from showy women.

Levine is aware of the tenuousness of positing an innocent America before "prime-time TV," as in "Coming of Age in Michigan," but this is part of his job, and he is compulsively drawn toward it. The younger Levine spoke in his prose of the lies of America's founding myths, while his poetry spoke in part against the reality; the older Levine has

bought into a new myth—of unheroic, negating paralysis—
that is altogether removed from the founding myths.

The "simple truth," in the collection by that name, is the
final stage of domestication, where other men, foolish and
deluded, act out the American Dream on the poet's behalf,
while the poet participates in the conservative political
culture's construction of the artist as oddity, a mimic-man
at best, with not enough independent soul in "Soul" to
constitute a sufficiently stable narrative even to last him
the day. In "The Trade," mundane events are glorified,
raised to the level of transcendence, before mockery takes
over. In "Out By Dark," the mythopoeic infusion, without
context, without urgency, is another reflection of the need
to crush any signs of romanticism, so that the weakened
man may find some place in the new economy, without ever
complaining.

"Getting There" is the summation of Levine's
present enervated aesthetic. On the road here, there is no
companionship, no male bonding, no risk-taking. Every
hint of whatever used to constitute the myth of American
freedom is denied, destroyed, in the persona of the city
boy who never complains, works without stint (does work
make free?). The working-class male's obsessions—the
brother-in-law Joseph, in "Blue," with his talk "all day and
all night of beer / and pussy"—are no match for comforting
domesticity. Levine is celebrated for his empathy toward the
working class, but his conservative sneer toward his origins
is evident in "Blue and Blue," where the sustaining myth of
upward mobility is denigrated, even desecrated, as he does
also in "The Spanish Lesson."

This anti-Whitman now offers us the impossibility of
communication across class or other divides in "Dust and
Memory," the founding legend having been reduced to
debris. His vaunted memorialization of place is actually
only to use the wasteland as convenient code or symbol.
Reminding us of Olds, in "The Escape" we proceed
through various stages of infantilization of the self, as the
poet becomes at twenty-six a "woman" after first making

love, having until then been a child, and as escape for the harried urban man becomes an impossibility. The myth— "I'm an American, / even before I was fourteen, I knew I would have / to create myself"—is quickly shattered in the destruction of the adventurous man. Demagogues all utter simple, indisputable truths, guised in the cover of plain speech; Levine's new man, denatured and deromanticized, occasionally even achieves momentary peace, as he voyeuristically watches his sister in "Listen Carefully" (echoes of Olds), the pretense of unfiltered memoir hiding his discomfort with ordinary work, and also in "My Father With Cigarette Twelve Years Before the Nazis Could Break His Heart."

Mercy (1999) gives the impression that Levine is scraping the bottom of his barrel of memories, as he brings up an aunt or uncle, a fellow worker or departed soldier, to offer yet again the same persistent whine about the grief-proneness of all human exchange. The memories being thinner, the poems are pro forma, the characters having assumed roles Levine expects them to play. Levine doesn't even have enough energy left for his previous shadow-dancing around doubt and certitude. There will be no deviation in his form and content. Not this poet. *Breath* (2004) is his slightest performance to date. "The Esquire" is a story without purpose, concluding with his typical grief-bathed faint epiphany: "None of that matters now. The sun rose on time / over the great parking lots, empty now / that we're all too old or too dead to work." In "Dust" he takes a stab at realistic humor, but his heart isn't in it. It is characteristic that just when he is most out of breath, he should present this late effort as a collection of sacralized breath.

6.

Billy Collins represents a different tendency toward escapism. Naïvely trusting a childlike imagination, Collins's poetry at first glance appears to be free of the whining and complaining. But Collins's exercises in metaphysical reconceptualization don't really refresh ordinary experience, lacking the mystical glow. Apparently avoiding the trap of writing about trivial experiences as a child, a spouse, or parent, Collins still leaves the reader with the impression that his field of observation is not broad and expansive. His form of poetry betrays yet another type of insecurity toward the big, bad world. When he talks about death, he does it almost flippantly. When he brings history into the equation, it becomes implicated in his own banal preoccupations. Most recently, he has begun to pontificate, in his position as America's biggest-selling poet of serious intent. Having had a taste of celebrity, Collins has stepped easily into the myth programmed for him by the literary circuit.

His determination to shun greatness perhaps reflects the final stage of believing too strongly in one's own genius. Collins is disturbingly content even when raising the subject of death, his glee at managing to pose intellectual riddles overriding the tragic impulse. Collins is like a happy adult solving the Sunday paper's crossword puzzle, having skipped the front-page headlines, the mayhem and chaos on the planet. His search for stability has led him to devising single-mindedly predictable imaginative exercises. This is the ultimate stage of risk-averseness.

In *The Apple That Astonished Trees* (1988), Collins establishes his signature move: begin with a trope or event or reality we take for granted, alter one or more of the initial variables, and see where that takes him. Typically, we're made to realize the arbitrary nature of the setup conditions, without feeling anxiety toward the force field within which our minds operate. The mental gymnastics lead to soft landings. Collins's exercises are usually aimed at small scenes, or if they deal with big subjects like death, they deal with small conceptualizations of them. Thus, Collins's apparent liberation from the straitjacket of circumstance and destiny imprisoning other poets is only illusory. In the end he is only a cultivator of the garden, not a world-wanderer.

Both *The Apple That Astonished Trees* and *Questions*

About Angels (1991) exemplify Collins's tricky fantasies. In "Questions About Angels," we are asked what else we should know about the lives of angels besides how many "can dance on the head of a pin." Other poems ask: What would it be like to walk across the Atlantic? What feelings might a troubadour have experienced? If the members of a creative writing class were to come back as citizens in a city, what roles would they play?

Collins's characteristic operation—an initial leap, followed by a long train of hypotheses, speculations, wonderments—is poetry candy. Although he appears to have departed from the self's nervous tics, he hasn't replaced this with anything more serious than cute intellectual puzzles. Collins turns out to be a one-trick pony, dealing only with harmless stuff, altering values where the changes don't affect the fundamentals of human life. In the poems from *Picnic, Lighting* (1998) and *Questions About Angels* not chosen for inclusion in *Sailing Alone Around the Room: New and Selected Poems* (2001), the poet slides easily into the role of jester. The seriousness that an Auden might bright to this sort of enterprise is missing.

The dominant tendency in American poetry is a pervasive anti-humanism; the human being, and the real world he interacts with, have been removed from the operation of the will. All one can do, if one were to go by Olds and Levine, is to take things as they come. A first step toward questioning this primitive—almost barbaric—attitude might be to get away from the poet as peddler of soft lies, machinations invented to lull us into an even deeper sleep than we are in. Collins fails to do that in "The History Teacher," from *Questions About Angels*, even as he suggests that he is not interested in sprucing up history to cater to our short attention span.

A claim made for much contemporary American poetry is that it lavishes attention to details: but the details upon inspection often turn out to be shortcuts, appendages to the author's bulging self, code words and synonyms, not objects appreciated for what they are. Collins's elegy, "The

Death of Allegory," from *Questions About Angels*, seems to argue that oblivion—practiced selflessness—lies in the observation of things as they are, not as we wish them to be. Yet his playfulness with the materiality of objects is so jokey that it becomes another form of moralizing, especially as Collins keeps obsessively returning to the art of writing poetry, wondering if an audience listens or if his words sink into the void. This, after all, isn't too far from Graham's suspicion of the ability of words to convey meaning; Collins is not a chic deconstructionist, but the prime quality of the serious artist, his conviction that he can communicate with an audience, is missing. The distance between the poet and material objects remains undiminished, even as Collins does take up these objects for imaginative dissection—but they lead him always back to his closed world.

In *The Art of Drowning* (1995), a transitional volume, Collins frames his claimed literary predecessors—Penn Warren, Moore, Verlaine, Baudelaire, Shakespeare, Cervantes—as correspondences to things in the natural world, often mice, or other animals. A poem like "Reading in a Hammock" makes us think that Collins will never lose his childish perception of the world, that his low-key rebellion is actually a comfortable harbor. Collins's diction may be democratic, his subjects workaday presences, but his method relies on the conviction that there are no fixed parables worth moral consideration, no particularly convincing narrative of modern life demanding allegiance. "The City of Tomorrow," the glossy, mechanized version of it in favor in the thirties, forties, and fifties, is not something "we would come to inhabit / but a place that inhabits us"— in that case, we are at liberty not to inhabit it, should we choose so. The truth is that modern urbanism heavily influences our choices. But Collins considers himself at liberty to imagine a city of the future full of natural objects. This is a curious sort of romanticism not founded in moral idealism, and it is a tendency that is rapidly catching on among American poets.

Collins may not like the epiphany commonly tagged

on to the ends of poems—in "Lines Lost Among Trees" from *Picnic, Lightning,* he decries it as "the little insight at the end / wagging like the short tail / of a perfectly obedient spaniel / sitting by the door"—but he can't resist the temptation himself. "Man in Space" and "Philosophy" even accomplish moralizing through silence. There may not be epiphanies tied to banal domestic concerns, but Collins is no less domesticated and academicized than the tendency he claims to be rebelling against. The mode most available to American poets today is a kind of hardboiled naturalism, a social realism that defies the organic development of the human body and spirit; in response, Collins, in the typical "The End of the World," magnifies the free-floating fear of apocalypse by suggesting that the end of the world, in "smaller endings," occurs all day, all the time. In "Some Final Words" Collins offers his version of the denial of history:

> the past is nothing,
> a nonmemory, a phantom,
> a soundproof closet in which Johann Strauss
> is composing another waltz no one can hear.
>
> It is a fabrication, best forgotten,
> a wellspring of sorrow
> that waters a field of bigger vegetation.
>
> Leave it behind.

Collins is so determined to find the uplifting moment in everyday ephemera that it appears as its own brand of dementia. In "Picnic, Lightning," Collins's clownish persona accepts death's arbitrariness and prematurity, as he tries to lend beauty to slow death, which occurs every moment. Collins's overstudied sense of proportion, in contrast to Graham's uncontrolled movement, has the effect of squeezing out the emotional charge of realizing human tragedy. In "Snow," Collins accepts the shifting alliances of things that come in pairs, makes peace with the arbitrariness of correspondences.

All things are always in instant decline, even in the moment they are occurring. There is no Golden Age for Collins in "Lines Composed Over Three Thousand Miles from Tintern Abbey," and the stabilities of narrative, in "Aristotle," not worth more than a self-deprecating glance. Collins stoops to the attention deficit disorder of American readers, evoking praise for himself in "The Flight of the Reader" in these terms:

> Is it because I do not pester you
> with the invisible gnats of meaning,
> never release the whippets of anxiety from their crates,
> or hold up my monstrous mirror,
> a thing the size of a playing field?

Readers of serious literature, as recent surveys have shown, are rapidly disappearing in America. Collins knows it and accepts it. In his *Nine Horses* (2002), which opens with a prologue called "Night Letter to the Reader," Collins abandons the effort to appeal to the ideal reader, and instead caters shamelessly to the low literacy of the average actual reader. The parables still don't end in flux, and the strength that comes from knowing his weaknesses and those of his readers has been taken to pathological levels in his most recent work, *The Trouble with Poetry And Other Poems* (2005). Any hint of celestial music has been silenced by imaginative tricks following predictable ends. Collins's willful self-deprecation extends to extinguishing beautiful nostalgic moments from his own childhood, or from places visited that we typically associate with excitement.

Whether he is busily rejecting domesticity, as in "To My Patron," or accepting writing as passage through necessary hell, as in "Writing in the Afterlife," it is difficult to give credence to Collins, because he too participates in the fashionable notion of the conditionality of ideas. True, his colleagues prefer morose seriousness, while Collins adopts a showy embrace of playful imagination, but in either case there isn't any full-blown relationship of the poet with his wider society. Collins simply does not have that kind of moral strength, and he has made a fetish and virtue out of it. He wallows in the insubstantiality of the everyday object, but finally there is not much poetry can do with it. In the concluding poem to *Nine Horses*, "Poetry," Collins describes poetry as "a field where the animals / who were forgotten by the Ark / come to graze under the evening clouds," whereas today's naturalists try to "set up / the three-legged easel of realism / or make a reader climb / over the many fences of a plot." Realist poets only offer cranked-up details, but "poetry is no place for that." Poets are "busy doing nothing" is Collins's version of appropriating the sentimentalism American culture accords to the poet's persona.

7.

There are minor geniuses today in the American poetry world, quietly writing away at the lower levels of the economic pyramid, but they don't represent a critical mass. Is the idea of periodic revolution in poetry a passé notion, now that poetry doesn't emanate from outside the academic establishment, but is fully integrated within it? Whoever heard of professors taking to the barricades, to storm down the house of politeness? And what would we do if we had genuinely revolutionary poetry in our midst? Is it possible for individual spirits to transcend the smallness of the zeitgeist, if the distance between the two is too great?

Why can't we have an Olds who takes family relationships as a starting point, not the concluding act to a life spent pondering disabilities? Why not a Graham, philosophically sane, who doesn't show off what she only half-knows? Why not a Glück with a romantic attachment to the natural world, as well as to history and myth, rather than a passion for reducing everything external to her own small dimensions? Why not a Levine who provokes existential crises in readers of all classes, his poetry issuing from the sad and happy realities of work as it exists today? Why not a Collins who reinstalls the individual at center stage as the maker of his own will?

Decorum is the single most missing quality in contemporary American poetry. Taste, decency, proportion, humor, good will, transcendence, balance, respect, all are out the door, whether it applies to the writer relating to his work, his forebears, or his readers. A shrill transparency of questionable motives is everywhere on display. The culture of indecorum overwhelms even the better, calmer voices. The new formalists don't seem able to write anything resonant in this culture of violent rap and ubiquitous trash-talking. They are too keen to remain quietly in the corners, satisfied to be read by posterity. Meanwhile, American surrealism has become gentler and gentler in tone, as if surrealism too must accommodate to the reigning populist mode.

One seeks originality in vain. The poets discussed here each have vast numbers of followers. Graham is by far the leading influence on the particular version of the avant-garde dominating the graduate writing programs, and so it is her style of poetry which dominates the university-affiliated literary quarterlies. Glück's type of perpetual grief, oriented in domestic disturbance, is the default mode for most "feminist" poets, when it is not Olds's defeat by biological fact. Collins has spawned Bob Hicok, and numerous others who perform mental acrobatics without moral purpose; in this poetry, self-deprecation is so steeped in irony it leaves an effect of vicious calculation. Language poets are another predominant faction, with their own publication apparatus; they think of themselves as the most hip of the crowd, scorning anyone who pleads for a sense of reality.

Disturbing new combinations of the existing sloth are proliferating. Albert Goldbarth and David Kirby have acquired a substantial following by now; they write in a sprawl of pseudo-scientific language, as if Graham had decided to adopt concrete instead of abstract words. Poets attempting longer narrative poems in the Olds or Glück victim mode deliver truly exhibitionist tracts, showing no mercy to the decorous reader. The vast resources of the Western poetic tradition remain mostly unused, as the majority of poets show little mastery of technique—as long as they can ironically smile at their vague discomfort, we have poetry! The highs and lows of contemporary global reality, in all their exhilaration and depression, go to waste as subjects fit for poetry. The poetry of exhaustion shows no sign of extinction.

IS THIS THE BEST AMERICAN POETRY?

The poetry avant-garde continues insisting that it doesn't get enough respect from the mainstream scholarly apparatus, when in fact it has been seamlessly absorbed into the academic machine. In the case of language poetry, one reason for its proliferation is that this is the ideal correlate to the poststructuralist theory fashionable in the academy since the early seventies. Poetry which takes language itself as the arena of political action, without any ideological content in the old sense, is perfect fodder for critics claiming to take the bourgeois world by storm. There has been no shortage of critics defending the vacuities of experimental poetry as the cutting edge of human creativity.

Marjorie Perloff, in *Radical Artifice: Writing Poetry in the Age of Media* and other texts, has become a key defender of avant-garde poetry. Her argument is that artifice, in the sense of poetry that is clearly derived from playful language games, in the supposed Wittgensteinian sense, is the only acceptable form of poetic expression in the modern age of media. Our selves are fabricated by the tissue of language games the media daily enact, and to engage with our selves means to play with these languages. Does this "procedural" poetry not become the ultimate legitimation of media manipulation of the consuming body, however? Why can't there be an authentic oppositional self not deriving meaning from forms of discourse and meaning aside from media languages? Perloff's answer is that disruption of the language routines is itself the most revolutionary act; she is rather vague on how the reader's discomfort after defamiliarization leads to any sort of political change.

The *Best American Poetry 2004* anthology reveals how badly things stand. This volume has been edited by Lyn Hejinian, one of the prominent practitioners of language poetry for the last thirty years, and an assiduous manifesto-producer, as is true of other leading exponents of this variety of the avant-garde. A key characteristic of language poetry manifestos is to insist on this school's marginalization from the mainstream. In fact, legions of journals and small presses exist only to promote this and other forms of avant-garde poetry, and their editors look down on poetry that accepts a stable subjectivity as fascistic trash. Yet like any ingrained establishment movement, the avant-gardists can function only by opposing themselves in Manichean terms against the traditionalists who won't admit their existence. Hejinian has argued, in well-known essays like "The Rejection of Closure," that the open form, "paratactical poetry," or what Ron Silliman has called "the new sentence," puts the reader at the forefront of producing meaning, rather than the old-fashioned authoritative poet himself. Bob Perelman has explicated the critical postures of Robert Grenier, Bruce Andrews, and Ron Silliman, each enacting various forms of openness. Yet after what point does production of meaning become purely arbitrary? If sentences follow each other in random order, making any sort of meaning out of them becomes as easy as the writing of such poetry itself. David Lehman, of the New School and the New York University writing programs, founded *The Best American Poetry* anthology in 1988, and has been series editor since its inception. His apologetics reflect the same self-positioning as Hejinian in her role as a leading spokesperson of the mainly West Coast language school articulates: the New York School is also marginalized, ostracized, not supported by the establishment, and in constant danger of annihilation through cooptation and compromise by watered-down schools.

The Best American Poetry series is one of the key legitimating tools of the poetry establishment; once an emerging writer lands on its pages, the path to critical acceptance is much clearer—not to mention the lucrative rewards of security in the teaching world. The series is an accurate barometer of the poetry being published in the majority of the nation's many little magazines, particularly the MFA-affiliated ones, and by extension of the state of poetry itself. The various schools of experimentalism have by now become frigid parodies of their own early intentions, and nothing of lasting aesthetic value is to be found in the detritus. Regardless of the volume editor chosen annually by Lehman, year after year the mediocrity rises assuredly to the top, assaulting the discerning reader with yet another collection of self-indulgent poetry, obscure and vacuous, in tune with the poststructuralist mode still dominating the liberal ramparts of the academy.

The obscurity in the volume under study is self-desired, fully programmed and coordinated, not by any means accidental. This is a far cry from Randall Jarrell defending the obscurity of modernist verse to its earlier befuddled readers, as obscurity has been made the primary fetish, any poetry that seems easy to read being dismissed out of hand as the product of a compromised subjectivity. Experimental writers like Bernadette Mayer, Charles Bernstein, John Taggart, Rachel Blau DuPlessis, Robert Creeley, Clark Coolidge, Michael Palmer, Joan Retallack, Nicole Brossard, Carolyn Forché, Ron Silliman, and Bob Perelman offer prolific defense of the new poetry, again and again making a virtue of obscurity because it supposedly forces the reader to be on his feet, instead of passively consuming poetry. But if meaning is entirely arbitrary, or if it is everywhere, isn't it really nowhere? Language poets believe that the subjective "I" of the lyrical poem as it has come down to us from tradition is a fascistic expression with no relevance to the contemporary world. Rather, it's popular media, advertising, politics, Hollywood, sports, the corporate world, public relations, and propaganda that really define the fabric of our world—the "I" of the perceiving self is inconceivable without the heft of these languages. A new generation of poets like Haryette

Mullen, Brian Kim Stefans, Leonard Schwartz, Jena Osman, Sherry Brennan, Tan Lin, and Juliana Spahr dismiss the old subjective lyric as unrepresentative of the wide dispersal of meaning brought about by the new media. The avant-gardist school in the MFA universe fights it out with the confessionalist school, still presumed to be in dominance by the rebels at the gate. A solid point of agreement amongst the language poetry polemicists is that the confessional workshop poem—the other staple of the MFA system—offers only false epiphanies.

In what they consider the paradigmatic Wittgensteinian move, avant-garde poets want to fragment existing languages, defamiliarizing the nature of individual absorption into the capitalist mode of production. Like their fellow poststructuralist theorists, avant-garde poets think of themselves as political revolutionaries, while shunning the grand narratives of the past leading to one or the other political allegiance. The obscurity of language *is the point* of the exercise itself—once the reader finds himself unable to work his way into an epiphanic position following from some discernible narrative of the progress of the self, he is presumed to experience an aha! moment, as the manipulations of the many operative modes of language become clear to him. This is the final revolutionary gesture for today's American avant-garde poet.

Hejinian, in her introduction to the anthology, argues repeatedly for her choices being engaged with what's been "going down" in recent years, without mentioning the events by name. The seventy-five poems chosen are dynamic and alive for Hejinian because they are products of our present divided culture. One might expect the chosen poets to be urgently compelled to bring about new syntheses of form and content because of the pressures of the moment. But our avant-garde poets don't work that way. They gladly plunder trash culture, borrow from junk moments and movies, steal from art works and great novels, comment on each other's work, remark on how sad and awful their writing lives have lately become, all in the interest of talking about the inability of language to convey meaning, the exhaustion of all known language routines. Their poetry is most often about the impossibility of poetry in this new age of anxiety—not that we ever learn from their poetry what exactly the sources of the anxiety are, and what might be done about it, even at an aesthetic level.

The poems all sound alike, prosy, overeager to make the point that they belong to the present cultural moment, desperately trying to convince us that the owners of the words are cool, hip, well-read folks who sympathize with the underdog and have correct feelings about race, nation, religion, and sex. Rae Armantrout typifies the attitude near the start. The neatest way she can establish her hip credentials is by talking about how words don't mean anything anymore: "the way we joke / by using non-sequiturs, / elliptical remarks / which deliberately suppress context / in advance / of time's rub-out." The "we" refers not only to the poets who use language in this particular way, but also to the authors of popular culture (now including politics), which has lost referentiality to anything but itself. Poem after poem repeats the familiar whine about how poetry is impossible. In "Wolf Ridge," John Ashbery says, "We came here with a mandate of sorts, anyway / a clear conscience… Everybody got lost / playing hide and seek, except you [Ashbery?], / who were alone." In "The Eye Like a Strange Balloon Mounts Toward Infinity," for Mary Jo Bang, "We were going toward nothing / all along," and later: "You were not alone." As in Armantrout's poem, she is distracted by a billboard, which causes her thought to plunge to a stop. Alan Bernheimer begins "20 Questions" with "What can be said of the unspeakable that has not already been unsaid." The poet as lonely communicator, using lapsed tools: we hear much of that, too much.

The prose poems take it to an extreme, but our lonely communicators try to communicate (not that they would admit this motive) by playing with words. Far from insinuating some revolutionary political feeling as they disrupt the established modes of language, they come across as juveniles newly in control of a dictionary, and not knowing what to do with it. Thus, Charles Bernstein, in his string of ninety sentences masquerading as a poem, "Sign Under Test," offers: "When you say baroque you're barking up the wrong tree, which suits me"; "The station wagon stayed stationary at the station"; "Certain that this satin would intoxicate even Satan; the trips of the trade, the lisps of the frayed"; "If progress is a process, what is the purpose of purpose or the allure of allure?"; and most sillily, "Eugene Ormandy wore organdy. George Solti speaks in sotto voce. Toscanini dons a bikini. Neville Marriner slides down the banister. Herbert van Karajan had two carry-ons. Kurt Masur abhors clamor." Punning is carried to such an extent in the new experimental poetry that it becomes unable to strike an effect in the reader; it stabilizes language, contrary to its presumed intention. Jejune wordplay abounds in the rest of the collection as well. From Aaron Fogel's "337,000, December, 2000": "Tinterns and interns glint in the inner kiln / They call the court the melting geodesic / Dome the igloo aglow the banished rabbi…" Fogel admits that "parts [of the poem] were done almost by automatic writing." Fanny Howe, in "Catholic": "Through the door, an odor. A mystifying stiff." After some point, this stops amusing.

In prose poems like Mark Bibbins's "Blasted Fields of Clover Bring Harrowing and Regretful Sighs" the reader is challenged to find any sustainable train of meaning. Of course, the obscurity of meaning is precisely the stated intention of contemporary avant-gardists. This presents a strange conflict between Hejinian and other apologists' desire for a democratic readership of poetry, when in fact the most elitist rejection of ordinary meaning is everywhere in play. The idea is that it's supposed to be very cool to enjoy language at the level of superficial, random but not random, pleasure, to glory in the happy correspondences that seem to reduce all life to an inside joke, to which none, even the poet, however, can truly be party. The absurd genre, prose poem, trying to be two things at once and ending up only with a restless, attention-calling identity disorder, like a teenager who can't decide if she wants to refute her sexual identity or enhance it with cosmetic surgery, ought to be banished to the trash heap of failed literary experiments. Pray, what does this representative sample from Bibbins mean? "Stacked circles (rain down) say green it releases nothing. Bundled wires. Ellsworth Kelly strides from one red iceberg to the next. Each face projects onto antennae forcing a domain expressed as a skewered pod. Transparency behind a desk elusive plunge. A dissection of thought into its components the weight of meat up the wrong street the wrong backdoor. The blazer missed too as the wiry one observed. Someone slipped him diet Orangina and he went ballistic." And on and on ad infinitum. These are unfortuitous phrases assembled together, in an abomination of automatic writing, leading to no greater insight than that the speaker is worried, fragile, in danger of losing his mind, and suspicious of the reader's act of devouring his stray thoughts. And that the vague feeling of terror the poet feels is somehow worthy of shame and pride in equal parts.

T. J. Clark's "Landscape with a Calm (from a painting by Poussin)" wants to stand aside from the bedeviled gnostics parading their wares in the rest of the anthology. A professional art historian, Clark's observations on Poussin's classical landscape remain true to the original, trying to recapture some of the spirit of restrained tranquility without rupturing the connection between the painter's time and ours. But others in the anthology only seem to cannibalize works of art to show that whatever the visual artist intended, the present moment requires a violent imposition of our unphilosophical time upon his symmetries and balances. More representative of contemporary intellectual poetry, which bears closer resemblance to an underappreciated scholar's marginalia and footnotes than the weighty substance of scholarly labors, is Michael Davidson's "Bad Modernism," where his intent, he claims, is to "deal with more problematic or embarrassing aspects of modernism—its will to power, its racism, its imperialism—from within particular 'voices' created within modernism." Poets today declare extreme discomfort with classification and categorization, taxonomies and hierarchies, rankings and degrees, all the alleged blowback of modernity. Yet they never seem to understand that standing outside the tradition of reason and logic puts them in the undesirable posture of backing up with hallucinatory dreams and disconnected thought the rationalized destructiveness of today's political actors. It seems appropriate that a particular target of ire for the new surrealists is Andre Breton himself, and indeed any of the older surrealists who can be linked to a programmatic political ideology, rather than the vague fulminations against "capital" that today's American avant-garde offers. The poets seem to say with one voice that they are skeptical of reason, because it is often utilized for totalitarian purposes. But without the backbone of reason, not even the solace of fighting totalitarianism remains, only resignation to it. Art as handmaiden to primitivism has been overdone, and a retreat to classical proportion wouldn't hurt.

The poetry in this volume is not surrealism with a political agenda—the displacement of the hierarchical and hyper-rational with more egalitarian communicative potential—but surrealism without any agenda, other than pointing out how inappropriate it is to have any agenda. In Linh Dinh's accumulation of sentences, "13," futility is inscribed thus: "In the men's room of a small town bus terminal, you discover your oil portrait in a trash can. You cut the canvas out, then stuff your folded face into your back pocket. Later, you notice with irritation that where your nose should be is a clay pipe, and your mouth is just a hole." We've seen this picture before, in the work of Magritte and Ernst and the great surrealist painters who were responding to the totalitarian horrors of the early part of the twentieth century. But what is Dinh responding to, other than his private exhaustion, his inability to make sense of himself as professional poet in a bureaucratic environment? It is false to claim that poets like Dinh stand with feet grounded in their world. Their narcissism is pure: "You cannot understand the story of a youth who falls in love with his own reflection in a spring. Where you are, water does not reflect. Nothing reflects. One's view of oneself is made up entirely of other people's verbal slanders."

They borrow and they borrow, and then they borrow some more. They steal and plunder and piggyback and maraud. They are merrily living out Stephen Greenblatt and the school of New Historicism's belief that all art is intertextual, that the social circumstances use the author as mouthpiece, without his intentional knowledge. Old hat by now, this declaration of the death of the author, but our poets keep writing as if this were a brand-new discovery. That language can sometimes lead to unforeseen consequences, that it can be manipulated by tyrants, that it seems to have its own logic beyond the purpose of the writer, remain unfathomable truths to them. So they state their disallegiance to reason, and pastiche and parody and merge and collage to their hearts' content. We are supposed to be impressed by their nirvana of knowingness.

Rachel Blau DuPlessis says, of "Draft 55: Quiptych," that her use of the title "draft" suggests that "these poems are open to transformation, part of an ongoing process of construction, self-commentary, textual examination, and reconstruction." Arguing that this process has its parallel in the Hebrew genre called "midrash," she is pleased that her poetic practice seems to be a cross between "essay (in argument), story (in length), and poem (in heft and mechanism)." We have here as pithy a description of the poem in twenty-first century America as we're likely to get: it resembles what used to be poems "in heft and mechanism" only. Obsessed with Gertrude Stein's remark about the dictionary and the country, DuPlessis says in her poem (although this could just as easily have come from her blurb): "I want history told as transition between dream / and waking, my random dream, the cultural dream. / Of course I'm interested in 'the essay as from.'" Not essay as form (since all creative work is always subject to reconsideration, making form an unsteady platform), but essay as *from*, meaning from an uncertain subjectivity, who chooses words from the dictionary "in random curiosity." This project of poetry as "essay as from" makes the poem over into a "multiple fold for carrying" that can yield no "climax," but is only a "grid, a quip, a contour map, from where, / with paper folded so, you see a section of the country." As she says in her essay, "On Drafts: A Memorandum of Understanding": "I work with textual conventions and their critique—punctuation, capitalization, the look on the page, the page space itself, the notion of 'poem'" (143).

The poetry so far is mostly about the poet wondering how she writes poetry. Hejinian may have prefaced this anthology of the best of the best as suggestive of the rupturous tensions that have roiled this country in the first years of the new century, but so far we've read nothing of what's actually going down in the social environment, only what's going down in the poets' burnished souls, which are nonetheless incapable of telling stories. Everywhere the traditional art of telling a story is mocked, its great practitioners fodder for poetry's version of late-night comedians' quips. What else can we call this typical portion of Kari Edwards's "short sorry":

"AD." "and I" and before that "came" esp., et al's and fact that we are . cond col of the crt so nb the gigo dacrim cpiauxbf mfa's and tgif...Lt's who frEq frwy's and fx env's "to grip" "s"t "wit" here to and "it." "Wit." wit or without it, "It was something fit for" a bit-o dinner for four or a chicken pot pie make for "the clan's voodoo hoodoo," after... "of" "which the four Horseless," all taxi drivers stood and looked..at all the "Wonders." "As" if one was the other's assumption which "they opposed" as an anything to do w/ the answer 'all of the above-or none of the rest.' so, the lords, and ladies of the near . east end stopped doing drag_ and became other people's..people. and sat and wondered "of the Comet and" other parts.

It goes on in the same vein. Of "short sorry," Edwards tells us: "as if all points in the positional grind brought their own narrative to describe one's life; 'short sorry' is as if the autobiographical rhizome of everything in one's life is/was caramelized to a non-narrative narrative, neither nor or not, a poem or story or narrative or not-not." Storytelling is defunct in the workshop. Sometime in the sixties we were told that it leads to complacency, which we need to be jerked out of. Well, today's complacency is of a sort that Paul Goodman and Ivan Illich's most loathed targets were incapable of in those high years of the culture wars. Even earlier, in the twenties, we were told that language needed to be disrupted from its ordinary pathways, to open up foreclosed possibilities of meaning. But our contemporary poets disengage from new possibilities, any possibilities. Their motto is Kenward Elmslie's line from "Sibling Rivalry": "Counterfeit samenesses in virtual reality center my innards." At least, they don't misunderestimate themselves. Here again is the central conundrum: to borrow from media as though to subvert media, and yet be limited by the tactics of media. For a critic like Perloff, this is all to the good.

To rupture trained patterns of thought requires commitment to the world outside, such as a Breton might have been able to muster, but our poets can claim no emotional maturity. A religious, sexual, scholarly athleticism repressed into nonexistence is implied in the primal "Nostalgia of the Infinite," Barbara Guest's response to de Chirico's surrealist painting, where the tower of the infinite prompts her to regret the loss of detachment. Yet no greater feeling seems to be evoked by the painting than pervasive detachment, of all diverse entities from their opposites, or even parallels. The infinite is reduced in Guest's aesthetic to a small moment, of touching hands and bourgeois smiles.

A baby is the most narcissistic of creatures; it knows nothing of complexity. So is today's poet. Carla Harryman's excerpts from *Baby* suggest that the baby stands in for today's poet, the pure narcissist:

Baby has discovered a primal land of no name narcissism not because she knows the meaning of narcissism and wants to convert self-adoration into something invisible, filthy, eager, peppery with sweat, and universally altruistic. Not because she even means to love herself. Intention switches places with the disquisition of lungs bursting with her smarts withering future word balloons. Next baby is in hiding. She is going to praise something not worth knowing. No worth. No verdict. Salty lips wrangle with mist. Clotted clouds devour a sky. The goodness of good words of Kantian aesthetics blow amongst flimsy detail for the round world amplifies a life of its own, a life on its own, an anti-aesthetic with revolt a wish list or one and one and one steeped in spikes, fingers, and holes.

At best, the muse is a distant voice, that can't be trusted. The poet, in treating the baby-muse, knows that she is a "lazy and even abusive parent." The poet processes knowledge "in the argument machine" whose driver is "a god with the face of a man and the body of an inkbottle." Automatism, in all its meanings, is implied in this discursive processing of knowledge of the real world. Meanwhile, the poet is made uncomfortable by the reminders of the age of tragedy (which has been replaced by today's virtual heroics), the other poetry that can't quite be made to disappear: "The other baby [the great poetry of the past] ridicules and ridicules. You are left left left there. Left and thrown down and the other baby gets under you and licks the wounds that gird the fine figure you cut when you are hiding the truth: you are just a baby. The other baby who has ridiculed and tormented you and who now soothes you with tongue and a special silence abandons you, goes to work, mercilessly."

The educated American of the twenty-first century represents a departure from his boorish predecessor. He is shamelessly proud of his ignorance. That's what we're seeing in this new poetry. For Jane Hirshfield, describing "Poe: An Assay (I)," "The real work may be done off to the side, while the hands—like a magician's—are always seemingly in plain view. And that, and not the trick's ostensible outcome, is the point." But is it? Isn't the artifice of art supposed to remain hidden? Wandering the grounds of Yaddo, Hirshfield realizes that Poe's stories were written to engage "with the horror of an increasingly darkening time." But Hirshfield has a difficult time being Poe-ish because not only can she not bear to see the horror of our time, but she can ignore it too, by her omissions. Avant-garde poets today make a mockery of systematic acquisition of knowledge. Poe's tales hint at the sorrows that can befall private parties when they refuse to partake of common public knowledge. The two aesthetics couldn't be more different; hence the falsity in our poets appropriating the supposed omissions of the tragic writers of the past, thinking that latching on to their inconclusiveness will somehow elevate the thinness of their own poetry.

The avant-gardists seem unaware that whenever the writer is ostensibly removed from the scene of the action, so is the reader. The reader's presence is inconceivable without the presence of the writer. Lehman, Hejinian et al. may argue all they wish for readerly involvement in the "open" text, but openness without writerly authority is an invitation to the reader's alienation, not democratic participation. A clear contradiction opens up when avant-garde theorists claim, taking Tristan Tzara's line, that the writerly self emerges in the most random constructions. Then is there something more worthwhile about the unconscious writerly self as opposed to the conscious one? The intent in this kind of poetry seems to be to suggest that poetry is always mere annotation, an unnecessary marginal exercise, and that philosophy or science might well be what the poet would have done had she been more attuned to these mental processes. Poetry, our best of the best are convinced deep down, lacks an audience (despite all their polemics that their poetry is reader-centered). Without a specific audience in mind, only trust in serendipity counts, and that's not enough to produce lasting works of art, with an authentic effort to reason things out behind them.

So in "To an Audience," John Koethe says, "If my thoughts were thoughts that you alone had had— / The reality would be the same." Quitting "this theater of dreams" means joining the unpoetic reality, undisciplining the writing self that daily confronts the empty mirror. Koethe says in his commentary that he thinks "of poems... as forms of talking to yourself (though . . . [he's] pleased if readers want to come along for the ride)." The audience is a useless construct for the modern poet; one can play with the notion by conjuring an objecting audience, for that is all an audience really is, and then retreat to the stupor of the self. The age of reason demanded a specific audience for art and science, and it was duly produced; the age of millennial anxiety demands an Arcadia of the musical, distinguished, pastoral self, steeped in attacks on logic. The curious assumption seems to be that a utopian feeling can somehow be produced by ravaging the trash products of the dystopian media.

In Sean Manzano Labrador's "The Dark Continent," Ann Lauterbach's "After Mahler," Nathaniel Mackey's "Sound and Cerement," and Steve McCaffery's "Some Versions of Pastoral," truth is a republic of one, the agora has been smashed to smithereens, and philosophy is as inscrutable as the Dow Jones Index. As usual, modern art is the great inspiration—or rather, it isn't, but only the surroundings in which it comes encased. So Labrador says in his explanation that "When I go to the San Francisco Museum of Modern Art, I don't care about Chagall's cats. I care about the sixty-plus-year-old Pinay and Pinoy Guardsmark guards guarding Chagall's cats." For Labrador, all the agents in the theater of art and ideas are collaborators in their own invisibility. Not far removed from the sentiment of Ann Lauterbach, who used to work in art galleries: "I had been thinking about the failure of hearing/listening in a culture that privileges visual over verbal communication, and how that failure is acted out as deafness to other cultures."

Echoing DuPlessis, McCaffery writes, "The man takes a walk from dictionary to landscape / turns away in Old

French / nothing happens." Why would anything happen, when the preface to the poem begins with this string of indecipherability? "Et in Arcadia ergo points to everywhere. Semantic stability laid smooth across cyclic ridden-epoch pages of remainders. It is the theorized ambrosia and all that's deaf against light among the swamps of somewhere. Chapter gathers grey did I live in it? Fleece of the place changing name to four-footed high-forehead country chin." McCaffery acknowledges interest in Crabbe, Goldsmith and others who wrote what has been called anti-pastoral poetry, pointing out the dark underbelly of rustic idealization, but in his version of the anti-pastoral the self remains impenetrable against the onslaught of history. The poets' immersion techniques remain all-important: "Perhaps Paul Celan is the crematorium built especially / for Language Poets. Perhaps / no things but in ideas."

Our contemporary poet is ever alert, like an Echelon system of the mind, to sweep up whatever cultural debris he might utilize for his next cannibalistic poem. Paul Muldoon wrote "The Last Time I Saw Chris" as an assignment, with "six end-words...chosen at random by six members of the class [at Princeton]," leading to the discovery of a gallery called Crazy Monkey in Amagansett. Alice Notley wrote "State of the Union" from the obvious source. Bob Perelman simply chose to recast his own earlier poem, "Here," in "Here 2," leading to the predictable discovery of the writer's lost moorings. Having woken up to Proust dipping "his Krispy Kreme into Kafka's coffee" and the author's only "parachute...the poetry map" he'd "stitched together" gone, his "writing...ripped open," and having to greet the nightmarish morning, with news of ongoing history in the form of loops that the world is taking without the poet's permission, the poet can only blame language: "because inside a language / everything sounds more or less the same." Convenient scapegoat, indeed, it's all language's fault—"the problem is one of basic structure"—not that of the user of the language. The last hope of "credible inquiry" was surrealism, but that logic petered out in "snores issuing in apnean revolt."

Primal screams of horror at their helplessness issue often and loud from our best American poets. Carl Rakosi's "In the First Circle of Limbo": "Liberate me, / Muse, / from this encirclement / of categories. / Your themes / are plein-air / endless / sad. / Put some wit / and compassion / into this pen!" This liberation doesn't seem anywhere in the offing for poet or reader, because the poet is overwhelmed by the limitlessness of real world material to write about, which paralyzes the storytelling instinct (probably because such writers were never good storytellers to begin with, much as they may choose to blame the structures of language). Carly Sachs's "the story" consists of unreadable broken syntax, whose stanzas read like this: "and was my thought hands body / where that I maybe saying white / hearing was and hallway be who / why and this wasn't did sure / were was oh angel in / need so my then saying making / that's when must there I in / United States do have he." Jennifer Scappettone constructs in "III" three columns of parallel doggerel; whenever there's parallelism in our poets' universe, we know we'll be looking for clues to meaning in vain.

In this matrix, where poets are implicated beyond their ability to wiggle free, we might include Ron Silliman, who begins "Compliance Engineering" with "Our true form is the blurb," later suggesting that "Language / poetry…[is] understood / as a problem of nostalgia." And we might include Bruce Smith's "Song of the Ransom of the Dark," for the speaker of which *"Poetry had failed me / …slowly poetry had failed me / …first as grace, then as skin, then / …as woman as terminal being…"* Also firmly entrenched in this matrix is Edwin Torres, who proposes in "The Theorist Has No Samba!" a "New Instantism," which would be "a language of tangent = / tanguage > ambient funguage > there is a modern path / > invented through accidental spontaneity + of mock / language sport = fractured intelligentsillys > there / are sage athleticists + important children farmed out / to the furthest reaches of nowness > …> …>" Torres's proposed aesthetic will pluck "spontaneousness out / of the ether" and deliver it "into the throes of the wild / screaming bastard maggot that IS poetry!" The poet will "refuse to comply by the aged / fumblings of mere MEANING and instead descend into / mere HEARING." We can be grateful that "The Theorist Has No Samba!" is what Torres claims to be an "unchanged" email exchange. We may not understand it, but we're glad that he was able to let off steam about his "Futurist bafflement of possible theory." The poetry in this volume is often indistinguishable from the poets' blurbs at the end, from where the last statement comes, and the reader of this essay might be occasionally confused whether a quotation is from the poem or its blurb. If this is the case, Silliman's point stands.

So much desire to be allowed to listen, in a culture so dedicated to producing noise! What is going on? If everyone makes noise, including New Instantaneous Poets, how can anyone listen? The poets all think that they're in love with "precise language," as Paul Violi does in "Appeal to the Grammarians" (another euphemism for today's poets?), but they're anything but. David Wagoner, in "Trying to Make Music," is closer to the state of things today, where poets bend and crumble under the burden of making music and meaning, unable to grasp their "native tongue," with the result that there is a pervasive *"Lock-down and Body Search! Silence and Lights Out!"* About the only poet with a light touch in the anthology is James Tate in "Bounden Duty" where he acts out the President's instruction to "Just act / like nothing's going on. Act normal." This obedience, however, does not take place in a recognizable world, but only in the poet's imaginary relations with his fellow citizens.

We've seen, over and over, the refusal to make meaning of the material of the world, even as this desire is stated to be the summum bonum of the poet's existence. We've heard poets shouting at the tops of their unrhythmic, cacophonous voices that they desire to be relevant, to mean something to the culture, to figure out some way of making language the useful tool it was in prehistoric times (by which they mean something like four decades ago). We've seen them posture, and preen, and prance, and dance around in all states of dishabiliment and undress. We've seen them argue with political phantoms, philosophical quandaries, and scientific indeterminacies, which they're eager to reproduce in more prolix forms than ordinary human endurance can stand (particularly when they turn their hand to the late, great prose poem). What we haven't seen in this anthology is the poet pursuing the art of poetry as something other than churning validation of his profession qua profession. Strong poetry demands a strong audience, which these poets aren't willing to grant.

INDIA ABROAD:
HOW NOT TO ALIENATE THE WESTERN READER
WHEN WRITING ABOUT THE INDIAN DIASPORA

BRICK LANE BY MONICA ALI. SCRIBNER, 2003.

THE NAMESAKE BY JHUMPA LAHIRI. HOUGHTON MIFFLIN,
2003.

As highly praised as Monica Ali and Jhumpa Lahiri's novels have been, they both present unrealistic, distorted, and one-dimensional accounts of the South Asian immigrant experience in Britain and America respectively. Ali settles for fixating on a working-class family, sheltered in an immigrant ghetto in London, that never engages dynamically with the rest of British society. Lahiri is unable to bring into the picture anyone other than comfortably middle-class professionals, steadily building their version of the American dream in the Northeast, with no experience of prejudice or injustice.

To read Ali is to be immersed in a tiring exposition of South Asian culture that passively backs off when faced with Western modernity; the immigrant culture's very resources of interpretation and accommodation seem borrowed from media schlock and kitsch, its cumulative historical legacy summable in secondary personal tics that seem no more valuable than the latest Western diet or fashion fad. And Lahiri would make you think that the process of assimilation for the Indian immigrant among prosperous American cadres is as smooth, frictionless, and banal as the rapidly readable, omnipotently calm, programmed and programmable quality of her writing itself; again, the surface of Indian culture comes off as having been vanquished by the merest touch, the most unassuming gesture, of the alien host. Neither writer dares say the least unfashionable thing among liberal circles, giving the lie to realism even as their writing is accoutered in realism's outward trappings.

To begin negatively, a short list of what Ali and Lahiri (both of Bengali heritage, both having grown up in the West) *don't* talk about, shocks us into a recognition of how much is missing. Ali's book has no substantial British character at all; apart from the occasional mishapful encounter Nazneen, the heroine, might have with a pedestrian or authority figure, it is as though the Indian immigrant lives in an impenetrable shell, immune to give-and-take between herself and the host country, except in the most mundane of financial transactions. So in what sense can *Brick Lane* be an exposition of two cultures in intermediation with each other if one culture is entirely missing?

Let us then praise the book, if we must, for being a claustrophobia-inducing, limitlessly static step into a familiar corner of the river, its repetition a guarantee of a certain kind of intellectual death for characters and readers alike, but not as a contribution to understanding what happens when two cultures collide. Indeed, when Nazneen and her family, late in their immigrant career, witness on television the hijacked planes penetrating the World Trade Center, this event quickly becomes assimilated into the existing surreal private family drama of the husband Chanu wanting to return to Bangladesh after thirty-plus years in Britain, with Nazneen and their two pubescent daughters, Shahana and Bibi, to tag along.

The parallel to this is Ali's depiction of Bangladesh, which seems impervious to dynamic change brought on by Western influence. If the imaginative life of the Indian working-class in Britain is bound by the grandiose rhetoric of Chanu, the impoverished auto-didact who goes about collecting certificates and diplomas as if they were so many talismans, the extent of intellectual understanding of the Bangladeshi working-class, represented by Nazneen's younger but more beautiful sister Hasina, is contained in the broken English (an evocation of the English spoken in Britain by the most illiterate of subcontinental immigrants) in which Hasina writes her letters to Nazneen over twenty years. These letters are an unbroken chain of misery—rape and domestic violence, sexual and emotional abuse, exploitative work conditions (in where else but the legendary garment industry?), starvation and illness, wife burning and dowry blackmail—in short, the full catalog of suffering in a black hole of the imagination, the very "basketcase" Chanu understands as the West's only perception of Bangladesh.

There is no cultural, political, or economic progress of any kind in Ali's Bangladesh. The country might as well be where it was more than thirty years ago, at the time of its independence from Pakistan, one small mishap from mass disaster. Even if on some levels this reflects reality, what about the pockets (some might say vast reservoirs) of development toward a more humane, liberal, tolerant society, not as susceptible to the broken clichés of Allah and Muhammad, and Qur'an and mullahs, that Ali insists is the totality of working-class Bangladesh? As with the late-night documentaries of starving African kids with distended bellies that after a while numb and disgust for their shameless exploitation of human sentiment, Hasina's letters also provoke anger at Ali's savvy manipulation of cheap Western guilt.

And what does Lahiri exclude from her story of the Indian immigrant experience? Everything that doesn't fit into the private saga of professional and family success narrowly defined—that is to say, race, class, and gender, not to mention nation, religion, and civilization broadly understood to include existential dilemmas that rip apart an individual's sense of stability and wholeness.

If you're an Ivy League-educated Indian of upper-middle-class origins, a Brahmin preferably, and your whole life has been propelled by the faithfully lived out premises of hard work, austere habits, and rigorous study, and you now bear the fruits of this effort with a nice home in the New York suburbs, a pretty and tasteful Indian or white wife, and kids in private school, then you'll be right at home in Lahiri's world. But if you're a South Asian cab driver in New York, harassed by the police, shacking up with ten other immigrants to save money to send home, then Lahiri's readers wouldn't know about your existence (but then again, neither would Ali's, in any meaningful sense of the word).

Journalist S. Mitra Kalita, in *Suburban Sahibs: Three Immigrant Families and Their Passage from India to America* (2003), has described immigrant experience at different class levels. Here is the ambiguity of response toward cultural origins and challenges, the daily, incremental overcoming of roadblocks and resistance, in ingenious and socially informed maneuvers, that is missing from Lahiri's fiction. The real fun in fiction happens when classes interact. But when Americans accommodatingly cater to your ethnicity, painlessly shortening your name from Moushumi to Mo, and when your greatest source of emotional turbulence over your thirty-two years of life is deciding between your "pet name" of Gogol and your "good name" of Nikhil, wondering which will let you assimilate better with your classmates and lovers and fellow workers, you're in fictional melting pot land which, if it ever really existed, surely went out the door in the last few years of nationalist turmoil.

In a sense, Lahiri resists risk-taking to an uncanny extent, succeeding so well in limning the daily life of the elite crust of the Indian diaspora in America, in all their magnificent isolation from the more repellant chores of the working-class to merely subsist and survive, that her fiction takes on the aura of denial and fantasy. This is reflected in the easygoing fluidity of her prose, which moves from building block to building block of sociological characterization, unstoppable in its momentum by any risky philosophical adventurism that might question the premises of the fiction (by contrast, Ali's prose is unrestrained, repetitive, in great need of editing and shortening, probably meant to mirror the helter-skelter survivalism of a working-class family, but no less arrogant than Lahiri's language in its presumption of the writer's ability to encompass all that is worth telling).

It is no accident that Sonia, Gogol's younger sister, is only sketched out by Lahiri in the barest essentials, only there as filler, or occasional complement to Gogol's small identity conundrums; for to deal with Sonia in a realistic fashion would have required Lahiri to admit the greater difficulty of female Indian assimilation in American society, where certain brutal facts of gender discrimination in Indian culture cannot but be daringly confronted to emerge healthy on the other side. Instead, we only get Gogol's mother Ashima (a bourgeois version of Ali's lower-class Nazneen), ever-grateful to her husband for providing her a secure existence as a professor's wife in the Boston suburbs, and worshipful of him in eternity after his premature death of a heart attack in early middle-age.

One might argue that Moushumi, the Bengali girl who lived in England until thirteen before moving to America, and who goes through a rebellious phase by abandoning herself to sexual rapture in Paris in her twenties, before settling down to a Ph.D. in French literature at NYU and nailing Nikhil-Gogol as a husband according to both their mothers' expectations, represents a complex vision of piece-by-piece female integration into a more liberal definition of self and attitude. But Moushumi doesn't evolve from something into something else; she is who she is from the beginning, a gentle slap to the face of Indian complacency, even cultural arrogance, without in any way threatening the foundations of that self-satisfaction. She seamlessly integrates with Manhattan's artistic and intellectual arrivistes, taking her dutiful place as a slightly more exotic specimen from another world not in need of being understood or even explained. So, ultimately, Lahiri elides the whole issue of what it is to be a woman facing resistance to self-expression, since expression and the success following from it come so easily to her second-generation immigrants.

Consider these two brief passages from Ali and Lahiri as indication of the limited arena of their imaginations:

Gogol has been to the house before, a bit too frequently in his opinion. Astrid is a friend of Moushumi's from Brown. The first time he'd met Donald and Astrid had been at his wedding. At least that's what Moushumi says; he doesn't remember them. They were living in Rome the first year that Gogol and Moushumi were together, on a Guggenheim that Astrid had gotten. But they've since moved back to New York, where Astrid has begun teaching film theory at the New School.

And on the next page, continuing the description of Moushumi's friends as seen by Gogol:

He recognizes a few familiar faces tonight: Edith and Colin, who teach sociology at Princeton and Yale, respectively, and Louise and Blake, both Ph.D. candidates, like Moushumi, at NYU. Oliver is an editor at an art magazine; his wife, Sally, works as a pastry chef. The rest are painter friends of Donald's, poets, documentary filmmakers. They are all married. Even now, a fact as ordinary, as obvious, as this astonishes him. All married! But this is life now, the weekend sometimes more tiring than the workweek, an endless stream of dinner parties, cocktail parties, occasional after-eleven parties with dancing and drugs to remind them that they are still young, followed by Sunday brunches full of unlimited Bloody Marys and over-priced eggs.

And from Ali, this passage, which is exactly the same as any other in the constant stream of letters from Hasina:

Shahnaz is only bit older one two year than me and she gone very far along in school. Most day she talking about match. Parents have pick seven eight boys but Shahnaz refuse all. And she disagree to dowry. "Why should we give dowry? I am not a burden. I make money. I am the dowry." We have grow close. She show me how she apply her cosmetics and she teach how to make eyebrows less ugly by pull out the hairs. She try some rouge on my cheek but wipe it off. My coloring is not good for rouge. It make look cheap.

Oldest of us is Renu a widow. She was marry at fifteen to old man who die within three month. She go back to father short time he throw out. All the life she has to work but she the one who do not wish for this. Despite she have only two teeth she eat anything at all. Hard gums she say. "I can break bricks on these gums." Every lunch hour she is chew betel nut. It ban but Renu have no care about it. I asking if she marry again. "Who will marry these bones?" She wave her arms but no bones showing is bracelets from wrists to elbow. "My life! My life! Over at fifteen. Might as well be Hindus. His grave was big enough for two. Why did I not jump in?" She spit too as well never mind spitting is ban. She say there is no one to protect me. I must go here and there always alone. Anyone say anything they like because I am woman alone. I put here on earth to suffer. I am waiting and suffering. This is all.

It doesn't seem accidental that the plot of either novel can be summarized so easily and quickly. Ali's Nazneen is a villager plucked for an arranged marriage by Chanu, who went to Dhaka University and has been getting by in London on a council job. Fat Chanu is a flat character whose task it is for almost four hundred tedious pages to expound on the superiorities of the Bengali nation and his adopted nation's lack of appreciation for his talents. Nazneen, speaking no English (a virtue she more or less retains until the end of the book, after twenty years in England), is a complete stranger to British ways, disoriented and overwhelmed by an early short trip to the business district near the Tower Hamlets apartments, their immigrant ghetto. There is no emotional appeal to the novel after Nazneen's young son Raqib dies. One gets the distinct impression that all that Ali had to say about immigrant working-class life in Britain was already said at that point, and that the ensuing plot manipulations come about only as the result of a contractual compulsion to finish the novel.

The remaining two-thirds of *Brick Lane* is therefore populated with more stock characters, serving to fill out the picture of the "immigrant tragedy" (as Chanu would have it), to meet the reader's expectation. There is the money-lending Mrs. Islam to whom, inexplicably, the apparently practical Chanu and Nazneen seem to pay thousands upon thousands of pounds to pay back a loan for a mere sewing machine and computer. There is Nazneen's sordid affair with Karim, a middleman who supplies Nazneen with clothes to sew and fix; this affair dissolves in its own sweet way, never coming to Chanu's attention, leaving him undisturbed to bloviate on the virtues of Bengali language and culture. And following Zadie Smith's celebrated excursion into these realms, there is Nazneen's brief flirtation with the delusional local Islamic fundamentalist community, of which Karim is de facto leader, constituted to fight the skinheads, and presented by Ali with all the conviction of an academic or journalist assigned to the job, with inward disgust at her own lack of strength to resist such a task.

Not a single character in *Brick Lane* evolves. Dr. Azad, his wife, Nazneen's alternately frivolous and serious friend Razia, the daughters, the money-lender, Karim and his gang, all remain absolutely unchanged from beginning to end. It is as if once Ali puts a character to pen, she no longer has the capacity to do anything more with it except describe made-up events, usually of calculated and small magnitude, that leave the character fundamentally unmoved. Nazneen, it might be argued, evolves into greater self-awareness and independence, but the change, after hundreds of pages of tedious suffering, is inauspicious and suspicious at best.

All conflicts dissolve into nothingness by the sheer movement of events, rather than coming to a head. Raqib dies, preserving Chanu's unchallenged status as man of the house. Mrs. Islam leaves Nazneen alone after she refuses to pay anymore. Karim's gang of fundamentalists and the opposing skinheads enact a comical apocalyptic scene, complete with arson and looting, but Nazneen moves through this scene unscathed. In the end, Karim simply disappears (where? To an al-Qaeda training camp? One suspects, nothing so dangerous crossed Ali's mind), solving the problem of the affair for Nazneen. Chanu does return to Bangladesh, but he is unhappy without Nazneen and his daughters, and we suspect a happy resolution not too far off in the future. Just as there is no economic mobility for the hard-working migrant in this (floundering? Progressing?) Britain, there is no point at which the real conflicts between civilizations become exposed to the surface.

For Lahiri too, her peculiar stylistic consistency excludes drama resulting from characters really crossing over from one mode of being into another. Plot is a mere encumbrance secondary to the momentum of language rocking the reader into hypnotic appreciation of the ease and validity of random but destined events. Ashima, a middle-class nineteen-year-old college student in Calcutta, is chosen for marriage by Ashoke, a doctoral candidate in engineering at MIT. Unlike Nazneen, she does speak English, but her sense of alienation, her absolute commitment to the verities of Bengali Hindu culture, echoes Nazneen's own adherence to lower-class Muslim folk culture (there is no flirtation in Lahiri's book with the attractions of Hindu fundamentalism for the alienated among the diaspora, despite militant Hindu fundamentalism having taken over the Indian state—probably because this is not at present of concern to the Western consciousness, unlike Islamic fundamentalism). In the Boston suburbs, as Ashoke moves up the professorial ladder, Ashima also gives birth six years later to Sonia, the girl who remains an appendage to Gogol's story.

And Gogol's story is mostly about how minor identity issues play out around the choice of names. His father Ashoke decides to name him Gogol on the spur of the moment for the purpose of getting a birth certificate from a Boston hospital, while they await the arrival of the "good name" from Gogol's grandmother in Calcutta. The choice of Gogol is because when Ashoke was in a train wreck in India at twenty-two, he was in the middle of reading Gogol's stories. It was on that train journey that Ashoke had met Ghosh, a businessman regretful of returning to India because of his wife's preference. Ghosh invites Ashoke to see the world before he loses his freedom. This superficial incident, this slight connection to Ghosh, rather than any striving for intellectual or economic freedom, is what motivates Ashoke to emigrate to America. The whole plot, in fact, is made up of such insubstantialities, rather than a search for the deep springs of human motivation. Exile is for dummies; emigration leads to the securities of citizenship.

On his first day of kindergarten, Gogol sticks to Gogol while his father wants him to assume the good name of Nikhil. On his eighteenth birthday, just before leaving for Yale, Gogol has his name officially changed to Nikhil, which is the name he retains throughout his college and professional life. The one thread tying the book is reflections on the meaning of the choice of name for Gogol's destiny, but these meditations are laborious and tenuous in the extreme. Beyond the guess that Gogol represents lack of seriousness and Nikhil full maturity into adulthood, one fails to understand why the dilemma of the name requires such a to-do. The explanation for this obsession of Lahiri might be that rather than dealing with substantial issues of identity conflict, such as what Gogol-Nikhil might face were he to be confronted with barriers in the way of economic mobility, or challenges in the way of love because of class or racial or religious differences, she hangs her whole weight of novelistic gravity on a trivia of identity.

Indeed, identity, in the prosperous American milieu of the last decades of the twentieth century, seems nothing but trivially negotiable in Lahiri's imagination. Ashoke and Ashima resolutely perform their rituals and devotions in the company of Bengali Hindu friends in their suburban home at 67 Pemberton Road. Gogol easily loses his virginity to a white college girl at sixteen by claiming to be a freshman at Amherst by name of Nikhil, finding in this lie a boost of confidence.

After Yale, as an apprentice architect in Manhattan, Nikhil-Gogol is more or less adopted by the upper-class Maxine and her artistically inclined parents, their elite preferences in food and other lifestyle issues contrasting favorably with Gogol's parents' middle-class stringency.

When Gogol's father dies abruptly, Gogol finds it difficult to include Maxine in his grief, and this is the merest shred of motivation whereby their relationship ends. There needs to be no confrontation between Gogol and Maxine on what sets Gogol apart as an Indian immigrant; this would take us into the brutal territory of fundamental incomprehension, of which Lahiri wants no part. Soon after Maxine, Gogol is drawn to the Bengali girl Moushumi, and marries her, presumably to live up to the Nikhil part of his name. But when Moushumi becomes bored with Gogol's practicality and has an affair with an unemployed Russian academic, Lahiri spares us even the scene of confrontation between the estranged couple. At the end, Ashima, used to being a widow, decides to spend six months out of the year in India, and six months in America—an eminently reasonable solution to the immigrant dilemma. Gogol, packing up his things for the last time at their home at 67 Pemberton Road, expresses just about the same degree of emotion, which is to say not much, as when he traveled to Ohio to identify his father's body at the morgue.

What, then, are we left with as Ali and Lahiri's sum of contributions to understanding the nature of adjustment involved in the Indian immigrant's transition to the West? And transition here might be the best word, rather than more existentially freighted terms. Ali presents hard-working South Asians, both in Britain and in Bangladesh, as no more than economic units, able to appreciate their value as such—no more and no less. This attitude defines Hasina as much as Chanu, the money-lending Mrs. Islam and the entrepreneurial Razia, and finally Nazneen and her two daughters. The future of the daughters, even if they cross over into the middle-class, or at least acquire some of its scaffolding, is destined to follow the script whereby they are primarily economic actors.

In Britain's more racially divisive milieu, Ali has looked away from the challenge of full-blown realism by engaging with her characters as singularly driven money-makers.

As for Lahiri, her vision of America as land of opportunity for the upwardly mobile professional, arriving here with impeccable English and Franklinian rectitude, seems less and less relevant to the progressively declining social origins of Indian immigrants arriving on these shores since the floodgates were first opened in 1965. Lahiri's enactments of identity struggles, if that is what they are, occur strictly within the family, within different expressions of Indian culture itself, differentiated by slightly greater or lesser degrees of emphasis on separation from mainstream culture, but ultimately only segregated by trivia. The constant preoccupation with food as signifier of identity—this is true not only of Ali and Lahiri's books, but the whole genre of Asian immigrant writing as well—is a pretense to realism. If only identity were that simple; if only the choice of names so deterministic.

Imagine if Ali had chosen to have Nazneen have an affair with a British man, of any class. Imagine if Nazneen's daughters had stopped loving either of the parents, the insufferably voluble Chanu and the self-sacrificing martyr Nazneen, rather than taking slight issue with their cultural obsessions, but steadily loving them. Imagine if Chanu had fallen into poverty after giving up his council job for not being promoted (how does the family survive? Britain's generous welfare provisions must be the answer), his perpetually sanguine if complaining character suffering an erosion into something truly threatening. Imagine if Karim and his gang of fundamentalists, instead of being the vaguely perceived clowns they are, had terrified the reader with their determination and logic.

And imagine if Lahiri had killed off Ashoke before he had succeeded in providing handsomely for his family, while Gogol was still a child, Ashima still a newcomer. Imagine if Gogol and Ashoke ever had a confrontation (not to mention Sonia with either of her parents) on any of a number of issues that constitute ineradicable cultural divides, rather than the mere shred of a conflict over the choice of names. Imagine if there were a single financially insecure character in *The Namesake*. Imagine if Moushumi's parents weren't so understanding about her sexual freedom, if she wasn't a specter conjured to make a vague point about the heavy emotional price of American individualism. Imagine if there were a dark underside to the Hindu rituals Gogol and his band of second-generation immigrants willingly undergo, to please their parents. Gogol or Nikhil, in the end he is no more than a plastic surrogate for the kind of easy mobility and transparent back-and-forth that certain among the diaspora elite are able to manage, but increasingly less so, and almost never with the panache and lack of resistance from other threatened elites Lahiri suggests.

Neither of these novels is true to the reality of the multiplicity of experience among the Indian diaspora in Britain or America. While the authors might argue that their job was only to present a particular slice of such life, restricted to one class or category of immigrant, one gets the inescapable sense that hard choices have been shunned, and a kind of patronizing fiction, where the author presumes that nothing unspeakable remains outside the enclosure of storytelling, has been unfairly promoted as somehow authentic and boundless.

WHITE AMERICAN MALE PLAYING IT SAFE:
THE GROWING PHENOMENON OF THE "KIRBY POET"

**THE HOUSE ON BOULEVARD STREET BY DAVID KIRBY.
LOUISIANA STATE UNIVERSITY PRESS, 2007.**

The Kirby Poet exists only in the present moment. While empire is experiencing its last death blows, he presumes a millennium of untortured imperialism ahead. As art in America plumbs to its lowest depths, he proclaims its widespread dissemination, democratic acceptance, and inherent stability. Because there isn't a revolutionary history for him to contend with, not to mention egalitarian will, he can preach from his academic pulpit, taking the whole world for his audience. He cannot visualize an America different from today's ugly highways, fast-food drive-throughs, private healthcare, and convoluted election primaries, so he doesn't bother. When there is no past or future fundamentally different from the present, an imagination deluded by its chanciest gestures emerges to claim timeless logic. This breed of poet writes for an audience presumably identical to him (or to Billy Collins or Albert Goldbarth, his close cousins). All the exuberant froth of Western civilization— Bacon, Dante, Cervantes, Rembrandt, Voltaire, Sterne, Beethoven, and Darwin—has been brushed off, so that only the characteristic equanimity and superhuman confidence about his own privileged status remain.

Kirby's speech is utterly genial, pleasant, avuncular, demotic, approachable, wholesome, friendly. This is the source of the threat to the art of poetry, his perpetual affability, which wouldn't be the case if he were brooding, melancholy, threatening, elitist, prophetic, Olympian, unlovable, boorish, recondite, detached. Kirby's poetry is the epitome of apparently artless, spontaneous, immature, wishful language, which presents itself to us as though in the process of being thought out. A finished product can only be articulated with great pain in politics or culture, since to do so is to presume superiority over the unformed masses, who have neither time nor inclination to devote single-minded effort to such matters. The artlessness comes packaged in an innocuous smile, even as it sacrifices every value of humane civilization. New media work in one-sided fashion: the barrage of jagged cuts, impromptu stabs at thoughts and notions, comes at us in a unidirectional stream; we do not have input, only the apparent ability to do so, yet we feel joyful as would-be participants. The new media never speak down to us; to do so would be to violate the code of friendliness.

These premises of communication in a communicationless society apply to Kirby's poetry. He has mastered the art of speaking with such rapidity—hence the total absence of any stumbling blocks in diction or rhythm—that the discourse becomes entirely one-way. We are not given any time to think about what Kirby is actually saying. Feeling deluged by the flood of words, we are content to keep our heads above water. The flow of words cannot pause to take stock of its own movement, or it would be compromised. Speed is of the essence, in this madcap accumulation of convenient symbols and signs, whose vitality has never been less real than now. Even as middle-class America vanishes, its status codes must be given timeless validity. Kirby has called his poems "memory poems," but these aren't memories so much as ideas about the substance of memories: while they have all the specificity of memories, we always doubt whether the incidents happened. This doubt keeps the whole enterprise an airy, floating, ephemeral one: transcendence is being denied even as its forms are being inscribed.

The House on Boulevard Street is divided into three parts: jejune college hijinks, misadventures of an American in

Europe, and spending time with his wife—or as Kirby calls them in his Preface to the book, "the heated restlessness of youth, the mixed blessings of self-imposed exile, and the settled pleasures of home." Kirby gloats: "For the life of me, I can't recall a single minute in hell and have passed many a day that comes close to being paradisal." Remarking on the uniform appearance of the poems, Kirby says: "All of the poems are marked by fixed-length stanzas and a sawtooth margin, effects intended to help with the sense of what one critic [Peter Klappert, in a 2000 *Southern Review* essay, "The Invention of the Kirby Poem"] calls in these poems 'the whole motion of the speaker's psyche: like a pendulum, it swings in one direction with an enthusiasm or passion, momentarily comes to a point of rest, and then swings back the other way.'" In fact, Kirby never strays far from his point of origin, a Midwestern, middle-America death-in-life, which revels in lack of elegance and beauty as credential elements of American selfhood.

In the title poem, his marriage has collapsed, but we don't know why: does it matter, when he always has the opportunity to play the field, and move on from the debacle to a more wholesome constitution? We will never find out what was incompatible with the first wife, or what is so compatible about the current one (Barbary Hamby, fellow poet and teacher at the same university). He has no hesitation giving out family members' or lovers' real names and details; this is not confessionalism, this is only personal anecdote. We are invited to get familiar, but we can never know the first thing about the mind and soul of Kirby. He is in the process of laughing off his failures as a man, and we're meant to applaud him for his bravado. The white American man must never appear enamored of masculine virtues; this is the only way to maintain empire these days. He must present himself as the most benign of creatures. His first marriage collapses, and what does Kirby do? Not indulge in fantasies of revenge, not go on a fucking spree with younger women, not set himself up as heroic and somehow undeserving of the treatment, as any normal man would, but absurdly quote from Mandeville and digress to when he fantasized about being a beefcake male as a teenager. He speaks of "marriage, betrayal, self-betrayal" (this is pretty much the substance of the first marriage we will get to hear from Kirby), none of which was anything like "the golden world of *As You Like It* / where gentlefolk fleet time carelessly!" Literature is useless because it deals in extremes of emotion. Elias Canetti is not a character in literature, he is a fellow poet, but he is saturated enough by Old Europe's narcissistic grotesqueries that he is worthless as a model for imitation. As are Shakespeare's gentle comedies, whose pastoral beatitudes are not for the worldly poet. In his brief odyssey of melancholy, Kirby hasn't broken a sweat—he simply skips from Elias Canetti the sadist to Elvis Costello the crooner to Bolívar the liberator to Tsvetaeva the dissident and arrives at "the little fox" as the culmination of his intimate cycle. From here on out, nothing but marital bliss is possible (as indeed Kirby will demonstrate in the next two sections of the book). This rapture is the sum of Kirby's poetry. The Kirby Poet isn't dominating through any intellectual pyrotechnics: he simply presents conquest by his dull mind as a fait accompli. There is no defense being mounted here of any philosophy of life. Something orders of magnitude more descriptive than bourgeois complacency is indicated.

The white American male's tonic self-referentiality is his liberal card these days instead of any ideological commitment: as long as he can speak of himself as sole inhabitant of a world created each day ex nihilo for him, he is secure in feeling above the fray of nasty politics. Kirby's poem "I Think Stan Done It" was written in response to the mistitling of his earlier poem "I Think Satan Done It" by the editors of the *Poetry Daily* website who wished to reproduce it. "I Think Satan Done It," a paean to a formative rock-and-roller—"Jerry Lee Lewis is the undead, only cooler"—brandishes Kirby's hip credentials; his poetry is speckled throughout with references to Little Richard, Johnny Cash, Elvis Presley, and other liberators of the bonded, fifties white man. We don't understand what Lewis's music meant for its times, only that it kicked him into a frenzy of self-appreciation; the music is outside time and history, it borrows from no other form, and its compulsion not to transcend its limitations is what is coolest about it. In "I Think Satan Done It" (the title refers to the singer's exclamation "when an amp goes out") Kirby describes a concert at Florida State University, the closest he is likely to get to Bacchanal frenzy in his lifetime. When a woman whom he asks where she got her "Killer T-shirt" from tries to peel it off for him, he is afraid "Dean Don Foss" of the university will gleefully pounce on this "misstep."

Kirby yearns to procure a rebellious T-shirt for his wife; marital bliss is the one constant for Kirby, his youthful indiscretions being but necessary preparation to appreciate the omnipresent Barbara. This is not love as we have known it from any romantic literary form; it is not passion or consummation, delirium or engrossment; the wife is like a controlled aspect of the self: ubiquitous and consistently reflective, she is the gloss on the margin, the content of the page, the page number, the spine of the book, the dust jacket, the blurb, the preface, the acknowledgment, if never the heroine of the tome. He must keep mentioning her to remind himself of his own solidity. The Kirby Poet has recently made a fascinating construct out of single-minded monogamy, which apparently outlasts death itself: once the spouse is dead (preferably prematurely, of cancer) the project to memorialize her can begin in earnest (the prematurely dead poetess ideally gives her husband a head-start on the project, by writing of her own impending death in her last months), although of course passion must not rear its head even at this late stage. If she is alive, as Barbara is, she is the one woman who suffices for all of his needs, even his specifically masculine ones. She is not so much soulmate as solipsist's maid.

The substance of "I Think Satan Done It" is Kirby's attempt to convince "an editor at a big-city northern newspaper" to do a piece on Jerry Lee Lewis. Thus he proves with "factual / irrefutability *and* rhetorical power" the ability of Lewis to fire up melancholy Old Europe healers (French hospital workers). His earnestness toward the cultural artifacts middle America claims with unthinking pride is as sincere as his love for his wife. As his political contentment is his gift to the world (both old and emerging democracies), so is his collective cultural production a blessing to the troubled men and women of other countries who have not been so lucky as he has been. Rock and roll has its provenance in the agonies of black music in its various forms, and if it has an upbeat tempo, it is really the close counterpart of a pervasive melancholy; its bravado is closely related to pessimism. But Kirby is interested only in the finished product, not where it came from, or if it might have more ambiguous meanings than he can synthesize for an "800 words" piece for a newspaper.

Kirby goes on to equate Jerry Lee Lewis with Shakespeare. Nothing his rock idol does is throwaway, lacking material for reflection. At the end of the poem Kirby must reconcile with Lewis's promiscuity—"Mr. Lewis has married six times"—and the failure in general of rock singers to be role models to the younger generation; if he doesn't address these anomalies, he might be seen as too keenly on the side of the counterculture's transgressions, whereas what he really wants is to borrow the rock-and-roller's mutinous attitude without any of its punch. So Kirby describes Lewis's marrying six times as somehow subordinate to his singing about these failed marriages. Kirby repeats Lewis's defense that he "never claimed to be a role model," while emphasizing that Lewis did exactly what he wanted to in life, and "when it didn't work, he blamed the devil." He wishes Lewis to "have as much fun / in hell as you did getting there," imagining a frenzied auditorium in hell: "you swivel on your stool and look out as though seeing the audience / for the first time and jerk your thumb toward / the back of the auditorium and say, 'Them doors swing both ways.'" So in his aesthetic rock-and-roll has been emptied of political content. It is mere self-expression for

Lewis, as poetry is for Kirby. Lewis is evaluated strictly as an individual artist (or rather, the art, in Kirby's conception, flows from the unique constituents of a person's selfhood, and therefore is in no need of explanation or justification), and nothing that doesn't fit into this paradigm is referenced. The poem gives the appearance of being free-flowing, able to synthesize diverse inputs and sources, whereas in fact it is the most claustrophobic, self-enclosed, walled-off artifact imaginable.

But Kirby tops it in "I Think Stan Done It." The threats in his universe are either utterly trivial, reduced to the specificity of zero, or so abstracted, expanded to the scope of the universe, that in either case he has no meaningful sense of the choice between security and liberty. He must either trivialize or exaggerate, in both cases depriving the world's assorted dangers of their solidity. If only Satan were named Stan, the world would be different. Kirby describes the legend on the ceiling of a Gonzaga duke's castle: "*Forse che si, forse che no,*" meaning "Maybe yes, maybe no." Some claim this applies to the fortunes of war, others that it refers to love. Kirby is "betting on war." It doesn't make a difference to him, and neither does the exact meaning have any bearing on the eventual outcome, since the Italian forts are all equipped with holes at the tops of the arched gates where the defenders can pour on the attackers boiling oil or candy, take your pick. He then connects this with his own family history: "My parents dealt in both commodities, I think" (love and war? "After-dinner mints" and "rusty nails"?). He recounts a joke about how "Miss Josie called Dr. Tommy 'Earley' whenever / he forgot a car payment or left the milk bottle / in the kitchen sink, Early being the simpleton / of the little farm town she grew up in." We are to imagine the child Kirby and his brother rolling on the floor in laughter as they imagine Dr. Tom as the "drooling half-wit," who while his neighbors ride into town to sell their produce, stands at the courthouse "masturbating with one hand / and picking his nose with the other." Remember that these are "memory poems" as Kirby understands them;

but they are so in the sense that history lessons are for our forty-third president. Kirby asks, "What kept them together, my dad and mom? Answer: / nothing. Also, everything, and plenty of both // at the same time."

The climax of the poem is either after-dinner mints or rusty nails, depending on our interpretation. Kirby tells us that "Blaise Pascal said that if people / knew what others said of them, there wouldn't be / four friends in the world." This is how families really work: "we don't have the slightest idea about what we're doing / yet manage to do it anyway with a kind of / *Così Fan Tutte*-ish unarticulatable grasping at as much // of the truth as we can wrap our lunch hooks / around at any given moment." This is the substitute for wisdom, steeped in jokes, empty tourism through lands and literature, and hyperventilating (because disguising the loss of expressible masculinity) associationalism, that is supposed to be the payoff for putting up with his childish whimsy. So of course he must end with the joke about the carpenter who shows up at the gates of heaven and when God wants to know why he should be let in, answers that he did raise "this son who's really, really different." When Jesus leaps to exclaim "Daddy!" the carpenter stutters, "P-Pinnocchio?" In this poem that started off with an omitted "a" in a previous poem of Kirby's, we are led through a wild-goose chase: the Freudian implications of verbal slips; stale jokes about prudish English spinsters; a variety of names for the penis; an enigmatic quotation on a ceiling which could mean anything; an empty memory of childhood; and a joke about misunderstanding at heaven's gates. All of this adds up to nothing, even though tied together by the theme of the intentional misunderstandings we commit in order to allow life to proceed with the least amount of friction. Kirby wants us to believe that it is better to allow the innocent mistake to proceed, to go playfully with the flow and hope that things will work out. There must be a high degree of capitalist redundancy for there to be no consequences to misunderstandings (whether physical or verbal).

Kirby's primary self-conception is of a verbally charged tourist, walking without feeling any emotion amidst evocative or depressing landscapes, whether in his own country, or in France and Italy, where there is no compulsion to learn even the rudiments of the language, as Kirby teaches in those exotic landscapes, suitable only as backdrops and occasions for merriment. The manifesto poem, "Stairway to Heaven," elasticizes the term "memory poem" to the point of meaninglessness: "Even the term / *memory poem* isn't mine, since Byron had used it / for some autobiographical poems of his own." He also mentions a "review I'd written / of a collection of Hayden Carruth's essays / called *Reluctantly* in which I'd said, / "these essays...start abruptly and ramble / purposefully over the landscape before concluding / in a way that is both surprising and appropriate." Yet it is clear that any beginning, middle, and end will yield this result to the poet's satisfaction.

The kernel of the theme is present in each poem to the degree that it permits coherence of a certain kind—as though paint of a certain color were scattered haphazardly over a floor and walls, to give it a certain false unity. In "Dear Derrida," it is deconstruction; in "The Fugawi," identity; in "The Crab Nebula," teaching; in "The Ghost of Henry James," gothicism; in "Heat Lightning," puritanism; in "A Fine Frenzy," married sex; but these themes are in the nature of faithless promises. Wisdom is clothed in flippancy, indifference to the mighty struggle for virtue and justice: Kirby identifies as his real failings, in "Everything You Do Is Wrong": "not gloth and sluttony and the other five / but *my* sins, my tendency to avoid people / at parties if they're not more important / than I am, for example, for the pleasure I take / in the bad luck of my friends." The musical, cultural, political, personal, and commercial references are invariably middlebrow: this is to create a degree of friendliness toward the author, to reassure us that he has no airs, no pretences, that he is bedrock middle-America, whom we can trust for his witty parley for the duration of the poem. His treatment of

Europe is as a tourist escapade, in the worst senses of the word, but this isn't surprising, given his distinct otherness toward all forms of creation not strictly himself. In the last poem, "Borges at the Northside Rotary," he and Barbara get on the wrong train in Paris, and are surprised when "out of the dark / swaggered four Tunisian teenagers," who of course turn out to be friendly and harmless. But the racist presumption is always present, and there is no shame about it; it is simply how he conducts himself in the world.

Kirby's book of essays, *Ultra-Talk: Johnny Cash, The Mafia, Shakespeare, Drum Music, St. Teresa of Avila, And 17 Other Colossal Topics of Conversation* (2007), is his prose version of speech without purpose. A number of fertile subjects, particularly those having to do with his touristic forays in Europe, are undertaken, but none is pursued to the point of communication between author and reader. He'll explain to us why Shakespeare is so popular: "the most original of writers is the least original," besides being like Jackson Pollock in his speed. Whitman has been falsely categorized as an "American original, as cosmic loony," when he is better pigeonholed "as dithyrambist, as citizen of the 'old, weird America.'" Emily Dickinson's poetry is displaced sexual frenzy. Touring France, he comes to this conclusion: "With Rabelais and Montaigne as my guides, what I was learning was how willing the French are to embrace opposites: they like to think big, like Rabelais, yet they're as keen to split hairs as Montaigne is." Though he concedes to making sure "to see at least a couple of movies" whenever he is in Paris, he dismisses the European art film, because the "problem with detailing human nature is that it tends to be unchanging," whereas a "well-turned [Hollywood] plot . . . is never predictable." Observing growing religiosity everywhere, Kirby stays calm in his bubble of moderation, noting that "Christianity has been an indispensable spur to excellence in science and art" (not hesitating to rely on the racist Charles Murray to buttress his argument), and concluding that "arguing for or against religion, especially on the basis of whether it is good or bad for us, is like arguing for or against automobiles or ice cream or sex." He will pursue Dante and da Vinci's paths, but we get lost on the trail. He remains calm in the middle of exploring NASCAR frenzy at Talladega, Alabama. He empathizes with his son when he is part of the *Big Brother 2* CBS reality television show cast shortly after September 11, concluding, "Ours is a country of many freedoms. The greatest of these is the freedom to be dumb." Take him to the cradle of Western culture, and he will come away with nothing but scraps of his own selfhood retailed back to us, without story, enthusiasm, logic, finitude, romance.

The Kirby Poet has equally defanged the Enlightenment and Romanticism; history is a dead word to him. A man walks around in his past and in other lands and confronts only his banal persona, already represented to him by commercialized art. His guise is always friendly and benign, which makes him a more severe danger to happiness on earth than the dour jackbooted thugs of the past. We want to share a beer with him (as with Bush), but he will kill our imagination (or put us in a camp) with a smile always on his face. He is always a tourist, never a traveler; always desiring a laugh-track, never understanding. He is new: Lowell and Berryman were self-critical, not treading softly against their lost masculinity, let alone denying it as Kirby does. If this type's hegemonic rapture lasts much longer, the planet is doomed.

BOULEVARD SYMPOSIUM: "THE YOUNG DO NOT READ NOVELS ANYMORE."

On or about July 2, 1998, human nature changed—again. This was the date of release of *Harry Potter and the Chamber of Secrets*, the second Harry Potter book. It quickly rose to the top of the self-declared reading lists of college students, where the series remains today. From Breton and Henry Miller and Kerouac and Plath and Vonnegut (or even Hesse and Salinger) to J. K. Rowling? Even for the famously insipid young, this is a plunge of monumental proportions. Too much can be made of demarcating generations; yet mine is a definitely identifiable one, with its unique talents and anxieties, but quite unable to leave a record of itself, since its illiteracy gets in the way of context and history.

This is the most passive, confused, disoriented, malingering, abstract, ignorant, brainwashed, unified, coddled, meaningless American generation ever, and it shows in its reading and writing. It is also the most tolerant, self-sufficient, understanding, empathetic, multicultural, uplifted, vocal, articulate, knowing, ironic, sensible, pragmatic, disciplined, ambidextrous, wholesome generation on record. The two tendencies cancel each other out, leaving a zero entity.

Its strengths are the mirror image of its failings, both rooted in the complete disconnect between the private and the public selves, the personal and the political, which my generation (increasingly aware of its own marginality) sees no way of bridging, and hence has given up on the project of self-fulfillment. What it reads is trash (when a classic is processed by a trash compactor, it comes out as trash nevertheless); what it writes is equally ephemeral (it has no desire to attain immortality through art; it seeks a knowing kind of preemptive mortality, an orange alert of the soul, if you will, before pen is put to paper).

At a September, 2007 John Kerry event at the University of Florida, a blabbering student was tasered by the police. The students in the auditorium sat passively while the cops did their business. Later, Stephen Colbert (one of my generation's prime idols) commented on the audience: "You don't need a Fox body language expert to tell you that kid in orange is bored. He's probably thinking something like, 'I wish they'd stop tasering this guy so I could go home and watch this guy getting tasered on YouTube....The kids in that auditorium who sat idly by as their fellow student was seized, thrown to the ground, and tasered didn't lack the courage to help....They're just so used to watching videos like 'Crazy guys thrown out of lecture hall' that they didn't know how to help other than to link to it. I'm sure that guy in the orange is going to spring into action as soon as he gets home and fires up his blog." This about sums up the political instinct of the young.

The technologies of virtual expression, and the mass psychology of the young, seem to have blended into a perfectly complementary whole, so that the seams by now are impossible to detect. This generation has disappeared into the media ether, so the question of reading and writing meaningfully doesn't arise. The YouTube/iPod/Facebook/ Wikipedia generation has been sold a bill of goods masquerading as the pursuit of life, liberty, and happiness. It takes the entire production seriously—or so we can assume, since any comprehensible voice, aside from the media miasma itself, isn't detectable.

Gore Vidal used to talk about the passing of the novel as a meaningful cultural artifact, the crucial modern mediation between the individual and the mass. He lamented that "we are at the end of a great, great literary art, the novel, [at] the end of a rather weighing-down culture," that novelists are "on the periphery" now, and that the "audience for the novel is demonstrably diminishing with each passing year." Academics write and teach the "University Novel," in contrast to the public novel of before; it is an instrument of disconnection, not connection. All the verbiage of the present generation (things have become immeasurably worse since Vidal's protests of a quarter century ago) expresses its desperation to connect; all the means at hand result in further disconnection.

One might say that the problem *is* that the young continue to read and write novels; only, one wishes, they didn't, since they read wrongly and write wrongly, and perpetuate the illusion that a lively literary culture is still in existence, which is a further disservice to their sense of reality. But in fact they thrive only on delusions; reality in any of its forms is indigestible to them. Things are real only when mediated and procured and brokered; direct apprehension of any phenomenon leaves them reaching for overstretched metaphors handed down from more creative earlier minds. The soul has never before been so well assimilated in the technologies of production, to the detriment of individuality. The lines between mind and body, present and past, art and being, imagination and fantasy, have never been so fluid before (to my generation, the very source of its strength; to a Plato or Keats looking from on high, the source of its misery). The collective stream of consciousness for the first time produces the ideal capitalist subject, who actively participates in his own subjugation at all levels of existence. How can the most individualist of activities, the assimilation and generation of real art, take place when the necessary boundaries have been broken? Officially, there is no class, not even race and gender; the result is literary garbage. There isn't a single nameable man of letters among them, unlike Vidal; they have perfected an anti-intellectual practice of creative writing, compartmentalized from thinking; they operate in minute subdivisional niches of single genres, untaught in the arts of rhetoric and criticism. Never before have there been such narrow-minded writers.

Donald Allen's landmark anthology *The New American Poetry 1945-1960* (1961) included Olson, Duncan, Creeley, Guest, Ashbery, Ginsberg, Kerouac, Levertov, O'Hara, Snyder, Schuyler, and others. Michael Dumanis and Cate Marvin's anthology *Legitimate Dangers: American Poets of the New Century* (2006) includes Dan Beachy-Quick, Dan Chiasson, Nick Flynn, Jennifer Grotz, Terrance Hayes, A. Van Jordan, Ilya Kaminsky, Srikanth Reddy, Larissa Szporluk, Karen Volkman, and Kevin Young. The *Granta* Best of Young American Novelists list of 1996 included Sherman Alexie, Madison Smartt Bell, Edwidge Danticat, Jeffrey Eugenides, Jonathan Franzen, David Guterson, Chris Offutt, Stewart O'Nan, Mona Simpson, and Melanie Rae Thon. The 2006 list includes Daniel Alarcón, Kevin Brockmeier, Judy Budnitz, Jonathan Safran Foer, Nell Freudenberger, Uzodinma Iweala, Nicole Krauss, Ratawut Lapcharoensap, Yiyun Li, Maile Meloy, Z. Z. Packer, Jess Row, Akhil Sharma, and Gary Shteyngart. The earlier *Granta* list doesn't exactly contain my favorites (it was composed in the already degenerate mid-nineties, after all), but there are ambitious writers there, like Danticat and Offutt, striving to break free of the prisons of language and identity. The new list contains an uncannily high proportion of my current bête noires, writers of my generation against whom I have a visceral reaction; the emotional frozenness of their narratives can only come from unhealing scars, wounds so deep they can't admit they exist. The workshops and the publishers have trained them well to produce writing that seamlessly merges into the massive cultural output, leaving no traces behind. Are these Vidal's nightmare readers/writers, or what? They would say, in their defense, that capitalism's zombies are how today's Americans are, so why not reproduce reality? This is first of all a distortion, because zombies are only a part of the reality, and second because all art requires both a representational and an ideational component; practicing only the first, and at its narrowest base at that, is to collaborate in one's own annihilation.

A strong case can be made that these are the last days of the American republic; even if we return to normality in some shape or other, it still won't give us back the relative innocence before the days of torture, renditions, secret prisons, preemptive wars, paramilitary forces, faith-based science, mass deportations, military tribunals, border walls, cultural genocide, and all the instruments of fascist oppression. Habeas corpus might come back, but will there be a corpus to habeas? It would seem that these incredibly stressful conditions, for which no exact parallel is discernible in American history, would constitute the most propitious circumstances for the production of strong art. Consider what the modernists of the twenties and thirties did with comparable materials, and then consider what today's generation is doing with the stuff of reality it confronts: all of Huxley's and Orwell's final nightmares realized in a day-to-day degeneration to barbarism, and what we get are Jonathan Safran Foer and Gary Shteyngart, laughing at their own death, because this is what they are paid so well to do. What happened to the self-appointed postmodern site of resistance, located in the academy of the nineties? When push came to shove, and the fascists came to power, it was revealed as merely an entertaining component of capitalism's confidence game.

One can only conclude that Homo Americanus has entered the final phase of the authoritarian personality; in its American version it has a cute face and ready laugh, it has a fine sense of timing and correspondence, it is smart and businesslike and ruminative and professional, but it is empty of a soul. It conceptualizes itself as the hyper-alert postmodern generation, which doesn't let anyone get away with bullshit; it is actually a medieval cohort, beset by superstitions about its own central place in the universe, which it thinks still revolves around its assorted agonies and trepidations. Vidal and Updike, and Pynchon and Gaddis and Mailer (I am not fond of the last three, but offer them as examples of vast ambition), sought to reinscribe themselves in the continuing flow of history as active agents, as visionaries and prophets; the current generation has been taught to read only for entertainment, not even Ivy League breeding getting in the way of viewing the whole world as a playscape of blurred ideologies and beliefs, which only leads to their reconstitution as subjects of their own fear, their only subject. Mimicry, plagiarism, theft, imitation, these are the characteristics of a benighted colonial population; they have made a resounding comeback among young readers and writers.

The collective idiocracy needs a hard slap in the face, a reminder of how stupid it has become. Unfortunately, that requires real reading and writing, real pain. Those among the older generation, who know better, can't administer the punishment because the culture industry nomenklatura are reliant on the output of the young to fulfill the quotas of literary production— so Vidal's circle has finally closed, and there is no escape.

THE BEST AMERICAN POETRY GETS BETTER

THE BEST AMERICAN POETRY 2005. PAUL MULDOON,
EDITOR. SCRIBNER, 2005.

THE BEST AMERICAN POETRY 2006. BILLY COLLINS,
EDITOR. SCRIBNER, 2006.

What's with the American poet today? Is there nothing that can jolt him out of equable philosophizing? Must he accept every load of trouble with grateful bows, flattened heartbeats? Has he finally left his humanness behind, to play only insider-games? Is he like a child, immersed in playground horseplay, as the family fortune crumbles, or the father goes into exile? Can nothing pull him away from his entertainments?

In the first years of the twenty-first century, as present and imminent calamities gather steam (the overt blooming of the relatively quiet American empire into an aggressively nationalist-militarist one, the reversion to feudalistic practices of law and order all around the world, the desecration of the final remnants of the humanistic enlightenment project, and technological society's inability to grapple with the resource and demographic challenges), American poets have taken a hands-off approach to every disturbing reality, retreating into their academic shells to produce a poetry that is uniformly escapist. When we talk about a "best" American poem, we are talking about a poem that makes its isolation from untidy reality its ultimate aesthetic fetish; it refuses to subject its own streategies to criticism, removed as it is from signposts that can affix it in recognizable reality.

Discounting its suave apologetics of objectivity, the *Best American Poetry* series has actually become an accurate barometer of the ideal poem as validated by establishment circles today. Thus, two editors of quite divergent personal styles, Paul Muldoon in 2005 and Billy Collins in 2006, arrive at astonishingly similar selections of what they consider to be the year's best poetry. Whatever linguistic wildness pervades Muldoon's selections, or whatever formal tranquility prevails in Collins's choices, they are in the end overwhelmed by the singularly calm refusal to engage with the world at hand in both editions. Series editor David Lehman has succeeded in adding his legitimation to the grief and nostalgia-saturated memory and anecdote poem as the epitome of the art form. Editors change from year to year, but the choices remain reaffirmingly close. *The Best American Poetry* series has become a fairly interesting model of what happens to a dying art's plaintive apologizers when the death throes are palpable to all but the most committed insiders.

Muldoon's 2005 selections seem to have been made with a disturbingly high quotient of the self-celebrating trivial in mind. The inside jokiness, tempting apprentice poets to follow the easy path, is evident from the start, and never slacks off. A normal human being, with normal feelings and recognizable attitudes, would react differently to "congestive heart failures" and "brain tumors" than A. R. Ammons in "In View of the Fact." Ammons finds in terminal leave-taking "love that can grow brighter / and deeper till the very end, / gaining strength / and getting more precious all the way." Similarly, for John Ashbery, in "In Dearest, Deepest Winter," "living in this mild occasion" (aren't these revolutionary times?), "What calamity on the second floor could flood us / here on the fifth, and not be gone before morning?" One presumes none, unless the laws of physics (and poetics) are reversed, so we shall be safe. Jennifer Michael Hecht, in "The Propagation of the Species," asserts fatalistically: "There is no way to parry ordinary disaster. / There are no odds worth playing."

What is the view from the second floor, in deepest winter, in these poets' social context? For Catherine Bowman, in "I Want to Be Your Shoebox," machine poetics generates such impossible demands as "I want to be your paradox / I want to be your pair of socks / I want to be your paradise" and on and on for two pages. Where is the lover who'll yield so much? These are fact-fantasies, wish-making lists as ends in themselves, and must be treated with weary applause to keep the poet in good mood. Christine Scanlon's "The Grilled Cheese Sandwich: An Elusive Essential to Social Success" is another exercise in the same mode. An initial emotion— envy in the case of Stephanie Brown's "*Roommates: Noblesse Oblige*, Sprezzatura, *and Gin Lane*," hate in the case of Julie Sheehan's "Hate Poem"—mechanically generates a host of related reactions, one tumbling after the other, the poet's restraining silence on hold.

Game-playing serves its own ends in Andrew Feld's "19__: An Elegy," Stacey Harwood's "Contributor's Notes" (if possibility is postulated as infinite, as the decade of the hyper-commercialized nineties falsely promised, then no self-definition is possible—irony is by definition excluded, especially when its inclusion is so loudly notated), and Samuel Hazo's "Seesaws." Love the poet for his cuteness, or else.

Increasingly pervasive denial of reality is reflected in the comfortable habitation of a fantasy scenario, a "what if" mind-maneuver played to pleasant conclusion. What is being celebrated is the lack of aesthetic sophistication imputed to Americans by early European visitors, a criticism now internalized and regurgitated to self-satisfaction. Richard Garcia's "Adam and Eve's Dog," Jessica Goodheart's "Advice for a Stegosaurus," Vicki Hudspith's "Ants," Sarah Manguso's "Hell," D. Nurkse's "Space Marriage," and Matthew Yeager's "A Big Ball of Foil in a Small New York Apartment" exemplify this trend. The "what if" game— inserting incongruously charged emotion into a fixed small place of the imagination—has recently been perfected and popularized by Billy Collins; his imitators have run away with it as apparently the only alternative to self-focused grief; it's still no closer to the realities of postindustrial warring America.

For the poet to maintain composure—and the poetry chosen by Muldoon is all about the poet's sanity, never about the reader's needs—he need merely perceive or recall a slight and correct it instantly. This late in the day, the demiworld's everyday language is terrifyingly complicit in fascist expression, presumptively making the term "irony" a lie; the poet can always claim at least cattiness or jocularity to defend against the charge of gratuitous viciousness. Is it ars poetica or arse poetica, when the screw is made to turn in finite directions, in Arielle Greenberg's "The Turn of the Screw"? Poetry, it seems, is being force-fed its own crow, its emotive sources vampirized to the extinction of blood. Jane Hirshfield, in "Burlap Sack," claims that "To think that grief is the self is an error," but everything in this anthology militates against this sentiment. Galway Kinnell, in "Shelley," denies his original attraction to Shelley; the sordid facts of biography trump fantastic inspiration.

No change in aesthetic seems to have occurred since the go-go nineties, when identity was supposedly in perpetual flux, subject to hallucination from the self's ordering mechanism. Thus, Victoria Chang, in "Seven Changs," sings to a march disappearing in on-command victory. In the last decade of the twentieth century, big ambition was severely curtailed, in favor of changes so small incrementalism got a bad name. Stephen Dunn's "Five Roses in the Morning," Edward Field's "In Praise of My Prostate," Donald Justice's "A Chapter in the Life of Mr. Kehoe, Fisherman," Heather McHugh's "Ill-Made Almighty," Louis Simpson's "An Impasse," and Gary Snyder's "Waiting for a Ride," typify the new small poem conjuring conviviality. Such happy, happy marriages—and such happy, happy remembrances of old relationships—scattered all through the volume. The men-women war, apparently, is at an end. The memory of internment camps does not anymore interfere with sound-bite paradises. Nixon is an almost harmless buffoon in

Rachel Loden's "In the Graveyard of Fallen Monuments"—
the anger, the spite of that dark prince having melted in the
poet's restitutive penance.

In reality, the multicultural illusion of the nineties
has decidedly ended; but in the age of Guantánamo, Abu
Ghraib, mass deportations, data mining, and the suspension
of habeas corpus, a Zen-like peacefulness prevails among
our poets, as they contemplate the interaction of subcultures,
cultures, and civilizations on the local or global scale.
Surely, one of the functions of establishment poetry today
is to perpetuate the pretense that America remains a society
where individuals of any origin and means can pursue the
dream of personal happiness; the roadblocks in the path of
this aim are purely personal (mostly medical or physical
tragedies, that can always be dealt with, if the right attitude
of resignation and fortitude is available).

The actual mode of elegy is so far removed from the
faux elegiac poems in Muldoon's selections that only the
poet's wishfulness can come across, as in Amy Gerstler's
"Watch." Everywhere the attempt is to convey the
impression that the poet is in touch with archetypal angst,
even as the temptation is always to tame the nightmare, as
in Leonard Gontarek's "Blue on Her Hands." The ekphrastic
mode becomes a gesture of claiming identity at the mirror-
level the poets don't seem to have earned the wisdom to
capsulize, as in Terrance Hayes, Mary Jo Salter, and others'
poems in this volume dedicated to movies, painting, and
music. Elegy is the mode of lamentation for a superior style
of life; it can be argued that American literature has never
been elegiac (unlike European literature, in continuing
waves almost since its origins, and ever more so since the
Great War), with its incomplete grasp of history; least of
all is it elegiac now, when the present and future appear so
overwhelming that history as an explanatory force has been
washed out in the turbulence of popular culture. What we
get when poets succumb to the prevailing refusal of history
is narcissistic self-appraisal (usually with an uplifting
epiphany) masquerading as elegy, and "appreciation" of art

works without sadness at the passing of genius that seems to inform most such dedications in the great poetry of the past.

Whimsical address, to Dolly Parton, as in Steve Orlen's "Song: *I Love You. Who are You?*," or to the owl in Eugene Ostashevsky's "Dear Owl," functions to suggest that the poet's idiosyncratic desire has no normative value: it is a thing of beauty in itself, forever reducible.

To appropriate modes of revolution—even political—external to the American grain, and swallow even those in our machinery of hasteful replication, is perhaps the most blatant imperialist gesture. These poets are very, very good at it. One does this by placing oneself in the position of the minority (or woman, or foreign) subject, and speaking through its persona as if its every ratiocinative impulse was accessible for dissection: in effect reducing the mystery of human rebellion and integration to sequential steps of assimilation, nothing more.

The ubiquitous list-making exercise, in Maura Stanton's "Twenty Questions," has as its purpose only the defeat of the arsenal of interpretation the astute reader brings to poetry: Don't try to think of answers. In David Wagoner's "For a Man Who Wrote *CUNT* on a Motel Bathroom Mirror," a reading of the immediate past is offered that excludes the possibility of illiteracy on the part of the original recipient of the CUNT message. It would seem we readers are all literate CUNT message recipients from the tyrants at large, and arse poetica doesn't even need to pretend to help us out in the act of interpreting the assault.

Collins, in the 2006 edition, seamlessly picks up from Muldoon. In his Foreword, Lehman anxiously lauds Collins for his crossover appeal to mainstream readers (the poetry world seems to have a difficult time believing that one of their own could possibly have a wide audience). Collins, the former poet laureate, then does his public duty by declaring the state of poetry to be sound and healthy. As usual, what he declares he won't include is precisely what gets included. Collins says he'll reject poetry that seeks to elicit a stranger's instant sympathy for the poet's private tribulations, or poetry that wallows in family nostalgia and recollection for its own sake. Yet it is precisely poems that fit this mold that get chosen, over and over. True, the poems may have a polite attitude in not blurting out their angst (much as is Collins's own method), and they may not use the list of banned signifiers ("we used to," "the old Motorola," or "Dad's fishing rod") to get past Collins's gatekeeping, but they are still very much in the falsely sentimental nostalgic (never elegiac) mode. Collins says that he likes poems which narrate an incident without the narrator quite knowing where he is going, the element of surprise the poet himself feels in the process of thinking out loud appealing to him; again, very much as is his own mode of writing. The problem is that with Collins his transcending emotions, starting from small steps, remain only trivial in significance; and so it is with these poems. Collins is somehow affiliated with the movement to return to "form," and so he must mount a defense of form in the selected poems—but the most fleetingly superficial resemblance to form (regardless of the absence of meter or rhyme or any of the traditional constituents) is enough for a poem to fall within form (Julie Lario's double abecedarians, which seem to be playing with the form for its own sake, will suffice). This is form as Muldoon would understand it, plastic beyond meaning, beyond any stability—the antithesis of form, in fact.

The first three poems set the tone for the volume. A number of poems play with clichés, received wisdom, conventional language, without there seeming to be a point behind the playful reversions; the play itself suffices. Thus, Kim Addonizio's opening "Verities"—followed by Tom Christopher's "Rhetorical Figures," Mark Pawlak's "The Sharper the Berry," and others. Similarly, Charles Harper Webb's "Prayer to Tear the Sperm-Dam Down" only results in unsuccessful irony, his reversals of received opinion falling flat.

The faux nostalgic mode (we might say, nostalgia minus the substance of experience backing it up) makes its appearance in the second poem, Dick Allen's "'See the Pyramids Along the Nile,'" and later as well, as in Terrence Winch's "Sex Elegy." (Often, in these poems, nostalgia comments on its own vapory thinness, its own impossibility, without considering any aesthetic alternative other than nostalgia, as in Gerald Stern's "Homesick," John Koethe's "Sally's Hair," where both Sally and her hair are questionable as independent entities, or Dorianne Laux's "Demographic," which manages to romanticize the usually sordid business of riding an urban bus.)

And Craig Arnold's "Couple from Hell" launches the Collins narrative (or might one claim that the epiphanic narrative poem is now generally the mode of reflection for the American poet?), beginning in a trivial experience, hesitatingly suggesting transcendence, and finally eluding meaning. Stephen Dobyns's "Toward Some Bright Moment" is the quintessential Collins poem of inaction and paralysis, an expiation of guilt at the poet's nondoing. The poet sees a woman kicking a dog on a city street, does nothing, and later chews over this incident to justify his ways to himself. On the surface this would seem to be the kind of poem Collins admires: event leading to reflection, the poet not quite knowing in the course of the narrative where he is going. Yet we know that the return is always to the content, paralyzed self: there is no mystery here.

Elsewhere, there is the only the merest hint of the actual world of turbulence and crises we inhabit, only lyrical puzzles to work out. In John Ashbery's "A Worldly Country," the rubble is "quiet," and why "peace had subdued the ranks of hellishness" seems a matter of afterthought. The poetic gesture of easily claiming peace has gained dominance over the romantic's difficult struggle with matching the inner and outer worlds in some semblance of harmony. In Krista Benjamin's "Letter from My Ancestors" any substance the old-world ancestors might have claimed in terms of their trials and tribulations is eschewed in favor of their confirmation that they lived and suffered and died so that the poet may have "the luxury of time / to write about us."

That is all we need to hear about what they actually did: this is the ultimate in narcissistic self-enclosure, where every attempt to empathize with another's life turns into an affirmation of one's own choices. The serenity in this poem — as if the entire twentieth century were being dismissed for being too full of disturbance—is violently offensive. Carl Dennis's "Our Generation"—the poetic counterpart to the avalanche of boomers' journalistic self-praise in the last decade—repeats the putative accomplishments of the poet's generation, which seem to consist above all in wanting and achieving the very things people of prior and succeeding generations will also want: "Children and lawns and cars and beach towels." Something of this same denial of the passage of time (this time in terms of beautiful women refusing to notice an aging poet) is apparent in Mark Halliday's "Refusal to Notice Beautiful Women"—the poet's version of the mid-life crisis that used to result in impulsive purchases of fast cars?

Exhausted by the compressiveness of the small Creeley poem, poets today have become enamored of sestinas, villanelles, and other European repetitive forms; the uses to which these patterns might be put in bridging the gap between the artist's presumed innocence and society's corruption are obvious. Instead, poets manage to squeeze out the disconcerting trains of meaning these forms almost impose upon the writer, in favor of mere self-expression (the quality Collins avows to exclude in his Introduction), as in Laura Cronk's "Sestina for the Newly Married" (in her note, she misapprehends her use of the form resulting in "a kind of address that is private and public at the same time."). The mature poet incarnated as teenage prankster is evident also in Daniel Gutstein's "Monsieur Pierre est mort" (one wonders what "form" Collins would categorize this poem under). R. S. Gwynn uses the limerick form in "Sects from A to Z" to miss an opportunity to satirize religious denominations: the object seems to be to evoke the gentlest of acquiescing laughs. There is little acknowledged distance between poet and subject; and hence little room for judgment.

A consistent characteristic of contemporary American poetry is the flattening of history in the individual's private agony. Laura Kasischke does this in "At Gettysburg," which manages to contract, not expand, our understanding of the nature of war. The answer to Kasischke's question in her note, "Which one of us, I wondered, does not truly understand the nature of war?" is that no one does, or that it is the poet's job to make herself and us understand, not to take understanding for granted.

The machinery of imagination is efficiently put to work, as in the 2005 edition, with list-making (the antithesis of narrative, plot, story, history) as an end in itself, as in Megan Gannon's "List of First Lines." What is the sensation upon reading such a poem? The vague reflection that language is infinitely permeable to diverse uses, given changeable motives? Why is this observation intriguing, in this simplistic form, at this late date and age? Not even the grim adolescent determination to ask the unanswerable questions pervades these superficial exercises. A fascination with encyclopedic knowledge as an end in itself has recently found obnoxious prose expression by several know-it-all narrators (such as A. J. Jacobs in *The Know-It-All: One Man's Humble Quest to Become the Smartest Person in the World*), who seem to take seriously the notion that mere immersion in indiscriminate knowledge somehow makes one brighter. Amy Gerstler is fascinated with the 1910 *Encyclopedia Britannica*, using tidbits (which ought to be horrifying) to entertain her auditor, in "For My Niece Sidney, Age Six." Don't worry, little niece, nothing in the world can't be processed by your teensy-weensy grade school brain (would 1910 be the same year Virginia Woolf thought human nature had fundamentally changed?).

Aging, mortality, chronic illness, loss of friends and family—these are what the nostalgic mode again and again seeks to overcome. When the poet confronts these "tragic" manifestations directly—as in Jim Harrison's "On the Way to the Doctor's," the result is bathos—not the disorientation the poet presumes he is accomplishing on our behalf. Both poets' and readers' minds have become so desensitized to description of these kinds of everyday "tragedies" that each further attempt to bring the horrors home only reduces the cumulative impact of this particular spectator sport. Perhaps the most trite poem in these two collections, Liz Rosenberg's "The Other Woman's Point of View" (was a poem even necessary, once this title was set down?), comes tagged with the self-congratulatory note: "About this poem I have little to say except that such poems are difficult to write…. Part of poetry's task, it may be, is to break that silence, even when painful."

Everywhere, poets wonder what they might have said in the moment had they had the courage (this seems to be a way of bringing themselves down to the prosaic level, perhaps seeking to embellish their Average Joe credentials, by declaring that they too suffer from lack of decisiveness, and are as culpable in the forces of mass degeneration as your next-door rancher or carpenter). Terrance Hayes's "Talk," which describes missing an opportunity to take offense at a racial slur by a middle-school basketball teammate, seems to be a form of racial guilt turned inward, when the subject ought to feel outraged at others' insensitiveness. This is a curious move, but juxtaposed with Joy Katz's "Just a Second Ago," which contemplates tossing a "drink across the visiting poet's shirt," the varieties of conjuring faux melodrama—"It's amazing: Traffic stays on its side of the road" (is it really?)—seem endlessly inexhaustible. In her note, Katz talks about the "unbearable fragility of love and order and being alive," which speaks volumes about the fantasy of disorder as a controlling check on the potentially fascist personality's slavish adherence to actual tyrannical order.

David Kirby's characteristically uncontrolled logorrhea in "Seventeen Ways from Tuesday" (no attempt is made to search for a meaning beyond the incident being recounted in numbing detail), also builds from a scrap of conversation overheard. Kirby's self-amusement bothers. It's almost as if the "best" poems don't have independent lives of their own, but can only sustain themselves if they are parasitic in every way possible. The poets frequently make an issue of their parasitical existence (is any other self-conception possible in the predominant living-off-the-MFA-programs model?), commenting on the futility or indirection of their poetic endeavors, as does Jennifer L. Knox in "The Laws of Probability in Levittown," where the facile borrowing doesn't even seem to have celebration as part of the impulse. The Collins-like preoccupation with the poet's status is also the theme of Richard Newman's "Briefcase of Sorrow," Mary Oliver's "The Poet with His Face in His Hands," and J. Allyn Rosser's "Discounting Lynn." In "Tonight," Mark Kraushaar imposes a television police car chase over a loved one's battle with cancer: what a winning combination! It's as if the derivation from popular culture were the only way to give life to death-dealing cancer. (Again, the rage at the unfairness of life—"It struck me...how utterly arbitrary and unfair it seemed," says Kraushaar's note—points to the potentially fascist subject blooming into maturity.) Sue Ellen Thompson's "Body English" (where she tries to tackle the grief of her mother's death from cancer "by focusing on a single gesture") and Allison Townsend's "What I Never Told You About the Abortion" are two poems that misappropriate the public nature of elegy toward purely private ends, dissipating the emotion even as it is in the process of being described.

It will be observed that there's less and less need, as the years go by, for the authors' explanatory notes at the conclusion of the volume; the poems speak for themselves, and the glosses only serve to make them more banal. It's also remarkable how often the quality of the notes seems more memorable than the poems themselves, as if whatever was unique about the lyric poems had leaked out of them to leave them vacant. Collins argues in his Introduction (this is a common tactic among poets defending their art these days) that multitonality is characteristic of the poems chosen, but in fact there is only a singular tone of placid removal from the pain and hurt of everyday life. The deviations toward humor or depression are slight, and in the end always lose out to the (presumed) happy endings.

Collins might praise accessibility as a desirable quality, but what we get when the search for accessibility comes without a verbal charge is the utter denotative banality of Betsy Retallack's "Roadside Special" (this is a compendium of numerous popular techniques, including list-making, repetitive fragmentary asides reverting to their own inconclusivity, and David Kirby-like uncontrolled long prosy lines), or Kay Ryan's "Thin" (the Thin American Poetry?), Vijay Seshadri's "Memoir" (a thin poem which states its desired emotion, "lacerating and unforgettable," without giving any cause for such a reaction, and which the poet describes as "a piece of literary criticism"), Charles Simic's "House of Cards" (which announces the death of narrative—"There's no more to tell," without us knowing the context for the fear), and Franz Wright's denial of death in "A Happy Thought" ("Dying, I imagine, / it will be the same deal, lonesomer maybe"—this, from a famously depressive poet)—all of which provoke numerous questions about what fears the poets are so intently barring from admission to conscious recognition.

Here then, are our "best" American poets, teaching us the lesson that in the new millennium the art consists of adopting an unvarying voice of blasé optimism in the face of calamity. It's not Muldoon's or Collins's fault; it's the poetry we must abide today. As Krista Benjamin writes in her note about her great-grandparents: "I believe they would be glad to know I am doing work that I love and that I don't have to spend the hours they did in the fields, the post office, or the shop in order to survive." Or as Charles Harper Webb declares, "If the sense of fun, excitement, and energy I felt giving birth to this poem comes through to the reader, it may become another argument for the worthiness-to-live of humankind." We're so very happy for you!

The Poet as Anti-Narcissist

RIPPLE EFFECT: NEW AND SELECTED POEMS by Elaine
Equi. Coffee House Press, 2007.

Elaine Equi is a poet of immunities. She seems to have
inoculated herself early in her career from the temptation
to deliver wasted homilies to oneself. Her sharp wit cuts
through false guarantee that the private self is after all
accommodated some degree of freedom in a brutal consumer
economy. She redeploys the language of self-improvement,
commercials, diplomacy, biography, and ritual intercourse
to penetrate the fog of holiness surrounding us. She is
preserved from futile discourse about the insufficiency
of language as means of understanding by her touching
humor, which comes from a deep sense of self-assurance.

This edition collects nearly all her biggest hits from
previous volumes, particularly the explosion of creativity
that marked her emergence in the late eighties. Her early
work, from *Federal Woman* (1978) to *Accessories* (1988),
provides a lesson in how a poet may start off having most
of the elements of her quintessential poetry in place without
achieving complete realization. What was missing was
her later characteristic boldness in following the lines of a
paradox to its full consequences. She would go on to equip
herself for this task by developing not the typical rootless
irony of our times, but an epigrammatic, razor-sharp,
enclosing and enveloping humor, sturdy rocks in a swift-
moving sea carrying drowning packets of language.

Nearly every poem from *Surface Tension* (1989), *Decoy*
(1994), and *Voice-Over* (1998) is memorable, and many of
them have found their way in this collection. There is none

of the weepy confessionalism, the grindingly narcissistic, or the paralyzed self victimized by an indifferent public space in Equi's work. Instead, we find a woman courageously confronting the many hypocrisies which encompass an ordinary American's self-definition in terms which outstrip the actual mean reality by a wide margin.

In *Surface Tension*'s "A Date with Robbe-Grillett," Equi builds at least three different worlds—everyday perception of phenomena, romantic exaggeration of effects, and stripped-to-the-essence minimalist sensation—which somehow leave a dominant poet standing around to observe the intersections and remain solidly tangible.

Much experimental poetry suffers today from the disease of fragmentation, disjunction, and disorientation for their own sake, and therefore shatters into nothing upon close scrutiny. It is very difficult to make a poem like "Folk Dance" (quoted in whole) hold together:

1. Carrying a tray.
2. Using a camera.
3. An undetermined celebration.
4. Up and down the stairs like
   the chambermaid in *The Dead*
   who says "men are all palaver
   and such as they can get."
5. Asparagus peeking out from
   under the salmon.
6. Coolness outside. Sky by Turner.
7. A square scarf folded to make
   a triangle.

The musicality, essential connectedness (lightly deployed under an apparent randomness), and the sense of the unprogrammable calculator are all enhanced upon rereading. The fragments are not stuck in there because they sound good, or for the heck of it.

This leads to another excellent feature of Equi's work. Unlike most experimental poets today, whose work seems repetitive when taken in mass, Equi's work feels better in bigger doses. This can only be because individual poems are prompted not by some unsteady whim of the moment, but by a witty judgment that isn't easily shaken.

In "At the Mall," "In a Monotonous Dream," and "Surface Tension," Equi teaches how much can be accomplished by leaving things unsaid—the power of silence is not so much a cute tactic, but the very engine of these poems. Where concise imagistic poems too often these days seem parodies of an exhausted modernist ethic, in Equi's world, because the reimagination of everyday images is founded in a worldly understanding of the many traps of self-definition offered by consumerist culture, the images become sharper and sharper after contemplation.

Decoy's "Brand X" critiques capitalism's exploitation of women's bodies while pointing out the ways the poet herself might have fetishized desire. "I know you think / this is about sex / but that's only because / it's really about advertising." Sex and advertising are on comparable planes, the origins of the confusion firmly fixed in the named will toward violence. As we parade our bodies, to cater to the public gaze (especially when we think we're being most private), so we flaunt our writing, all creative work in danger of assuming its fatal parodistic aspect. For an experimental poet to deal with the subject of poetry-writing itself, without it turning into high narcissism, is a noteworthy accomplishment. "Men in Camisoles" begins, "All writing is a form / of transvestism," an epigram that a less skilled poet might have followed up with some false rendering of the possibilities of the independent writerly self. Not to do that, and yet refrain from bathos at one's expense, is difficult, and perhaps the essence of humor itself.

Equi's images belong to the world constructed around them in an essentially logical relationship—each one affixed in the right place at the right time, as in the conclusion to "Art About Fear": "Still searching / for that spider / that goes so fast / and travels far. // Its poisonous scratches / like those of a pen." Again, as in "Brand X," the flow of meaning travels both ways—we derive value from the whorish writing world as much as it does from the well-meaning poet, and yet this doesn't mean that critique is impossible, or that it need wallow in its own dirt.

Equi's precise images compel rereading of the poems to locate their true value; this effort is always rewarded, as in "My Father Sees a UFO," where he listens to "a sound / small as the ice melting in his glass," or in "Sometimes I Get Distracted," which ends with the Zen monk throwing a ball "standing in his garden / centuries away." Time and space are collapsible not as high modernism would have had it, as perceptual antidotes to the fixities of a bureaucratic regime, but as notions that are implicated in the very fabric of our self-definition as consumers and citizens and artists.

Experimental poetry makes much of the borrowed nature of all language, the public imbrication of private utterings. Equi's departure is not seeing this as an excuse to avoid a necessary moral posture. In *Voice-Over*'s "Monologue: Frank O'Hara," while "the words are never really ours for keeps," it's also true that "The music is certainly blue enough / but not without its own tenderness / like an arrow shot I know where." If we know beforehand exactly where we're shooting arrows, the mystery is gone; yet this is not an excuse for illiteracy. A fine illustration of this ethic is "Second Thoughts," which, like "Folk Dance," could easily have degenerated into nonsequential doggerel, but remains a pageant to artistic creation that rewards repeated readings. "Armani Weather," like "Brand X," synthesizes our incorporation into consumerist culture without making apologies for any side in the bargain.

Equi has an eighteenth-century rationalist, pragmatic, enlightened sensibility, able to tackle the horrors of the present time without succumbing to the siren song of narcissism. She is one of the premier feminist poets of her generation. Equi's poem from *Voice-Over*, "Thesis Sentence," concludes: "The poem is a small machine made of God." Sometimes, if we're lucky, the poet is a maker of Gods.

HONEST CLARITY

THE ART OF SUBTRACTION: NEW AND SELECTED POEMS BY JAY PARINI. GEORGE BRAZILLER, 2005.

In times of distress, the poet who keeps his heart intact is the most consoling (hence also rare to the point almost of extinction). Here there are no adolescent verbal pyrotechnics, no shoehorned metaphors worked in for their sensational value, no wasted words which devalue their unposturing neighbors—and neither traditionalism nor confessionalism rampage in these pages for their own sake. Yet this poet isn't cool or distant: his work is fiery hot to the touch, the apparent simplicity a form of high art whose final sum is the result of many turns of the subtracting hand.

If Parini's art has a constant register, it is the intellectual's search for sanity in a world that by definition lacks it when large numbers of people are involved. Because he doesn't make an outspoken virtue of his own sanity, we willingly enter his cautionary world, giving him credit for self-contained knowledge at each step of the way.

The selections in this volume from previous collections—*Anthracite Country* (1982), *Town Life* (1988), and *House of Days* (1998)—reveal the poet's progress, through childhood, youth, and early maturity, and as son, husband, and father, toward an intelligence—akin to his admired Robert Penn Warren's in "Swimming After Thoughts," from *House of Days*—"that cunningly preserves what's left to stoke / his engines further."

In the "skilled dismantling" in "Suburban Swamp" from *Town Life*, and in the thirst that is "briefly quenched" in "Rain Before Nightfall" from *House of Days*, there is a hint of regret that perhaps too many things have been subtracted along the way to self-sufficiency: the sense in the selections from the earlier collections is that knowledge is not always earned through pure rigor, that grace is often at play. The poet doubting the efficacy of his scholarly rectitude is the continuing thread in the new poems as well, although now he shows more confidence in his method of work.

The purpose of the opening section among the new poems, "After the Terror," seems to be to reinfect the debased language of today's demagogues with new vitality: the mere act of restatement—in "State of the Union," "The President Alone," and "In the Village of the New Century"—without recourse to poetical language, should be enough to do the trick. Any reasonably intelligent person is presumably in possession of the imaginative resources to understand, and expose to his own satisfaction, the emotional drives behind the impotent daily rituals prescribed by those in charge.

If one is willing to make this minimal effort—how difficult, after all, is it to see the truth-lie of "Everything has changed, though nothing has," in "After the Terror?"—if one can indeed respond with imaginative triumph to brutal rigor, then there is hope of moving on to a saner future.

From the second section, "Fish-Eye View," onward, things get considerably more exciting. There is a lot of Hardy here, and Frost, their serious-playful construction of the wise person's relation to the flux of the world in plenty of evidence. The poems in "Fish-Eye View" elaborate the hiddenness of things, the ever-regressing layers of meaning that depart from surface reality, whether in the natural world, as in "Crow's Nest," or the social world, as in "Old Teams." But the mysticism in this attitude is moderated: surely, the origins and ends of things are not entirely beyond recognition, are they? Or there would be all the room in the world for tyrants to fool us with their mumbo-jumbo.

There is admirable moral restraint in poems like "High School," "Family Reunion," "Covenant in April," and "Waiting Room," the poet never asserting his superior imaginative worth over his poor readers. The diction is as always spare, each everyday word enriched and magnified by the considerable weight it's meant to carry: in effect, this is a downward recalibration of language, in an age of pointless verbal excess. The imaginative conceits are similarly "simple"—understandable by those outside the academy, without access to poetic language—and yet for that very reason they sustain a high order of meaning. This is true of "Misjudgments," "The Imperial Bed Chamber," "The Living Rooms of South Rebecca," and the shorter poems throughout the volume.

Parini never makes a fetish of being oppressed, least of all by that all-determining bugaboo called History. The corollary to this realization of everyone's latent ability to be a participant who counts—a most democratic attitude—is the refusal to make a fetish of being elevated by Nature. Parini's romance is with the substantiality, the materialness, of the roots and branches of nature's manifestations, never losing sight of the fact that man is above all a creature compelled to move forward in his own history. Every covenant is either a natural offshoot of one's predominant mood, or it means nothing.

The third and last section of the new poems, "White Cane," is the most thrilling. This is a harbinger of the promised wiser future, where language and meaning are capable of being restored to orderly correspondence. In "After the Big Bang," Parini's own consistently followed motto is succinctly stated: "Meaning follows from a certain burst, / the blunt initial blue-struck blade, / the bid for help, the consequential word." In "Mind," the comparison is to the restlessness of the wind, which "knows nothing"; in "A Short Address to the Academy of Silence," we learn that disciplining the overreaching urges of rhetoric, so that solitude is found even in kindred company, is the way station to a knowing mind: "We must form academies of silence, / classes where the only sounds occur / when empty pages flutter in the gust / as tinny leaves rehearse their crumbling." Any delusion that the hiddenness of things has finally been understood is punctured, however, in the immediately following "White Cane."

To what purpose, though, the stripping away of excess language—and by extension excess emotion and interpretation? In the remaining poems of "White Cane," we get a fish-eye view of the poet's work seeing the poet: the vigorous man slaving for "the work itself, its laughter and its tears, / this snake that eats its tail and disappears," as in "After Hours." After all, aren't all manuscripts lost (even if refound), from the first moment of creation, as we get the sense in "The Lost Manuscripts?"

"By the Light of Morning Snow," "Large Projects," and "A Life Sentence" illustrate Parini's aesthetic ideal, language having been stripped of redundancy to an almost unbearable extent: what remains after all the necessary subtractions is the poet as the sum of all the passengers on "The Heaven Train"—Jesus and the apostles, Peter and Luke, Judas and John, Mark and Matthew, and above all Paul. But Judas, in his questioning of loyalty (to a God whose rituals are boringly predictable) isn't far behind as the essence of the model citizen-poet: in "Judas in His Cups," how could we not fail to share Judas's sickened view of Jesus's hey-presto miracles? For this poet, disenchantment—as in "The Pope on the Subway"—need not lead to despair. The poet as "Appleseed" doesn't need miracles, when "[h]is life's his deed."

The real miracle, which one hopes comes unannounced by pomp and ceremony, is to be able to "subtract the last things" one doesn't need, as Parini shows in "The Art of Subtraction." The lesson for aspiring poets is the immensity of honest clarity that can be added after ruthless subtraction: the life and the art become twining folds of simplicity in this most daring of formulations.

FEMINIST POETRY, THE WAY IT USED TO BE

LOVE BELONGS TO THOSE WHO DO THE FEELING: NEW AND SELECTED POEMS (1966-2006) BY JUDY GRAHN. RED HEN PRESS, 2008.

Judy Grahn takes us back to the raw energy of early second-wave feminism. Today's post-post-feminist poetics has radically downshifted to accommodate the failures (real and imagined) of the women's movement, but Grahn returns us to the thrilling point of origin, as dreams were being hatched, patriarchy was being clubbed to death, and a new world seemed within grasp. Grahn's poetry is rooted in the most essential old English rhythms. Hers is verse worthy of memorization; it is not prose masquerading as poetry, set off by haphazard line breaks. Every rhyme, every break, every surge, every pause is earned. Grahn's prosodical skill results in a high-energy verse, fused with its political aims. This is a faithful marriage of high art with political purpose, a potent combination sorely missed today.

Grahn's style, fortunately, has not shifted for the worse as the fortunes of the feminist movement have ebbed. She remains as hyper-charged a bard at the end as at the beginning, giving nothing to cynicism and lassitude. In "Some Ways of Knowing This Is a 'Judy Grahn' Poem'" we are told that "it has craft and musical sensibility, meant both to stand well on the page and to be satisfying to read out aloud or perform." From the oral vitality of *Edward the Dyke and Other Poems* (1966-1870) to that of the late poems "Forest, forest" and "News" there is no lapse.

"A History of Lesbianism," an early poem, sets the Grahn

pattern, a dialectic that works by composing the subterranean voice as the inveterate enemy of ideology. Thus,

> How they lived in the world,
> the women-loving-women
> learned as much as they were allowed
> and walked and wore their clothes
> the way they liked
> whenever they could. They did whatever
> they knew to be happy or free
> and worked and worked and worked.
> The women-loving-women
> in America were called dykes
> and some liked it
> and some did not.

The gritty ordinariness—working-class lives persisting despite invisibility—is dynamited by the ending: "The subject of lesbianism / is very ordinary; it's the question / of male domination that makes everybody / angry." In "the big horse woman," we read: "red was above the mountain / and red was in her eyes / and red the water running / on the big horse woman's thighs," but the poem concludes: "this poem is called / how Naomi gets her period," again a disruption of the comforting rhythm by descriptive rationality, a pointer to how we undermine spirituality by relentless classification. When the "Vietnamese woman speaking to an American soldier" says: "make children play / in my jungle hair / make rice flare into my sky like / whitest flak / the whitest flash," we hear a voice that we've never heard before.

The Common Woman Poems (1969) are seven of the classics of American poetry. The common woman is common as "a nail," "a thunderstorm," "the reddest wine," and in the most famous poem, "Vera, from my childhood," she is common as "the best of bread / and will rise / and will become strong—I swear to you / ...on my common / woman's / head." The second of these poems, "Ella, in a square apron, along Highway 80," reads in its entirety:

She's a copperheaded waitress,
tired and sharp-worded, she hides
her bad brown tooth behind a wicked
smile, and flicks her ass
out of habit, to fend off the pass
that passes for affection.
She keeps her mind the way men
keep a knife—keen to strip the game
down to her size. She has a thin spine,
swallows her eggs cold, and tells lies.
She slaps a wet rag at the truck drivers
if they should complain. She understands
the necessity for pain, turns away
the smaller tips, out of pride, and
keeps a flask under the counter. Once,
she shot a lover who misused her child.
Before she got out of jail, the courts had pounced
and given the child away. Like some isolated lake,
her flat blue eyes take care of their own stark
bottoms. Her hands are nervous, curled, ready
to scrape.
The common woman is as common
as a rattlesnake.

Survival, in Grahn's world, comes without frill and frolic; it is not the luxury elite memoirists have made it out be.

The *She Who* (1972-1974) poems signal an increase in confidence, the common woman's will increasingly manifest. In "She Who increases/what can be done," the speaker says: "I shall grow another breast / in the middle of my chest / what shall it be," and as we find out, "breast number three / is She—Who—works—for—me." "The enemies of She Who call her various names," "She who bears it," "bowl of blood," and "The woman in three pieces" are early examples of expropriating demeaning vocabulary, reassembling disassembled parts, restarting a forgotten vocabulary based in honesty. "Carol and her crescent wrench," for example, begins:

Carol and
her crescent wrench
work bench
wooden fence
wide stance
Carol and her
pipe wrench
pipe smoke
pipe line
high climb
smoke eyes
chicken wire
Carol and her
hack saw
well worn
torn back
bad spine
never—mind
timberline
clear mind

The breaks accord with extreme pressure to deliver, if we only "let her." Similarly, "the woman whose head is on fire" starts reassembling the disembodied She Who:

the woman whose head is on fire
the woman with a noisy voice
the woman with too many fingers
the woman who never smiled once in her life
the woman with a boney body
the woman with moles all over her.

Grahn's ongoing project, a four part epic poem, two of which, *The Queen of Wands* (1980-1982) and *The Queen of Swords* (1986-1987), are excerpted, engages with the myth of Helen of Troy. Grahn says she has "taken the literary idea 'Helen' (as the beauty of all women) and splattered her as if she were an egg, except each splatter has a regenerative quality;

they are not identical but they have the same substance." In *Swords*, Grahn has "modernized Helen...by setting the scene in an underworld lesbian bar of contemporary times." Yet at no point in this "mythic realism" does Grahn lose hold of the vigor of her rhythms. The times have become more complicated, but as ever Grahn has her eyes on the prize which, according to "Like a woman in childbirth wailing," is "This industrialization / of love, of birth, // this is the last besieged castle."

Grahn should be required reading for poetry workshops, to demonstrate that a vital, accessible, politically necessary poetry from a woman's point of view can still be written, without any need to resort to narcissistic confession, willful obscurity, or language games. Before there were many niche feminisms (with a haughty academic feminism perched at the top and frowning on working-class mysteries), there was the discovery of the "common woman," deep as ancient myth, solid as the next-door neighbor, and Grahn, as much as any other poet, discovered her for us. As Grahn says in her Introduction, "Do working class and poor people have minds, and rich histories, and great capacity to engage in civic life? Or are we just objects of sympathy?" We must read her again to glean the answer.

HOW COMPETENCE HAS KILLED
THE AMERICAN SHORT STORY

BEST NEW AMERICAN VOICES 2007. SUE MILLER,
EDITOR. HARVEST/HARCOURT, 2006.

My continuing thought during this reading experience was, These stories are so very good, they're intolerably bad. Competence without genius has killed the modern American literary short story. These meet every last requirement of the well-made story, but there is no soul, no emotion worth speaking of. In fact, Sue Miller's Introduction takes note of Flannery O'Connor's comment that "the short story as a medium is in danger of dying of competence." The emerging writers showcased here, in this anthology representing the best of the writing programs, conferences, and colonies, have mastered the formula for successfully published and awarded literary stories, in much the same fashion that consumers of writing manuals first found success publishing stories with slick commercial magazines in the twenties and thirties. (The so-called "experimental" story, the other staple of the writing programs and the hippest of the literary quarterlies, is a separate beast with its own formula; but this is a subject for another essay—here, the focus is on the kind of realistic story the writing programs are choosing to package for broad marketing through this and other similar anthologies.) Sue Miller argues that there's "[n]ot a workshop story in the bunch," but in fact every single story fits the quintessential workshop model, even as it holds the promise (and this is the seduction) that it may turn out to be more. To walk the fine line between literary promise and compromise is really the art these fifteen emerging writers have conquered.

Let me define the standard American workshop story as I understand it. The narrative unfolds in a linear, chronological manner, with only as much backstory provided as necessary, the flashbacks working effortlessly to create just the right degree of tension—there's never too much information, nor too little, to either overwhelm or mystify us. Workshop stories accept a stable order of time and place, and stories occur within realistically identifiable milieus and settings; the Newtonian pushes and pulls are always obeyed, the deterministic logic of characters' actions always turning inward in the end, rather than radiating outward to affect their cultural context. In other words, this is a naïvely individualistic conception of reality, the declarations of America's founding fathers, or the enlightenment philosophes, taken at face value. The atomism is reinforced by history, politics, and culture serving only as background to individuals' private struggles, never as forefront of the story itself. No institution (a city, an organization, a company, a community) is ever the leading character itself; these external realities are subjectively processed by (usually a single) individual consciousness, so that a form of relativism is imposed on the available means of perception. The stability of context and relativity of perception are not really in conflict; holding the first steady allows the writer to easily toy with relatively shifting points of view.

Certain stylistic tics necessarily follow from these first principles of storytelling. In nearly all these stories, the time frame is neither extremely compressed (a few minutes or hours or days) nor extremely broad (stretching over decades or longer), but occurs over a "reasonable" length of time (almost leisurely, one might say); "dramatic" scenic moments are frequently interrupted by the blank white space indicating transition. Whenever a story flags, all a writer has to do is to insert the blank white space, and chronologically shift to a slightly earlier or later time, and provide some useful backstory, to fill us in on the characters' motivations. The impression (a hundred years after modernism) is of time facilely yielding to authorial manipulation. The point of view in fourteen of the fifteen stories here is either limited third person, or first person; no degree of authorial omniscience, in any of its classic forms, is ever exploited. Occasional poetic or lyric language is quickly subdued by attention-grabbing announcements (what I will call "information bombs"), again and again shoving the reader's face into the pungent earth of the writer's excavations; the poetic language functions only as a mood-setter, a rhythmic device, which must be balanced by the violent (always brief) expositional outburst. To Miller, the language in these stories might seem diverse, fluctuating from the "elegiac to wired, from elliptical to elaborate," but this is true only within the parameters of the workshop story; seen from outside its rules, the elegiac or exuberant tone is never anything but a means to near-complete closure (a decisive fact about all fifteen stories), the shutting down of metaphysical ambiguity, and the purely individualist epiphany to tie it all together at the end.

Enough of a general diagnosis. Each of the stories might easily serve the purpose of individual analysis with generalizable results, which again suggests that a formula is in place. Alice J. Marshall's "By Any Other Name" is about a stuffy suburban rosarian named Smith, who has deflected all his emotion toward maintaining the best rose garden in his neighborhood. His wife Marian is the device which allows him to indirectly socialize with humanity. When his neighbor Mrs. Martin starts undergoing chemotherapy, and can't take care of her competing rose garden anymore, Smith has the brilliant idea of maneuvering his way into taking charge of it. Smith, being the coldest of the lot, remains in the greatest degree of denial as he makes plans about the future (of Mrs. Martin's rose garden) when Mrs. Martin herself is liable to die. In Nevil Shute's novel of a post-nuclear holocaust Australia, *On the Beach*, people's inability to process the inevitability of doom, and their fixation with planning for a lost future, is carried to a peak. In Marshall's story, this point is acknowledged but subdued to the point of vanishing, as all the focus remains only on Smith's obsession with refuting Mrs. Martin's plan to nurture the difficult Jude the Obscure rose. We cannot miss the obviousness of the symbolism. Because the characters are so fully explained, the symbolism is a perfunctory adjunct to what we already understand from the first summarizing paragraph, rather than an invitation to import difficult meaning. Far from being a meditation on our denial of death, the story becomes a mildly pleasant account of Smith's comeuppance (a happy ending!). All the gaps among human beings' knowledge of each others' essence are resolutely shut down, so that when the story is over, the story is over (unlike, say, Tolstoy's "The Death of Ivan Ilyich," where the concentrically expanding circles of mystery associated with an individual's impending death are potentially wide enough to include everything in the universe).

Ellen Litman's "About Kamyshinskiy" is about a group of recent Russian émigrés in an eastern city (in these days of Homeland Security and an undeclared immigration moratorium, for Litman the only issue seems to be how immigrants handle themselves, once they pick up and leave their homelands at will), with one of the women, Kamyshinskiy's wife, having already died of cancer, and another, Seryozah's wife Olya, currently undergoing treatments. Litman shifts among different third-person limited points of view, but this device is wasted in her hands, since no ironic counterpoint is introduced; the story could easily have been told from an unshifting limited third-person point of view, which is essentially what it is. Like the other stories, this one begins from a low level of conceptualization (moving to America makes the Russians more likely to give in to hedonistic urges than in the old country) and remains there; the author is committed to a basically uplifting story of America bringing about a benign synthesis between tradition and experimentation. At the end, the moral is neatly summed up by Seryozha: "It's not America. It's them. America just gave them space." The story reaches complete closure, is never about the neighborhood or the community but only about individuals, and the moral strain of switching allegiance from communism to consumerism is never explored; it can't, in the bounds of the workshop story.

Lydia Peelle's "Shadow on a Weary Land" owns the theme with the most social potential (leftover countercultural types, including "the Musician," hunt for Jesse James's buried treasure, on a Nashville outskirt being demolished in the rage for development), so its undermining with a persistent lyricism is all the more disappointing. This story could actually have been about Brown's Ridge Pike, a natural refuge threatened by commercialism, but it remains one about the lack of nerve of the motley group of characters; because the author herself seems overwhelmed by nostalgia (rather than protest), there is little space to ask meaningful communal questions. The point is more, These folks had better get used to the inevitable, than Is what we think the inevitable really so? Whenever we're likely to get angry, in comes the first-person narrator with a lyrical passage, or an information bomb ("I used to be an inventor," "Since my stroke…" "Lacy's baby starts to show") is dropped to take us right back into a character's solitary background. It concludes: "Everything changes. Even in Brown's Ridge. Of course I know."

The thin substance of the new realism is suggested by how easily the stories dealing with suburban dysfunction shade over into belligerent parody, a hip adolescent tone which suggests the Reality TV smash-mouth influence on the young authors. A slight shift toward understatement of tone, in M. O. Walsh's "The Freddies," would have given us a standard suburban family drama, much as Ryan Effgen's "The Inappropriate Behavior of Our Alleged Loved Ones" (where *Happy Days* and *Guns & Ammo* intrude for their symbolism). We are our beastly instincts, is the point of these stories, as is Dan Pope's "Karaoke Night," where the setting is the concluding metaphor. How easily the themes can be foreshadowed, prognosticated, summarized! Viet Thanh Nguyen's "A Correct Life," which is about a handsome young Vietnamese refugee's coming-of-age (and homosexual awareness) in 1970s San Francisco, begins: "Liem's plan was to walk calmly past the waiting crowd after he disembarked, but instead he found himself hesitating at the gate, scanning the strange faces anxiously." The workshop rule of clarity has been so completely absorbed as to squeeze everything but clarity out of the stories, essentially leaving nothing in place. In this as in the other stories, nothing surprising happens, because the data must seamlessly correlate with action. The concluding paragraph is a masterpiece of reductionist binary contact (between America and Vietnam), heavy-handed symbolism, and the standard-issue forward-looking epiphany. Caimeen Garrett, while projecting, in "The Temperate Family," the current obsession with missing children back to eighteen-seventies America, fails to exploit the satirical means superficially at hand to explode the fetishization of children's innocence which began in the Victorian age (and has found renewed energy since the seventies). It becomes another individual case study of obsession, refusing to go beyond a certain depth, the promise of social exploration wasted with the requisite epiphany and full closure.

The new American diversity is apparently pulling the short story away from suburban dysfunction; the problem isn't the content, which does plunder the big subjects, but the style. In Fatima Rashid's "Syra"—where a working-class Pakistani immigrant is being deported, forced to leave a wife and child behind—because all the elements are formulaically in place, there is little emotional engagement. The deportee had crossed the Mexican border, hid his past from his wife, feels guilty for having let his sister drown in Pakistan two decades ago, and now finds his past catching up with him after immigration registration. The tone of the opening paragraph makes the end fully predictable (true of all the stories); "Syra" is like the other stories in the conventionality of the dialogue, the undisturbing balance between scene and summary, the stated and the unstated. The past, present, and future are seamlessly connected, leaving no emotional charge. This is equally true of Keya

Mitra's "Pompeii Recreated," which is about an Indian divorcée facing constrained remarriage options in Houston; all the narrative elements are assembled, the recurrent water symbolism conveniently spells transitions, the reader's stereotypes of overbearing Indian men and semi-assertive Indian women aren't challenged, and the reader is forced to note the parallelism in sacrifice among three different generations of women. The conclusion is utterly sealed.

Kevin A. González's "Wake" is steeped in the Natalee Holloway Aruba setting, *Girls Gone Wild*, and a whole array of Hollywood movies and popular music exploiting the coming-of-age potential of the Caribbean islands. The function of the setting is to bring out the theme (the conflict between the discipline necessary for success in the States and the freedom the islands' playscape provides), but it is merely introduced, not explored, leaving no point to the various characters' emotional callousness except as it echoes television anger, and easily parodies a superficial post-Bret Easton Ellis, post-Seinfeld cynicism. To make something happen, González either drops frequent information bombs (to appease short attention spans), or melodramatic interjections (like Uzi-wielding robbers "with black stockings over their heads" disrupting bar flirtation). The prose rhythm, the anti-style, if you will, is quintessential workshop: half Hemingway, half Alice Munro, a nonexperimentalism with language that journalistically replays realist conventions. Time past, present, and future seamlessly meld toward definitive closure, as all loose ends are tied up: "Our wake looks like the tail of a cloud: shaking everything up from underneath, unsettling the plane of the surface."

Exactly the same observations apply to Anne de Marcken's "Ashes" (like "Wake," the title announces closure) where journalist Louise (an extension of Marshall's Smith) exploits her husband Dan's request to scatter his ashes in the ocean as material for an article for *Home & Hearth*. Had de Marcken provided a sample of Louise's writing, that would have created distance between narrator and character. This would-be meditation on the current state of writing never turns that way, as blank white spaces suggest stable linearity, the logic of death remains subdued, entertaining interludes work toward closure, and the epiphany is immaculately set up. The panoramic sweep never spills beyond the grasp of the containing metaphor, the tight conceit. Robert Liddell's "Whatever Happened to Sébastien Grosjean?" is in the same mode, as the setting of a tennis match between overdog Roger Federer and underdog Grosjean at Houston's elite River Oaks tournament, watched by the corporate-trader point-of-view character and his upper-class friend Win (whose father, boxholder at the club, is dying of cancer), says nothing about class difference, has no point except to suggest that the upper classes might have a difficult time grieving. Grosjean can't make a comeback; it is inevitable. Can elegance and panache beat back death? That's not even the symbolic territory this exploitative story breaches.

There isn't in these workshop productions a single searing note of anger at the world's poverty and injustice, the vast bridge between classes and nations' degrees of affluence; American consumerism owns the world, and the narrative strategies of these authors smoothly reinforce this unalterable given.

VOICE IN FICTION:
A FAVORITE MFA/WRITING PROGRAM SHIBBOLETH

At the *L.A. Times* Book Festival, all they're talking about is voice: http://latimesblogs.latimes.com/jacketcopy/2010/04/literary-prize-winners-discuss-the-use-of-voice-and-language.html.

And:http://latimesblogs.latimes.com/jacketcopy/2010/04/selling-unstoppable-voices-to-the-highest-bidder.html.

Teachers of writing instruct: "Discover your own voice. You're not a real writer until you've found your own voice. Once you find your voice you're on your way. It took me years to find my voice."

Agents say, "Let me read the first fifty (or five) pages of your novel, to see if I like the voice."

Editors say they loved your plot and characterization but couldn't fall in love with your voice.

What the hell does voice mean? I'm clueless. This is just another of those fakeries writing teachers — or writers forced to sit on panels and not having the intellectual honesty to talk about the tough work of writing rather than writing as the festival or conference-goer sees it — pull out of the hat when they have nothing else to talk about.

It's like talking about tonality in poetry. It has the same kind of meaninglessness.

Did James Joyce discover his voice with *Dubliners*? *A Portrait of the Artist as a Young Man*? *Ulysses*? *Finnegans Wake*? Oh, I guess he shifted voice each time. What an asshole — definitely not a real writer. He didn't find his voice until he died, I guess. Maybe after *Finnegans Wake* he'd have found his voice.

What about Hemingway? He stayed true to his "voice" after his first successes. Maybe he shouldn't have.

I recently read Chang-rae Lee's four accomplished novels. He has a distinct voice in each of his four novels. Is he still discovering his voice? Is he an apprentice writer?

Voice is too vague to be useful for anything. I suppose it means each writer has a distinct style and he ought to stay true to it. Chekhov sounds like no other writer; early Chekhov we can legitimately dismiss as lesser writing, because he hadn't yet arrived at his style. The same goes for anyone else. The Faulkner style. The Graham Greene style. The Evelyn Waugh style. The David Lodge style. The Kingsley Amis style and the Martin Amis style. The Salman Rushdie style. And on and on.

On the other hand, Salman Rushdie wrote *Fury* (his worst book)—the "culmination" of his style? And his *Grimus* was not in his style, and hence unimportant. But what about *The Enchantress of Florence*? Are we really saying that his style in his new book is the same as in *Midnight's Children*? Hasn't he matured in the meantime? Style is about all he has read and written in the duration.

Talking about style is different—and much more difficult and off-putting. Style suggests endless experiment with technique, rigorous effort, deep training in the canon, elaboration and enhancement rather than sanguine discovery by subtraction, the possibility of change over time, crossover (positive and negative) effects between genres (Rushdie's essays versus his fiction), the linkages connecting one to the important developments in the reign of the language. The language itself changes—locally, globally—even in one's own lifetime, and that has everything to do with style.

Style, you see, is much less conducive to hyperventilation. You can't talk about how you spent twenty years soaking in Nabokov and Coetzee, but in the end arrived at something uniquely yours, yet utterly unimaginable without having absorbed these writers for decades. Your style is made up of the unique concoction of writers you most seriously absorbed. There is not some cuckoo-clock "voice" waiting inside you to pop out at 12:00 a.m., sounding like no other clock in the world.

Sometimes maybe you ought to sound exactly like someone else you admire—or even hate. Sometimes you ought to cheat, plagiarize, copy, steal. Sometimes that may be the best early training. And in cheating and stealing you may discover how hard style really is. Style doesn't await you every morning, finished, stamped with your name and honorific. It wants to escape you if you show so much as an iota of laziness. It is not yours to possess and claim as your own. It is shared property. You owe it to Shakespeare. You are nothing on your own. To think that you possess a voice of your own is delusional.

Voice you're supposedly born with, only to discover at some fortuitous moment in time, style you laboriously acquire over time—or really, something you can never finish acquiring, even if you're the greatest writer alive. Amy Tan has a voice editors and agents can recognize (or think they do); Coetzee has a style that baffles you from *Disgrace* to *Slow Man*. He has matured. Partly he has disowned who he used to be. As it should be.

Style is something editors—and writing teachers—are not qualified to critique; to critique someone's style requires you to be at least at the same level of accomplishment as the writer in question; but voice anyone can critique. How does one critique voice anyway? What does one say, except utter inanities? Your voice is too sarcastic. Your voice is too hallucinatory. Your voice is too boozy. But that's not how voice is critiqued. It's something, actually, beyond critique. You either have it or don't have it.

It's a subterfuge, allowing one to judge individual effort without making any real attempt to penetrate the infinite densities of style. It has the same philosophical value as the equally bullshit "Show don't tell" or "Write what you know."

Plot and characterization work integrally with language, and the writer finds the language to connect plot and characterization such that both seem utterly natural.

It may mean having a minimalist style, or a maximalist style, but can't that change over time, from book to book, or even during the course of a book? Is Lawrence Durrell, aside from *The Alexandria Quartet*, not Lawrence Durrell? Is he a fraudster? Does D. H. Lawrence change over time? Virginia Woolf? Nabokov?

Even once a writer hits his stride with style, he experiments with it all his life. That is, if he has any guts at all. I remember the Dave Eggers of *A Heartbreaking Work of Staggering Genius*. Now I'm confronted with *Zeitoun*. I guess Dave lost his "voice" somewhere along the road. Oh wait, there were also some really different other books along the way, so he's been floundering all along, hasn't he?

Writers need to be told to put aside the idea that they can learn writing by being told fancy concepts. Like voice, or tone. Or neat dictums like finding your voice under your ass, where you've been sitting on it all along, or in your condom wrapper or Ikea knife set or Peelu toothpaste or wherever it's been hiding.

Voice is for one-trick ponies. Not for behemoths like George Orwell. From *Burmese Days* to *Keep the Aspidistra Flying* to *Animal Farm* to *1984* to his great essays, where is the voice of George Orwell?

I hope I never see the day when I've found my voice. How is it possible to ever find your voice? Voice is mystical. It puts the writer on a pedestal. No writer worth his salt ought to want that.

P.S. In MFA parlance, voice may actually mean a hypercharged, galloping, contextless spree—such as in Junot Diaz or Jonathan Safran Foer or Colson Whitehead—choked with metaphors, overwritten, edgy, hip, cool, self-conscious, rapid-fire, disguising any honesty and sincerity in writing, or rather, covering up for the lack of it. Antonya Nelson and Maile Meloy write more "mature" versions of this voice. That's what they really seem to mean, if they tell you, Honey, I don't think you've found your voice yet. That's the reigning voice, the Michael Chabon, Jonathan Lethem off-kilter irony, Philip K. Dick with a lobotomy, and you better get with the program, the Manhattan-Brooklyn affectedness, or else. Also, a lot of graphic novels seem to represent this voice. The voice and the picture are merging. And they say science fiction is a con.

NEW RULES FOR WRITING FICTION

To presume knowledge on the part of the reader greater than the writer's own, in each and every visual image, in all instances of speculative metaphysics, is the new sine qua non of effective narrative. The reader's hostilities toward a world at once benevolent and repressive toward him cannot be contained in the nature of the self-contained artifact of old, with beginning, middle, and end. This goes beyond the alleged nonlinearity of the contemporary style of postmodernist fiction, initiated in the sixties: what is being called for is not that kind of rebellion, it is orders of magnitude greater than those early rumblings of discontent. Postmodernist fiction was a tame offshoot of modernism, when all is said and done, living by the old rules, handed down and turned over from side to side to extract the maximum benefit from the quintessential realism of the nineteenth century in all its various forms. The rules then still presumed a domestic sphere alienated from the political one. Now, the domestic as such doesn't exist, neither does the extraneous environment which breathes fire into it or pours water over it. To want to continue to write the old style of fiction requires continued belief in the old categories, but all those categories of being and existence have ceased to matter. The most interesting writing today comes from writers born in the developing world, or with a close orientation to it: they are still playing out the clash of classes in their thrilling narratives. Yet this too is only a partway advance toward the glories of the novel yet to come. There is a truly global culture in existence for the very first time in human history, every event anticipated and acknowledged and deconstructed before its actual occurrence (such as the current crisis over global warming) or the millennial year concern over terrorism (which bore post-apocalyptic fruit soon thereafter). Writing that is not far in advance of this fundamentally altered reality of the mechanisms of perception is writing that is stillborn, abortive, reprehensibly cute and precious, doomed to die.

1. Audience. Pre-eighteenth century, the audience was patronized, was the patron, small and elite and knowing, so the writer wrote as though for himself. In the two democratic centuries that followed, the writer's audience was the slightly more ideal version of himself, able to grasp verities just beyond his reach, confident, marching onward toward the glorious future. Now the future is here, and it is not anything anyone anticipated: it is a future where nothing happens, for the foreseeable distance, regardless of the rise of heretofore undeveloped countries to economic prominence. The back of the technocratic/mechanistic/bureaucratic beast cannot be broken, yet its beastliness is for the first time a historical fact. It wasn't quite so during and after World War II, because the last ideological struggles were still playing out; now that they have finally faded from the historical stage for the first time since the initiation of the democratic audience (no one takes seriously any current political ideology, not a single one), there is again a need to bring into being an audience which doesn't yet exist. The astute writer today addresses himself more and more to an audience not of the present (whether elite or democratic or avant-garde) but to an audience of the unseeable future. As soon as he lapses into addressing the present, his writing becomes immature, not sufficiently tragic, hardens into rote forms and gestures. Every writer will have his own conception of what the audience of the future will be. It forces one to come to terms with the future, which is all we have left.

2. Psychology. The entire psychological apparatus of the liberal-democratic era is dead. What motivates humans, and why do they feel happy or sad? These are questions as fresh as Locke's slate again. (Sociobiology is a final assertion of vulgar empiricism, a last gasp of the failed value system.) People are not political creatures, par excellence, as Rousseau might have believed, in search of nobility and dignity. People are not bestial naturalist machines either, as Zola contemplated, and as Freud and his followers elaborated. Certainly, Freudianism of all shades is utterly dead, and certainly also the cadaverous Freudian-Marxist combination, such an impetus for critics of the second half of the twentieth century. The field here is clear: the human being is again ready to be conceptualized, in an era when human dignity has become as cheap as it was during the Dark Ages. If writers continue to write as though the linkages between individual consciousness and family or social bearings were still intact, they produce an unreal substance, the cheapest product on the market. Once again, the individual is alive to the possibility of being enshrined as the center of the universe, a project repeatedly under assault since the French Revolution. It won't be a second coming of the enlightenment, but an intensification of the humanist creed. Authority everywhere is falling down. The second-hand writer clings to the psychologists' authority over human development, explicating emotions as though they were necessary and productive, in their benign or vicious forms. But again today we don't know the first thing about what makes people act the way they do.

3. Nation. The novel has been the dominant form of the modern era, the intuitionists' step-by-step building of nationality, taking account of regional flavor, yet reaching for the confident nation-state's universality of beliefs (coextensive with imperialism). For the first time since the Renaissance, the nation-state is not a viable entity. Other forms of globalism were merely precursors; this is the beginning of the real occurrence. The worst tyrants have not been prepared for this cataclysmic result. The greatest battle today is between forms of friction and forms of fluidity to allow the emergence of a world nationality, where the role of particular languages ceases to matter. This might sound like the recurrence of an age-old ideological battle, but it is new, because absent the newest technologies of communication, the world nationality was only a dream. The shrewd writer no longer locates himself within a nation-state, a region, a neighborhood, a national ethic and sensibility. If he does, what he produces is less than sociological document, since it doesn't even have the latter's stickiness for resistant fact. The end of the nationalist writer means new forms of narrative, where the individual seeks to assert his being not in relation to a national reality, but a transnational one, meaning that he is in dialogue with many different cultural heritages all at once. This is fundamentally different than the novel of growth as sought by either Dickens or Joyce, and it utterly complicates the old psychological routines (I do such-and-such, because I am acted upon in such-and-such ways): one perceives the possibility of shifting between cultural traditions, not in the comatose late twentieth-century version of cheap parody and pastiche (a la Barthelme or Barth), but toward purposes not yet clear (since the final political arrangements are not yet known, and can't be known).

From these few preliminary principles, certain facts emerge. The future of the novel has never been brighter than it is now, since we only have to multiply what was accomplished in one nation-state at a time, within one cultural tradition at a time, to a possibility where all nations and all cultures are simultaneously in competition to provide sustaining narratives for the first truly global audience, connected for the first time to the anticipation of a historical future, a future that gets written day by day, moment by moment, already commented on before its fatal slippage.

The world may yet end in barbarity, due to shortage of technological ingenuity and overexploitation of resources, but if this ends up being the case, it will come about in gradations of pain we will have felt beforehand at each step of the way. Fiction must incorporate large, undigested, indigestible chunks of knowledge from all forms of disciplines (since the social sciences, as conceived in the nineteenth-century cauldron of empiricist pressure, are at an end anyway, and have ceded all those facts of human interaction to the artist), in order to stir things up in a more wholesome diet of reality saturated with the flavors of imagination. At the moment, writers bargain with small chunks of reality, as though they were in a zero-sum or losing game, not willing to bite off more than they can chew. They guard the thresholds of consciousness, reluctant to admit newcomers without clearly stated credentials, who might perhaps bring in deadly germs and viruses to the already vetted inhabitants inside. But we are at the final stages of reality as a removable adjunct from imagination, playing out in the utter discrediting of forms of national and particular authority. An avalanche of reality is at hand; it cannot be credentialed.

Readership has been declining because the writing product addresses itself not to a global audience of the future but to limited niches, as per the dictums of the marketing mavens of the publishing industry. Niches are self-limiting, doomed to obsolescence as soon as they are categorized as such, always in danger of further subdivision. The true writer exceeds these niches in every venture of his, contemptuous of the notion of history as that which is already known. Niches are in love with their own status, or so they are told, but always restless to move on. They are the final stage of the mass culture, the mass breaking up in allegedly discrete zones of self-consumption, idolizing publics who hire worshippers in their own image. At some fatal turning point, niches dissolve. Then the old energies, so long in abeyance, are suddenly released, let loose on the world. Part of the appearance of this shift is the conspicuous dumbness of large segments of the world population, the reemergence of myth, superstition, folklore, ritual, religion, mystery, sophistry, illogic, perversion, redundancy. But this is a temporary reckoning. More crucially, the energies find writers willing to be overwhelmed by the universes of tragic pain betokened by the flood. The flood is universal, leaving alone only certain mountaintops. Those who have seen it coming have already prepared their arks, unbeknownst to the ordinary niche-makers. They have left behind the social science disciplines which had so far been making competing claims to superior insight about human beings, and they have also left behind their status as supplicants to an irresistible commercial culture. A darkness is at hand, when it's not outright twilight, the worst of all conditions for navigation. The beginnings of language are once again palpable. The future of the novel has never been brighter.

My Warehouse Eyes, My Arabian Drums

Kapitoil: A Novel by Teddy Wayne. Harper
Perennial, 2010.

Teddy Wayne has written one of the best novels of my
generation. Free of the traps recent fiction writers have fallen
into—uninteresting, paralyzed, dysfunctional characters;
inorganic plots stemming from too narrow an appreciation
of reality; overwritten language, pretending to be lyrical,
when it substitutes for clear thought—*Kapitoil* cuts through
our cultural moment as sharply as Evelyn Waugh's *Scoop* or
A Handful of Dust did for their time.

Is it possible to play non-zero-sum games—
among individuals, businesses, institutions, and above
all civilizations—given existing language rules? What
would radical liberation of language, and hence thought
and action, mean? Asking these questions through his
lovable protagonist, Karim Issar, Wayne totally upends the
conventions of the 9/11 novel, the immigrant novel, and the
Wall Street novel.

Karim, a computer programmer from Doha, Qatar,
is helping Shrub Equities' New York office with Y2K
debugging. The novel consists of Karim's diaries from
October through December of 1999. The highly compressed
time period suggests that American culture is not so dense,
subtle, and textured as natives believe. Karim masters
American language pretty quickly.

Karim's unique vocabulary is what makes him most
"Karim-esque"; it's a concoction of business jargon, rational
matrices, mathematical probabilities, and predictive
speculations. Karim diligently lists new words and phrases

at the end of each chapter; after first meeting his officemates Jefferson Smithfield, Dan Wulf, and Rebecca Goldman, he defines "book it, genuflect, kudos, minor league, piggyback, pod(mate), privy to, scintillating, vassal, you was robbed." When Karim shivers, he "vibrates"; when he gets better, he is "enhanced"; he often "reroutes" his brain. The novel begins: "The Atlantic elongates below us like an infinite violet carpet."

Conventional American slang is as artificial as Karim's book-learned cost-benefit analysis; it is merely a time-honored method to help smooth indignities imposed by the system. The clash between these two styles allows Wayne to bypass the language of familiar first-person fictional consciousness, and to create something entirely new. He opens up a huge new space between forms of thought, allowing him to redefine love, compassion, fear, guilt, and grief in purely Karim-esque ways.

Karim, as an outsider, is able to see tangential things that natives ignore; this quality allows him to write a program that can profit off oil futures, based on the predictive ability of noise, contained in news, that others have ignored. This program, Kapitoil, becomes a potential lifeline for Shrub Equities. The firm's legendary founder, Derek Shrub, wines and dines Karim, takes him to the World Series at Yankee Stadium, and invites him to his Connecticut mansion, ostensibly as a role-model for his disobedient sons—all with a view to getting Karim to sign over ownership to Kapitoil. Karim has other ideas; he wants to turn the program to epidemiological purposes, to help with disease in the developing world. His mother died early, and his beloved sister Zahira, a smart biology student, suffers from ulcerative colitis. Shrub is as generous with Karim as he possibly can be, yet this is not enough for Karim.

Kapitoil is also one of our time's great love stories, free of every cliché of recent literary fiction. Karim—a truly Stendhalian romantic hero—falls in love with Rebecca, becoming quite a humanist in the process. Rebecca introduces him to Leonard Cohen and Bob Dylan, and under her tutelage he makes the jump straight to a particularly Karim-esque humanist postmodernism (one of his later entries reads: "phallogocentric: I still do not understand what this means"). Karim interprets Dylan through Jackson Pollock, the original inspiration for Kapitoil—but our society can no longer accommodate such synthesizing humanists.

We desperately wish Karim and Rebecca to beat the odds and be together, but Shrub is an immovable wall; once Karim makes his final decision, Shrub warns him: "You are a cipher…. You don't exist…. People from your area of the world can encounter visa problems very easily…. Sometimes they can't reenter the U.S. after they leave. Forever." Confronted with the loss of Rebecca, Karim, of course, makes a uniquely Karim-esque decision.

Throughout *Kapitoil*, Karim's rational brain tries to make sense of the power configurations in various games: fantasy baseball, real baseball, racquetball, pool, Taboo, Scrabble; each has penetrable rules, as is true of our overall culture. Karim's sheer decency compels him to break rules again and again; his most touching encounters are with the black driver Barron, toward whom Karim shows no class animus, and with whom occur Karim's first and last encounters in Manhattan.

Why did 9/11 happen, and why do we continue to respond so blindly? Wayne answers these questions better than Mohsin Hamid and Joseph O'Neill, the best authors of this genre until now, since *Kapitoil* never needs to mention 9/11, even peripherally. There is no metaphorical overload, no figurative ecstasy, just knife-sharp narrative. The 9/11 novel ought to be doomed, since Wayne has fully kapitoilized on its premises—much like Karim deciphering the tangential to return unprecedented rewards.

Wayne gives due credit to the American corporate establishment; yet even in its best light, it cannot play a non-zero-sum game with the Karim-esque. And that is the undeniable crux of the matter. Wayne breaks up the equation fiction writers have grown comfortable with, to argue that: suffering must be earned; there is a clash of cultures, but not between the antagonists we believe; America will keep playing zero-sum games until complete extinction; we're too far down our path-dependent trail for internal or external rescue; there will be no second acts.

This is a lot for one novel to pull off! After reading *Kapitoil*, you might well agree that this young author's fictional algorithms are impossibly ahead of the critically accepted market signals.

INTERIM INDIA

BETWEEN THE ASSASSINATIONS BY ARAVIND ADIGA.
FREE PRESS, 2009.

It is difficult to build on a book as successful as *The White Tiger*, which won the 2008 Booker Prize, and is a substantial addition to the canon of Indian diasporic writing. *The White Tiger*, to recollect, is about a hyper-ambitious Indian driver who takes revenge on the unjust economic and political system. Set in the twenty-first century, it describes an India in the throes of globalization, amidst the milieu of international call centers and falling bourgeois values.

Adiga has written not so much a follow-up, but a prismatic shattering of the clear, one-sided lens through which we read *The White Tiger*. It is not so much an expansion of novelistic possibility, but a willful step back to explain the raw emotions that went into *The White Tiger*. Where *The White Tiger* is highly finished, voice-driven, and ferociously cogent and consistent, *Between the Assassinations* ventures into its *pre*-aesthetic, so that it is determinedly uncentered (despite its being focused in the South Indian town of Kittur, a device familiar from Sherwood Anderson's *Winesburg, Ohio*), resists completion, and lacks the idiosyncratic private voice that often characterizes the postcolonial novel now.

Where *The White Tiger* is a singularly driven, almost Forsterian novel, in its desire to complete itself as text and subtext, leaving nothing to chance, *Between the Assassinations* stifles closure, to use that unfortunate cliché. This makes sense because whereas *The White Tiger* is located in a moment where the fundamental decision, for India to switch to a capitalist economy, was already made, "between the assassinations" refers to that nowhere land of the late 1980s when Indira Gandhi had already been assassinated (ending a phase of national certainty handed down from Nehru) and Rajiv Gandhi, her more Western-oriented son, had yet to be assassinated. India truly didn't know, in those years, where it was going. The linked-story format—which always indicates that the propulsion isn't there to show off a full-fledged novel—serves this transitory context well.

Adiga, in the new book, tells the same basic story over and over. Often, someone from the village has come to the city to make his fortune, but inevitably finds the limits of caste and class stopping him dead in his tracks. Ambition is raw and abundant, but opportunity severely limited. We might view the book almost as a justification for the chaos of post-1991, post-economic liberalization India. Kittur represents all of India's linguistic, religious, and cultural diversity, with its Muslim, Christian, and Hindu neighborhoods organized around timeless principles of segregation. Often, a go-getter from the lower class hinges himself to a rich patron, only to discover that he is useful only as long as he can outcompete countless others striving to replace him.

In "Day One (Afternoon): The Bunder," a Muslim factory owner is unable to escape bureaucratic corruption, if he is to keep his workers employed; in "Day Two: Lighthouse Hill," "Xerox Ramakrishna," who illegally copies books, stands up against censorship by selling *The Satanic Verses*; in "Day Two (Evening): Market and Maidan," two brothers, Vittal and Keshava, consider the choice between abject but consistent employment, or taking a risk with a temperamental patron (Keshava is a forerunner of the protagonist in *The White Tiger*, *without* his luck); in "Day Four: Umbrella Street," Chennaya, the deliveryman, and in "Day Five (Evening): The Cathedral of Our Lady of Valencia," George D'Souza, the mosquito man, bash their brains to escape the bottom, but are thwarted. Adiga's avoidance of stylistic flourishes in telling these stories makes the denouements all the more powerful.

By objectively retelling the same essential story, Adiga assumes a position midway between patronizing exoticism and illusionary romanticism: we cannot get away from the fundamental reality of half the world's population getting by on scraps, yet we must not overlook their sheer determination either. Kittur is über-Darwinian; yet moments of compassion among the oppressed workers—the domestic servants, the small-time vendors, the cart pushers, the rickshaw drivers— arise organically from the narrative, and are central to how Adiga wants the privileged Western reader to reposition himself toward the enormity of worldwide poverty.

This is a worthy second book, and a tickling promise of what is sure to follow from this supremely confident writer.

CAN WRITING BE TAUGHT? THE SYSTEMS-THEORY RATIONALIZATIONS OF AN INSIDER

THE PROGRAM ERA: POSTWAR FICTION AND THE RISE OF CREATIVE WRITING BY MARK MCGURL. HARVARD UNIVERSITY PRESS, 2009.

Three major trends, "technomodernism," "high cultural pluralism," and "lower-middle-class modernism" define for Mark McGurl postwar fiction under the domination of the now 350 creative writing university programs, in what he calls the "Program Era"—egalitarian and systemic, as opposed to the elitist, genius-presuming "Pound Era." All reflect "autopoetics" (self-referring authorship). In his systems-theory analysis, McGurl sets boundaries to answer only what kind of writing is being produced. He states disinterest in judging the quality of the writing, or its political consequences.

McGurl's categories are problematic, muddied by cultural realities exceeding his systemic bounds. What McGurl considers lower-middle-class modernism (established by Raymond Carver) is actually middle-class anomie. The Program Era does not produce working-class fiction. McGurl shuns the hard questions about social influences. Is there more homogeneity in the class origins of program recruits than McGurl allows? Despite appearances to the contrary, do Sandra Cisneros and Jhumpa Lahiri produce the same restricted type of fiction? To understand autopoetics' independent basis outside the academy, McGurl would need to expand his system to the point of meaninglessness, encompassing everything.

Creative writing does not equal *writing*. It is a new form of writing. The rise of the Program Era is the single most important influence shaping American writing. However, it's possible that over time the massive output of the Program Era will vanish, superseded by the writing of those untouched by the programs' mediocre excellence (or excellent mediocrity). McGurl considers a program writer anyone who attended college (Updike, though he shunned teaching), taught writing secondarily (Philip Roth), or taught after being established (Toni Morrison). A different ranking would result if we separated those (like Bellow, Mailer, DeLillo, Pynchon) who aren't quintessential teachers. The ubiquitous campus novel is a way to expunge the academy's discipline, not the harmless exchange of energies McGurl presumes. Depending on the academy for a steady paycheck is not the only way to survive. Possibly the uniform model has emerged because of talentless people afraid to independently carve out a broad career in letters as used to be the case.

McGurl doesn't talk about publishing or sales, and he considers only fiction. This is for a reason. The Program Era may not be in steady state equilibrium, as McGurl implies, but may have reached homeostasis. Essential feedback mechanisms are blocked, and the programs are indifferent to markets. Program poetry has explicitly stated its disinterest in broad readership. It's never clear what lies within McGurl's system boundaries. If McGurl had performed a systems analysis on "theory," i.e., literature departments, the articulation would be different but the results, in terms of pluralistic indifference, would be similar. "Systematic creativity," contra McGurl, is still a contradiction in terms, though his whole brief is to argue against old-fashioned uncreated genius and the self-taught nature of great art.

McGurl denies interest in the "pros and cons," but his definition of creativity as whatever the system produces is a moral judgment. This flatness leads to a quagmire in his tripartite historical scheme to understand the last century of American writing, based on the three paradigmatic dicta of "write what you know" (1920s, experience, Tom Wolfe), "show don't tell" (1950s, craft, Flannery O'Connor), and "find your own voice" (post-1960s, creativity, Toni Morrison). These three divisions are meaningless, since in practice the programs follow all three simultaneously. The first two, "write what you know," relying on experience, and "show don't tell," relying on craft (improvement by subtraction, limitation, elimination, i.e., less is more), have been retained, even intensified, along with "find your own voice."

McGurl's benign posture overlooks toxicity in the system. His separation of self-expression from self-discipline breaks down upon inspection, so what we have is masochistic expression. Writing that reaches a broad audience (Updike, et al.) does not abide by "creative writing" rules. The academy is obsessed with the authority to speak (one can only write about one's own people; the use of imagination is forbidden). This is a negative consequence of "find your own voice." "Show don't tell" leads to abjuring history, because modernist narrative is proscribed. "Write what you know" leads to solipsism. All three operate intersectingly today, contradicting McGurl's presumption of a dynamically evolving system. The programs' recent reconciliation with genre fiction might have occurred because it's easiest for creative writers. McGurl mocks Joyce Carol Oates's revisionless prolificity ("useless as a model"); the cult of revision follows from pseudo-egalitarianism ("diverse aesthetic democracy"), the denial of genius. Minimalism (fiction stripped to verbal basics, shunning flourish and style), and McGurl's alternative category of miniaturism, are not so much genuine artistic movements as system grotesqueries imitating theory, creative writing's opposite ravenous beast. Literature departments and writing programs are corrupted by the same forces. Minimalism, like theory, is a form of obscurity.

McGurl designates creative writing as part of the liberal arts branch of the university, but doesn't view the university from a transcendent stance as ideological tool. Creative writing revels in the social engineering clichés of the moment; its three major directives instruct the student to be apolitical. Each dictum enforces masochistic self-disciplining (creative writers celebrate revision, pain, editing, slowness, scant productivity, socialization, teamwork), recursively forming the system's objectives. How much of creative writing is dynamic two-way flow, and how much is imposed by the system's needs? Self-imposed limitations are only accelerating with the system's exponential growth and complexity, further constraining expression, not liberating it. Armchair revolutionizing in theory and lacerating discipline in creative writing flourish in parallel.

McGurl eventually betrays his anxieties toward writing (exactly echoing the academy's anxieties). He buys into authenticity (excoriating Ken Kesey's appropriation of a Native American voice). He loathes Kay Boyle's revolutionary politics. Authenticity (as opposed to fantasy) is the ultimate self-limitation. Why is the university so invested in imposing this discipline? "Voice" equals strictly private voice, not a universal voice. The directive to "find your own voice" is rhetorical anyway (commercial publishing doesn't abide radical politics of any kind); it serves conformism to reigning social platitudes, whereas McGurl takes it at face value. Voice does not equal cultural difference.

McGurl's third differentiation, shame (the diffident minimalism of Carver) versus pride (the exuberant, expressive, excessive maximalism of Oates), completely exposes the fracture. Minimalism, the "discourse of beautiful shame," for McGurl "seems to have no politics." We could just as easily argue for shame as maximalism, or pride as minimalism. Can't Vonnegut's minimalism be seen as pride? Can't Updike's maximalism be seen as shame? Besides, the dominant value in creative writing for the last two decades has been neither shame nor pride, but *grief*, spilling over into memoir. There is no true maximalism in America (unlike Grass or Rushdie's); it remains a subset of minimalism (and minimalist politics), so McGurl's "affective dialectic of shame and pride" is false. Sandra Cisneros, as

McGurl points out, easily switched from minimalism (*House on Mango Street*) to maximalism (*Caramelo*); it's because both reflect the same defeated spirit.

Stripped of the jargon and diagrams, McGurl's book boils down to these assertions: only the imitable are taught, silence equals resistance, only affiliation is possible, the literary field equals the university, cultural pluralism reigns, all writers are self-commodifying, self-doubters like R. V. Cassill and Ronald Sukenick display "facile tendentiouness," and standardization is unavoidable.

A counterargument would stress that the greatest learning is derived from the inimitable, silence betrays cowardice, disaffiliation and indie culture give the lie to the unavoidability of affiliation, the literary field exists in many sites other than the academy, self-victimization is the reigning philosophy, program writers are more self-commodifying than the disaffiliated, the system purges internal feedback from dissenters, and the end of excellence is well in sight.

WHY IS IT SO DIFFICULT
TO WRITE ABOUT THE WORKING CLASS?

When one casts one's eye over the landmarks of twentieth-century fiction, the standouts are usually written by middle-class people about people like themselves meant to be read by people like themselves. This was the territory James, Wharton, Cather, Proust, Forster, Woolf, Joyce, Waugh, Nabokov, Greene, Cheever, Updike, Rushdie et al. felt most comfortable charting. One thinks of Lawrence, Dreiser, Lewis, Steinbeck, Farrell, and Wright, to name a few, who might be said to have addressed working-class characters, but there is a separate question of the intended readership. Moreover, the writer himself is by definition one who has broken through certain class barriers, if he arose from lowly social origins; otherwise, he wouldn't have mastered conditions enough to be getting published. Perhaps he feels some remnant attachment to his class, wishing to describe its travails to the world at large. But even then the writing seems to be addressed to a middle-class audience, the writer looking backward over his shoulder, writing defensively and reactively most of the time, rather than with the faceless confidence with which middle-class norms are addressed.

The working man is a curiosity, whose very makeup must be repeatedly elaborated, to free him from the panel sitting in judgment, whose opinion is very severe toward his likes (the middle class is always prone to hurling charges of inherent degeneracy against deviants). The same defensiveness is almost never in evidence when writing about middle-class characters, who are the ground norm of behavior, so to speak. Thus we find that working-class writers writing about working-class people for working-class people is almost an impossibility. At best we might have fiction about working-class people, even though the writer and the reader might not fall into that category.

To counter this argument, one thinks of Dickens, Hugo, Dostoevsky, Zola, and Hardy in the nineteenth century, but immediately the mind is overwhelmed by the example of Austen, the Brontës, Balzac, Flaubert, Eliot, Thackeray, and Tolstoy, whose orientation might be said to be more toward the middle class. (As soon as a Pamela was formulated, she seemed to give way to Elizabeth Bennett.) Even the example of the former set of writers isn't quite correct, because the social ideal is to be middle class, and workers are presented more as deviations from the norm than something to attain to. It was in the nineteenth century that the middle class was coming into its own, so this hesitation on the part of a writer presumably as well-acquainted with the working class as Dickens is easy to understand. We might even say that nineteenth-century fiction, more than any other cultural factor, assisted in the creation of the actual, living middle class, as important moral codes were translated from the realm of abstract philosophizing to the level of ordinary conduct. Perhaps the nineteenth-century novel as a whole was no more than a category of rules for conduct: how to be a bourgeois amid often trying circumstances, without losing your cool. A vast array of characters cohere together under this banner.

Capitalism emerged victorious during the course of the twentieth century, the story of the entire era consisting of its forceful imposition on the remaining resisting traditions. It encountered a bump on the road with communism, but this was only a hyper-accelerated version of capitalism, capitalism looking past its present dilemmas toward what comes after; and it fell at times into a warped embrace of its most violent tendencies, that is, fascism; but on the whole its progress was steady and irrevocable. The writer no longer needed to wonder about alternatives to capitalism.

Romanticism strictly speaking was no longer possible. The only thing to do was to take the thing at face value, and live with it: modernism, and later postmodernism, were the strategies of choice in dealing with the new reality.

Much more so than in the nineteenth century, the working class fell out of consideration. If one looks at the vast amount of quality writing in English emanating from the South Asian subcontinent, for example, one realizes that the overwhelming majority of it is about middle-class people, writing by and for similar people. There are one billion poor people—very poor people, who often live by traditional, even medieval, means—in South Asia, and another one billion poor people in China alone, yet there is almost a negligible amount of fiction about them. In English, one reads about families living in sprawling apartment buildings in Bombay—but that isn't the norm in India—and even if they struggle, they are leagues apart from the servants tending to their needs. There are love affairs, as in Western settings, there are divorces, there are aging parents to be looked after, there are scandals and mishaps and surprises and secrets, but it is basically a middle-class norm. When was the last time you read about the life of a factory worker, say, or a farmer, in India or China? Even when one thinks of the greatest of modern African writers in English, Chinua Achebe, one recalls the clerk struggling against corruption, not necessarily images of backbreaking labor. One imagines warring factions within tribes, relatively prosperous, but not accounts of famine or ecological disaster or mass death or genocide or extinction, or as bad, the relentless gloom of labor without adequate remuneration.

Among the structural reasons for the eclipse of the working-class character in twentieth-century fiction might be included the following: a) it has become difficult to conceptualize labor in humanistic terms, since it is part of the rationale of the social welfare state to redefine it in melioristic terms—the whole project of modern liberal democracy collapses if it is admitted that there is such a thing as unremitting cheap labor, without spiritual consolation;

b) an ideology of passive citizenship, rather than heroic struggle, is instilled at every level, from grade school to the university on through the mechanisms of artistic production and dissemination, which emasculates a certain sensibility of rebellion; once ingrained, it is difficult to suddenly argue one's way out of it in fiction; c) to actually read about the working class as it lives and dies would be a colossal bore, as nothing much interesting, by definition, seems to happen in working-class lives: not the love affairs and social fallouts of the rich and aspiring, certainly, but instead more drudgery than the human mind can comfortably process; so it is a question of the loss of entertainment value versus authentic representation; d) the working class itself doesn't want to be objectified as such, and the middle class has taken this as an easy way out from facing the most resistant social problems; e) to write about work as such, in its unrewarding, elemental, primitive aspects is to revert to a psychology retreating behind enlightenment progress, and moreover makes it difficult to construct convoluted plots, the very marrow of absorbing fiction; it makes the writer think he is underutilizing his skills at developing psychological complexity; f) major writers seem to have written about people of leisure, while only minor writers, like Henry Miller or Louis-Ferdinand Céline or Charles Bukowski, seem to have written about work; does one want to join the canon, or be on the margins?

Writers, being only part of the larger culture, are no less immune than anyone else to these tendencies. It will be seen that each of these elements has a component of social reality as well as individual reality, the nature of writing merging seamlessly with the nature of society to make it almost impossible to address work. Status is a central question in each of these tendencies, the difficulty of class relations in capitalism without ideological competition being that class has become inextricably bound up with cultural obfuscation. If the writer were truly honest about his own status as parasite on capitalist culture—his own position as dispensable worker, in other words—he wouldn't be able to function. A certain amount of dishonesty seems to have become indispensable for one to be a functioning writer these days.

The novel has become increasingly implicated in the lie that capitalism perpetuates, has always perpetuated, that there is no dearth of opportunity for any single person, given hard enough work and a measure of luck, to transcend his or her class origins. Without mobility, there can be no capitalist credibility, and by extension, no credibility in the novel. One wants to read about characters who overcome difficulties, who have a certain nobility of heart even if they find themselves in straitened circumstances. Jane Eyre is the paradigmatic example here, or perhaps Pip or David Copperfield or Jude. This seems to have always been part of the contract of the novel since its very inception, its greatest pleasure residing in the victory of the well-meaning over assorted social forces, not necessarily evil, but at least blind. In a sense, harmony is the desired goal of all novelistic writing, the return to equilibrium of positive and negative forces, so that the individual in the end finds himself more or less where he deserves to be. Too great a deviation in the negative direction, and we have the naturalistic novel, which couldn't last very long. Too great a departure in the opposite direction, and we have the romance, which has never been considered literarily respectable. It is simply more difficult to write credibly of people of lower social origins rising above barriers and hurdles, than it is to write about people already there. It makes for more realism.

To the extent that the novel is a realistic document, and it must also adhere to the need for growth and change leading in the end to equilibrium, the novel must be a story of middle-class people. If the working-class person stays in his position or even falls below it, readers wouldn't like it; it would be too drab a tale. If, on the other hand, he rises too high above his station, this is taken as a slap against realism. Realism is nothing but the story capitalist culture has told itself about itself, and if characters start playing fast and loose with what is possible for them as individuals to do or not do, the effect is too jarring to play well over time. We might say that the aim of all literary institutions is to minimize (ideally to abolish) precisely this jarring element, to ensure that the high-flyers are returned to earth, and the bottom-scrapers are taught to think a little higher, so that in the end society's story about itself remains as valid as ever. We cannot have stories of paupers becoming princes and vice versa; the reading public wouldn't stand it. Paupers might try hard and perhaps not have to beg anymore, but anything more is tasking the patient reader with more than he bargained for. The novel is the most elaborate artistic contract yet devised between producer and consumer, and failure to deliver a satisfactory product can result in its early cancellation—and the end of a promising career.

To revert to the institutional reasons for the avoidance of working-class situations, the writer would have to position himself outside the vanities of liberal humanism since its twentieth-century incarnation, long on promise but short on delivery, if he is to write persuasively about the truth of labor without any compensating reward, material or spiritual. The saving grace of capitalism is that it has delivered often enough on its promise of class mobility to keep the faith alive. The twentieth-century writer found the topic of relative class transposition uninteresting; there was enough reality to capitalism's story to even assimilate mass dislocations cut off from ordinary life, like concentration camps and forced labor and cultural revolutions and organized genocide. Capitalism has always resisted—despite the attempts of Adam Smith and the earliest (moral) economists—accepting labor in humanistic terms. It is the crucial driving force of capitalism, more than capital itself, yet it may not be talked about. It may be dealt with mechanically, as a necessary input, but it cannot be discussed in human terms. Twentieth-century welfare capitalism addressed labor at its most undignified zero state, in conditions of mass unemployment or rampant inflation, by means of bureaucratic programs aimed to smoothen the worst of the business cycle, but this is not the same as placing labor at the center of capitalist development. The savvy writer perceives the black-and-white dichotomy here, which militates against the kind of ambiguous honesty fiction thrives on. On the one hand are mute laborers; on the other are articulate liberal spokesmen; what is the common cultural ground on which the two cohere? None, to be honest, unless liberal capitalism were to accept its foundation on a modern form of slave labor, much like the Greek or Roman "democracies."

The writer in the developed society, like fellow members of the intelligentsia, is taught to think of himself as a cog in the wheel, not as a one-man revolutionary charge but as a minor contributor to a larger cultural process. This tendency is deeply ingrained, and the writer tends to think of himself as successful and even honest to the extent that he has internalized this "truth." Dissident heroism is out of fashion, and has been so for a long while; one might conceive of modernism as heroism without heroes, or the substance of heroism muted to mundane action— viz. Joyce's *Ulysses* as the exemplary case, or Proust's labyrinthine masterwork. By now, a deeply involved circuit of rewards and punishments extends from one's earliest conscious awakenings to one's mature artistic perceptions, all set up to work by positive reinforcement ideas of a lasting order, an abiding sanity, to the vast capitalist performance of which the writer is a small, though useful, part. In situations such as Stalinist Russia, where labor is too elevated, made the substance of heroism, a surfeit of prodigious energies results, an unrecyclable wave of romantic passion, if you will—hence the need for samizdat literature outside the bounds of socialist realism, which posits a heroic struggle against the blind forces of bureaucratic repression. But this situation doesn't last long: the tension within it is too great to be sustained for long, and it is too rife with multiple opportunities for bad faith in the writer and his intended audience. In the Western countries today, culture is the last great remaining abstraction, the last means of authority not yet fallen to discreditation from top to bottom, unlike politics or the economy or science. We live and die by culture; we are all makers of it, from the most inane blogger to the award-winning author; its magnification is so large that it is seen as immune to individual effort.

Something inherent in the ideology of fiction, since its very inception, says that it ought to entertain first; other values might well ensue, but without the entertainment function, fiction is useless. To have an interesting plot, reasonable class mobility is a prerequisite. Here, culture works hand-in-glove with its economic base, the perpetual lie enhancing and reinforcing both. One finds an astonishing correlation, over time, between ideas of mobility in literature and in the real economy—restricted, in the eighteenth century, quite fluid in the nineteenth, immensely fluid in the mid-twentieth, and more restricted again toward the end of the twentieth—to keep the story credible. Fielding could not have written of small entrepreneurs in rural England arising out of nothing but motivation and dreams of capital; Updike could not have written of serf labor in Pennsylvania kept under the heels of kleptocrats and plutocrats; and today Jonathan Franzen cannot write credibly of fascinatingly literate workers in New York organizing campaigns on behalf of clean food or subsistence wages. The novel, in short, has never consistently enacted a heroic struggle against material obfuscation, the myth that mobility can be anything but what it actually is in real time. Hence the vacuum must be filled with subsidiary entertaining values, like love and passion and scandal and grief—in short, the eternal search for (cultural) selfhood. Man finds himself above all in work; but the history of the realist novel suggests that this has never been accepted as the basic premise.

Is the writer a man of modern ideas, believing in individuality and freedom, or is he a man of the pre-enlightenment past, conservative in the sense of seeing no possibility for progress? Much of the most important fiction of the twentieth century was written by those conservative in every sense of the word. Why is this the case? It is because the irredeemable tragedy of work is something liberal writers have a difficult time processing; not that conservative writers—one thinks of Evelyn Waugh—necessarily do so either, but theirs is at least a tragic vision that allows the ultimately discomforting notion, that there might not be any progress when all is said and done, to dominate their vision. Optimism of the enlightenment kind has been under continuous attack, from 1914 onwards, amid all the senseless wars and man-made calamities of that duration, yet liberal intellectual culture dictates that one at least hold on to the fundamental myth that allows freedom of choice to the cultural agent, the writer himself. In Hitler's concentration camp, in Stalin's gulag, in Mao's reeducation gang, and most recently in the America of the globalization era, work has been idealized to the point of lunacy, being used to crush the human being's very soul and being; but to write about it is impossible in a way, since it first requires the writer to rethink his voice as not being part of the loud, optimistic anthem of progress and freedom.

To accept that the lie is true is impossible on its terms. Those who have done so have brought ruin on their reputations. There is a fine line between critique and paranoia, argument and invective, explanation and scapegoating, and many of the twentieth-century writers who seem to have had a natural affinity for the travails of work seem to have fallen easy victim to the charges of madness and hatred. The capitalist cultural structure finds it all too easy to define and redefine writers at will, easily caricaturing dissenting writers as madmen once they cross a certain line. After that, they may still be read by curious thesis-hunters, but as far as the public is concerned, they are forbidden entities, to be approached at great danger to one's spiritual health, and they will certainly never be part of the canon, so that in the medium term, at least, they are safely removed from consideration. Their only hope is to return to posterity's attention in the very long run, by which time conditions will have changed so much that they will be mere historical curiosities. Thus the writer is always forced to fall back on his ultimate need, that is, to be read and have a following, and most of the time he resolves to be read a little rather than being ignored completely. It is a bargain most writers explicitly understand, since each sentence comes down to a moral choice between versions of reality—whether to stretch it to help form a new reality, or to conform to its accepted parameters. And even if one stretches ably and well, one's reputation can be destroyed quickly, so that the ability to write more sentences that will be read at all can be quickly extinguished.

Of course, none of these inherent disadvantages necessarily decide the case. There are always exceptions to the rule, and fame and fortune to be made by taking up the ignominies of the varieties of exploitation, and even to keep the narrative entertaining as well as aesthetically pure. But these institutional forces, working together, are truly a massive detriment to writing honestly about the worker, the workplace, the idea of work itself. It is far too easy to become ironic about this thing, work, we all have to do, than face the situation head-on (viz. the vast amount of superficial writing about the inanities of the corporate workplace in contemporary America, all written without emotional content, without a tragic perception at work— mere glosses on comic movies like *Office Space*). Writing about work is to delve in a kind of filth civilized society has never acknowledged as being true about itself, and it takes a certain kind of immensely distorted personality, immune to criticism, to do it honestly. Such writers have been rare to the point of nonexistence in the ongoing phase of the novel's worldwide maturity.

Rehabilitating the Working Man From the Clutches of False Realism

WELCOME TO OAKLAND: A NOVEL BY ERIC MILES WILLIAMSON. RAW DOG SCREAMING PRESS, 2009.

For the reader used to anodyne fiction of personal travail—so-called survival from illness and marital woe, superfluous tragedies of affluence and mental rot (Eric Miles Williamson's first-person narrator mocks such prissy self-expression throughout the novel)—*Welcome to Oakland* will come as a slap in the face, a kick in the butt—a stab wound, rather—from which those of gentle spirit might or might not recover. This is the latest of Williamson's shattering novels of hardscrabble working-class existence in the Oakland of the 1960s, 1970s, and 1980s, as one of our most powerful writers attempts to rewrite the rules of literary fiction to take us closer to the truth we perpetually want to avoid—even in fiction.

Williamson, like no other writer working today, wants us to stare at the blood and gore and sweat—and the garbage smell, yes, the eternal sulfur—to which the rich consign the working poor, all the while coming up with abstract theories to save their souls, romanticizing their troubles and wishing away their deepest resentments. Every bitterness of the American male without a secure economic niche is made manifest, every revenge fantasy and survival strategy of his is related without fear or prejudice, so that we are left with a complete vision of life below the radar screen, beyond the surveillance monitors and census counts and sociological statistics and counseling offices, reminding us of how the other America lives. Williamson does it all in prose integrally linked in rhythm to the cycles of violence and satiety, the impulses of realism and vanity, and the surges of corporeal ecstasy and disgust. When Williamson reproduces the dialogue of his Darwinian men, who know little of correct notions of behavior and artfulness, it is with an inner ear no amount of artificial training can induce in a wannabe writer. To be any closer to the working man's experience of money and sex and play and anger would be unbearable; what Williamson has written is already on the verge of the unbearable, so that the pages one holds in one's hands constantly condemn our cowardice in staying away from these truths.

"I'm not writing for art fags," T-Bird Murphy, the first-person narrator, holed up in a shitty Missouri garage after two divorces, tells us at the beginning of the novel. T-Bird has managed to get himself in some unexplained trouble, leading to his banishment from the suburban, middle-class life he used to loathe in his early years. His expulsion from its securities and vanities is necessary and right. Even if he manages to leave the garage (as we feel sure he must, through sheer force of will), and regain a more livable space, he will never again fall for the trap of acting like the rich. *Welcome to Oakland* is very conscious of the prodigious volumes of dross produced in the name of art by the nation's middle-class and upper-middle-class writers, who have no experience of life below a certain level. The majority remains unspoken for; this is one of the great sources of Williamson's (and T-Bird's) anger, and it is as legitimate an anger as we have encountered in modern American fiction. It partakes of something of Richard Wright's fury, but it is many degrees more cutting because in some ways the white working class today is more invisible than the black minority ever was. It is forgotten, not written about, and when written about—say, in minimalist fiction emanating from the writing workshops—is devoid of the power which feeds revolutions, or even reinventions.

Following where he left off in *East Bay Grease*, in *Welcome to Oakland* Williamson tells us what happens to T-Bird as a young adult. T-Bird's Pop, who works at the Mohawk gas station, and lives in a trailer, has met a new woman Mary, who, though she sleeps around with many people, at least has the virtue of returning home by morning. T-Bird has to give up trumpet-playing because his front teeth are knocked out in a club melee, and drives a garbage truck for a living. He hangs out, with Pop and other vanquished males, like "Campos, Polizzi, Shapiro, Jorgensen, and Louie," at Dick's Restaurant and Cocktail Lounge, "the vortex of the sadness of the world." The regulars at Dick's stand up for each other, which includes destroying (or imagining doing so) anyone who messes with one of them: "*Please*, say the word," pleads Jorgensen, the retired Navy Seal. T-Bird's mother has married yet another rich guy, though she shows up at Pop's wedding with Mary at the end, only to break up into hysterics when T-Bird tells her about the gruesome deaths of his two brothers—Kent, for one, was dragged behind a car and ripped to pieces by the asphalt. T-Bird doesn't have a place to stay, so he ends up living in his garbage truck cabin, in the middle of a massive garbage dump. There is a lot of garbage in the novel. T-Bird begins the novel, "I'm always happiest when I live in a dump," and the most lyrical passages of the novel describe the earth reasserting itself in the garbage dump.

We encounter every sort of male emasculation in the novel, and every sort of distorted empowerment, including real or imagined retaliation. Both are aspects of the subterranean working-class life we almost never get to see. As for emasculation, work itself—not "eating fancy sandwiches and drinking wine," which passes for work, or rich people acquiring "life experience" by doing jobs they don't need to do to feed themselves, but real work, which leaves the smell of garbage deep into one's pores, or needs washing off by Ajax or dishwater detergent at the end of the day—is the greatest source of weakening. The rest—failed relationships, promiscuity, addiction, physical self-destruction, proximity and proneness to violence—

are only symptomatic of the debilitating quality of most work. Work, which only a handful of American writers in the last century have dared to confront in its physical unpleasantness, is Williamson's core specialty, his unique province. What passes as work in most other fiction, even of the gritty realist kind, is pleasant substitutes for work. The loss of power leads to perverse expressions of power, particularly in enacting vengeance against the fellow oppressed (never against the rich and powerful, though that may change, Williamson warns) and in performing petty acts of retribution (such as letting garbage trucks trail slime in the pretty neighborhoods of the rich, or ruining the car of some arrogant rich bastard who demands full service at the gas station but won't leave a tip). It is a trap enfolding generation after generation, except for an exceptionally smart person like T-Bird, who gets straight A's and loves to read.

The American male is in profound trouble, and Williamson wants us to know why. The reality of work—serfdom in new guises—has reduced him to cipher, and he knows not what to do except to lash out, ruin his body and mind, or at most assert a Darwinian survival ethos, even if it means being as cruel as the next person. Williamson explores in the novel various grown-up versions of male emasculation T-Bird faces (short of removing himself to art). There are abject males like Blaise, who must be watched for by sympathetic Dick's regulars, when their women leave them and take them for everything they've got, or when they're obsessed with women who are clearly no good for them. There are washed-out musicians, like Farrington and Oscar, who live on the rumors of past glories, but who suggest the only realistic end for careers founded not on elite credentialing but self-motivated creativity. There is the garbage engineer, the Dumpmaster Jones, whose philosophy of the dumps eludes the bureaucrats in charge of shaping landfills as the resting ground for fancy condos and golf courses. There is Pop himself, ribald and savvy (knowing of Mary's infidelities), having a good time at the

wedding, a powerful physical specimen whose imminent
decline we fear, since the uncertainty of life forgives no
one in Williamson's East Bay milieu. Compared to these
fellow sufferers are the weak, mean, spiteful, stingy, hollow
men who have made a Faustian bargain by giving up their
individuality in return for a trivial share of the economic pie.
One such example is FatDaddy Slattern, maker of designer
toilet seats, who cons T-Bird into mowing his lawn (though
the backyard turns out to be a jungle of impossible weeds)
for a mere seventy-five cents, and who then suffers total
misery as various tradesmen turn against him in sympathy
with T-Bird and make every part of his house fall apart. In
real life, of course, it is difficult to exact even petty revenge
against the likes of FatDaddy and his family, but do we not
think about it all the time? The narrator says at one point,
"Find me an American man who claims he does not want
to kill at least once in a day each day of his life, and you've
found one lying son of a bitch." These are the kinds of truths
we need to hear, and which are fiction's special privilege,
though lately we seem to be getting nothing of the sort.

Life and death acquire a rhythm bent to external stresses,
so that projects of self-improvement are meaningless in the
world Williamson gives us. The prologue is a salvo against
those who would tell the narrator to write by the rules of
genteel fiction. The first extended section, involving the
hapless regulars at Dick's, makes us expect a whining self-
indictment of the working-class male that never happens;
it borrows from anti-politically correct rants, yet what is to
follow utterly subverts this set-up, so that by the end of the
book we realize that our sympathy for the comrades at Dick's
is false, like all our programmed feelings. The next section
takes us to the spontaneous camaraderie among T-Bird's
friends and neighbors, young and old alike, who band
together, for instance, in exacting revenge on FatDaddy. It
is a pleasant interlude, which diverts us for a while from
the savage unpleasantness to follow. The section after that
involves T-Bird living in the garbage dump, as he speculates
that "some goddamn day there's going to be a really good

riot, a class war instead of a race war, and we're going to take them out, the fuckers." This, of course, is the ultimate revenge fantasy, and it is never going to happen; what remains to T-Bird is solitude of the most excruciating kind, which makes a mockery of voluntary solitude adopted by chic artist types. In the final section, T-Bird rejoins the community, as Pop's wedding takes place amongst escalating recognition of class division: "Poor people don't see shrinks. They get a fucking job." The only thing that will cure a working man's blues is revolution; but the revolution of the soul preceding the material revolution is nowhere in sight. The ending, with T-Bird proposing to Rhonda, Mary's stepdaughter, connects us directly to the prologue in the garage, so that the enfolded narrative assumes the quality of dream, hinting toward a collective future so bleak, for all classes, it eludes even the present narrator's courage. In these masterly movements from section to section, Williamson has done more than reverse the usual causation of beginning-middle-end narrative: he has encapsulated all future endings in his prolapsed beginning. He sharply individualizes working-class characters in a way we almost never experience, but always keeps the question of deindividualizing work at dead center, so that we cannot escape the one irredeemable problem, work itself. All his narrative strategies are geared to fulfilling this central authorial purpose.

How true are the perceptions of the working man when it comes to his joys? Here too, class realities (and resentments) complicate the picture to his disadvantage. Drinking, dancing, music, sex, breeding, a good physical scuffle, these all have to do with reorientation of the senses toward a higher experience, but they are bound by the reality of the body's mortality creeping in, faster than it does with rich people. Death, sudden and violent, is always around the corner, and it sullies the experience of physical joy. Not coincidentally, Williamson reaches the height of his descriptive powers in the passages where he describes living at the garbage dump, under the auspices of Jones, who is constantly building and altering a monumental junk sculpture. Man and machine are organically connected in *Welcome to Oakland*, in a sort of apocalyptic overturning of the Futurist manifestoes of the early twentieth century, reduced now to ineradicable filth and grime and sweat and dust. Man and garbage are also inseparably connected; sometimes it is difficult to tell one apart from the other, Williamson suggests. Jones says, about the hiss of methane, "That's the earth purifying itself, making itself clean again. Everything in the world becomes the earth's garbage. The animals, the plants, the people, all they make and unmake becomes the earth's garbage. And the earth, the earth don't care one bit, it don't. The earth just cleans its own self right back up." In passages reminiscent of Nathanael West at his apocalyptic best, T-Bird lights a thousand small fires in the garbage dump, after Jones has been fired by the bureaucrats, and has bulldozed his junk sculpture: "And when I'd lit enough, I climbed to the top of the mound beneath which Jones's sculpture stood and I looked out over the bay at the lights of the city, and I looked back down at the flaming dumps, each gas jet like a home, a campfire, a porchlight left on in welcome, and I sat down and I closed my eyes and I knew that I would never sleep again, not ever."

Young T-Bird is introduced to both Marx and Nietzsche by a sympathetic librarian. It's hard to reconcile the two philosophers. Marx wanted the rich people dead. Nietzsche wanted the weak to become powerful. Williamson knows that like Jack London—and Theodore Dreiser, James T. Farrell, and John Steinbeck—he inhabits both tendencies. The war between the contradictions produces devastating fiction, such that if George Orwell were around today, and surveyed the vast field of American fiction, Williamson is the one writer he might unabashedly endorse, for making us confront the physical core of brutality as Orwell himself did—without fear or prejudice.

Welcome to Oakland has a greater urgency and necessity than the much-acclaimed *East Bay Grease*, and deserves a wider readership. This is no less than a manifesto for early twenty-first century America, which has made a mockery of the American Dream for the working man, leaving him to inhabit the garbage and mortality we have so expertly banished from our sights. Williamson wants us to smell some of the forgotten smells, see some of the invisible blood, and feel truly and terribly bad about ourselves. His revolutionary asides are scattered all over the novel, sanctifying and crucifying the lost American male, giving resounding new literary meaning to the term "revenge fantasy." With this novel, Williamson's position in the pantheon of major American writers of the working class is secure, and we eagerly await the conclusion of the T-Bird trilogy, the years between his proposal of marriage to Rhonda at the end of *Welcome to Oakland* and his exile in the garage in Missouri. That should be a hell of a ride.

DECADENCE, AMERICAN-STYLE:
WHATEVER HAPPENED
TO THE AMERICAN SHORT STORY?

THE O. HENRY PRIZE STORIES 2007. LAURA FURMAN,
EDITOR. ANCHOR BOOKS, 2007.

BEST NEW AMERICAN VOICES 2008. RICHARD BAUSCH,
EDITOR. HARCOURT, 2008.

Recently, Horace Engdahl, permanent secretary of
the Swedish Academy, said that American writers are "too
sensitive to trends in their own mass culture." He added:
"The U.S. is too isolated, too insular. They don't translate
enough and don't really participate in the big dialogue of
literature. That ignorance is restraining." Not since Toni
Morrison won the Nobel Prize in 1993 has an American
received it, leaving partisans of Philip Roth, John Updike,
Don DeLillo, and Joyce Carol Oates to complain about the
injustice. The sheer volume of literary output in America
dwarfs anything produced by other countries. But how
much of it is of quality, and does Engdahl have a point?

On the whole, his assertion about American
literature's insularity is dead-on. Ironically, this seems to
have been less true prior to America's emergence as the
biggest global power after World War II, than in the days
since. This may have had something to do with earlier
American writers feeling insecure with respect to Europe's
literary accomplishments, and wanting to be part of the
great conversation, as Engdahl would have it. The short
story is arguably America's literary form par excellence;

it suits shorter attention spans, fulfilling the craving for concentration and economy. Until the sixties, Americans probably wrote the best short stories of the twentieth century, not only from writers better known to the world, but from a legion of masters of the short form who were regularly anthologized in the *Best American Short Stories* and the *O. Henry Prize Stories*, in the thirties, forties, fifties, and with evidence of high quality, well into the sixties. To open any of these ancient anthologies at random is to come across example after example of mastery of the craft, from writers like William March, Harvey Swados, Kay Boyle, Roderick Lull, Robert M. Coates, David Cornel DeJong, William E. Barrett, Jean Stafford, R.V. Cassill (interestingly, the founder of the Associated Writing Programs, the umbrella for the nation's burgeoning creative writing departments, who later advocated its abolition), and countless other masters. But after the sixties, writing became too professionalized, publishing too commercialized, and it became much safer — certainly more profitable — to wallow in the culture's narcissistic obsessions than to critique it in any substantial manner. America's 350 university writing programs compel callow graduates to produce enormous quantities of short stories, published by literary quarterlies so great in number that there is no parallel in the world. These truly meet the definition of insularity breeding on insularity. Removed from the arena of experience, the professionalized teacher-writer now gives us not the existential hero of John Cheever and Richard Yates, at odds with society, but the inarticulate slouch of Raymond Carver and Tobias Wolff. The steep decline in short story writing rather accurately reflects determining trends in politics and culture. The insularity is of a peculiar kind, insofar as it is premised on a sad masochism — a psychological retreat in the face of the nation's mastery of global economic and scientific processes.

To illuminate this retreat, I wish to postulate a theory of decadence to explain current American compulsions in literary fiction. The term typically applies to art and style of the last fin de siècle, but aside from the starkly absent fixation on pleasure for its own sake, the rest of the structure works well again today. Borrowing from C. E. M. Joad's *Decadence: A Philosophical Inquiry* (1947), and Henri Lefebvre's *Everyday Life in the Modern World* (1971), I see all American fiction today as representing categories of *victimization*. A stronger theoretician than I am would connect today's victim chronologies with changing modes of nostalgia in its temporal and spatial manifestations. All American literature now is self-conscious *pseudo-minority* literature (when did we have a majority literature, and what happened to eclipse it?). I will interpret the two anthologies with this reference point: What is the specific minority that consumes this literature (or is imagined to consume it)? American literature is obsessed in its search for structures of oppression, rather than liberation (this seems to me the indispensable element in decadence). Freedom now consists of all that used to be thought unfreedom. In the political realm, decadence appears in technocracy, conspiracy, and homogeneity. The narcissist is in love with his mirror image; the writers considered here make *private experience inaccessible* (like the consuming media ether), making the mirror opaque to observers. Decadence presumes *rigorous realism*, abstention from interpretation (Sontag's chickens come home to roost); this has led to investing boredom with inherent interest. Decadence returns to the *primitive*; hence the frequent idolization of childhood, perversion, drinking, self-destructiveness, and apathy in these fictions. Characters are at a lower intellectual plane than writers, since fiction lacks a moral object. Absence of character leads to *portentous symbolism* as weight-carrier. The conditions of the writing business today (specialization/ professionalization/academicization of the young in writing, before the occurrence of substantial experience) are premised on the equality of all experience; the focus turns to the *trivial* (art for art's sake), since writers lack experience. Nietzsche's definition of decadence would be the *desire for weakness*; this urge permeates fiction. The effect of consuming these anthologies is to leave profoundly enervated, weakened, apolitical readers. This actually seems the aim of the writers, who represent the flight to authority that began in the seventies; in mass clusters, writers have been congregating around the domination of the writing programs, disseminating weakness into the culture like a virus.

Turning to the "adults" first, the O. Henry anthology is bookended by William Trevor's "The Room" and Alice Munro's "The View from Castle Rock," as though to envelop the decadent style with foreign mastery (Trevor gets extended encomiums from Charles D'Ambrosio and Lily Tuck, two of the jurors; no other writer, save Saul Bellow, has been as lionized in recent years by the American establishment review press as Munro). It makes sense that an author like D'Ambrosio would adore this ridiculous tale of a woman standing by her husband for years, after she knows he killed his mistress. The tone is set for the narcissism to follow in the anthology, with hushed language that suggests earth-shattering issues were at stake, when in fact this is an abject tale of self-regarding characters it's impossible to care about. Do D'Ambrosio et al. only misread the tale, in finding its characters profoundly sympathetic? Surely, their project is more insidious: it is to redefine what we ought to, against our moral grain, find sympathetic. Moral judgment, the jurors tell us, would have ruined the story; in fact, its absence makes for a hollow core, enervating to the limit, Trevor's desired aesthetic effect.

Munro's "The View from Castle Rock" is about immigrants from Scotland traveling in a ship to North America in the early eighteenth century. Her language, like Trevor's, is at odds with the importance of the subject; in her case, she adopts a languorous tone that suggests nothing significant were at stake. It is a version of the immigrant's unavoidable loss for the decadent generation, implying that whatever they lost is ours to claim with impunity (for a radical contrast, a moving story of the immigrant's irretrievable loss, see Claire Messud's 2001 novella, "A Simple Tale"). The nostalgia in Munro's tale is so saccharine it makes us look for meaning in deliberately presented detail, because the mind must seek any foothold in a vacuum. They may employ different registers of language, but Trevor and Munro share the quality of skidding only on the surface, refusing any depths to probe; the shimmering, disappearing detail is held out as disembodied promise, as though an art lover were being seduced into physically caressing an impressionist painting, fingers seeking impossible secrets.

Elsewhere, enormous verbal fire is expended in trying to make us care—but we find we're being asked to care more for the writer than for his creations. Justine Dymond's "Cherubs" is not so much about the transgressions of American soldiers fighting in France during World War II as it is about how we might like to imagine today French decadence of a certain time and place, anodyne and harmless, restoring the presently shattered alliance, if you will; the glittering sheen of nostalgia (how does nostalgia triumph for those who were never participants in a given episode?) prevents direct confrontation with historical turnings. Eddie Chuculate's "Galveston Bay, 1826" imagines Indian tourists traveling South to visit a rumored lake, converting the whole thing into a made-for-TV spectacle, complete with a murderous Hollywood tornado (primitivism for the postmodernists, without its gory implications). Vu Tran's "The Gift of Years" is about a Vietnamese soldier caught in that country's wars, raising a gifted, intuitive, courageous daughter with a streak of violence, which ends in her murder of her abusive husband, a crime either real or imagined, depending on the reader's perspective. Is there a suggestion that war perverts nonparticipants, the future generations we invest our hopes in? Not really—it is simply what is, a quirk of the daughter's character. No moral consequences or connections are implied. History comes in handy to score points about our present decadence: its unquestionable advantage over superstitious systems (such as the antiquated enlightenment rationalism which buys into victors and losers in historical confrontation).

What happens to the coming-of-age story in the age of reawakened primitivism, experience without judgment, and weakness as the new strength? Richard McCann's

"The Diarist," beloved by the jurors, consists of a series of binary oppositions (the majority culture's signposts of stark masculinity, versus the eleven-year-old boy's inclinations to femininity) which imply that all of us are a little bit gay on the inside (the academically beaten-to-death thesis of the social construction of gender and sexuality); we are all potentially categorizable as minorities, crimeless victims, suffering from no one's delusions (the diary, after all, conveniently rescues us). The pervasive victimization, aided by the hazy language of backtracking nostalgia (it opens, "Here's one thing I remember, from all the things I never wrote down in my diary the summer I was eleven, the summer before my father died") from the child's perspective is rooted in the decadent-liberal phase of political understanding. One can spin out endless story scenarios from the basic McCann root: for example, the teenage girl who feels pressured to lose weight despite her boyfriend's supportiveness (or should we make it despite the antagonism?—either works). The degree of moral conflict, because of the location in the child's mind, is persistently low (as in the symbolism of tearing the lightning bug), and is aided by the droopy language, glancing back uncertainly at its own misgivings.

The companion to this coming-out story is Adam Haslett's debilitating "City Visit," where an adolescent Missourian boy makes a date with a man on the internet in New York, and while visiting the city with his mother, consummates it. While the online advertiser has presented himself as a real date, of course he is a prostitute. Haslett tries to draw us into sympathy for the initial innocence and steep learning curve of Brendan, but what does Brendan learn other than the futility involved in gestures of intimacy? The effect is to leave us drained, devitalized, impotent, cynical toward romantic love, resigned to a world where boys transmogrify into old men before our eyes. The most depressing story is Andrew Foster Altschul's "A New Kind of Gravity," where a young man works as a security guard to protect women and children from abusive husbands and fathers, a sort of MSNBC's relentless "Lockup" theme (harsh prison conditions as the ideal) for the literati. Many of the inmates are Hispanics (immigrants sharing in our innocence-as-victims, protected under liberal do-gooder auspices, while in the real world they are rounded up and deported, even when they have children who were born and grew up here), toward whom the narrator shows a brutal protectiveness. This story is paradigmatic for the Bush age, the coming out of liberal futurists enamored of surveillance and lockdown technologies, only this time for their own "progressive" purposes.

Most of the stories offer displacements of current anxieties into safe territory, a willed regression of the mind to more primitive sets of conditions. Munro's story must be seen in the context of recent near-genocidal levels of American xenophobia. Trevor so dresses up fidelity that it becomes enabler to murderous infidelity, whereas in the real world marriages break up easily, more and more often without trace. Susan Straight's "El Ojo de Agua" cannot but be read in light of the Hurricane Katrina criminality; yet she removes the flooding to memories of 1927 Louisiana, recalled by an old man overcome by much bigger present (personal) worries. Similarly, in the background of proven war crimes in Iraq and Afghanistan, Joan Silber gives us "War Buddies," safely displaced to Vietnam (equally war crimes-ridden, but who cares now?) in the late sixties, with a protagonist so innocent he doesn't know how unsafe Vietnam is when as an airplane engineer he accepts an offer to work at military bases there. The American "brand" has never been so sullied as now, so Silber offers us a whitewash for earlier war crimes; the two engineers, one a nerdy loner named Ernst whom the narrator admires for his untouchable reticence, are simply doing their jobs: "We were not, of course, in the shit with them [war crimes perpetrators]. We had by this time some inkling of what the shit was. Well, the whole world knows now, doesn't it, what we made soldiers do." The Sunbelt's prosperity (and associated rightwing politics) are premised on militant imperialism; why not remove the present stain by setting up a fantasy of Phoenix in the sixties (can it really have been as bucolic then as Silber presents it?), where hardworking engineers embody American innocence? To top it off, the narrator marries a Thai woman (more washing off of white imperialist guilt), a nurse no less. We can still win Vietnam (as John McCain would have it), we can still leave with honor!

Innocent grief compounds primitive emotionalism. For Ariel Dorfman, in "Gringos," all Americans (even immigrants) are innocents abroad, subject to exploitation or outright theft (as happens in this story), and the safest role for Americans overseas is to enact their quintessential character, to reduce the danger. Says the husband to his wife: "I didn't want him to know I'd realized he was a pickpocket. He could have done anything to us, to you, in that place. I played the innocent. He also played the innocent. The one role that we would fall for." Then adds later, "We speak Spanish. We're survivors. It wasn't meant for us, you know, that sort of warning [about thieves]." They then admit, "Maybe we're turning into *gringos*." This is their moment of awakening, realizing they belong to the gringo project of everyone being a victim of some sort. Rebecca Curtis, in "Summer, with Twins," suggests that a teenager's summer stay with rich, exploitative, narcissistic school friends is somehow emblematic of the irreconcilable class difference adults ought to inhabit as well; economic injustice becomes a matter of personal adjustment. Brian Evenson, in "Mudder Tongue," regresses his aging protagonist to a primitive speech disorder (how language begins, in children, with parts of speech out of sync), literally embodying the speechlessness of grief. And for Sana Krasikov, in "Companion," the multiplicity of choices for an attractive Russian Jewish immigrant leads to a sordid self-preoccupation (like Haslett's gay kid) that profoundly primitivizes levels of agreeableness in civilized society—back to a conceptualization of friendship (with manipulative dependency) a child might be theorized to possess (by utterly cynical psychologists).

The tyros in *Best New American Voices* aren't far behind

in catching up to the veterans' decadence. But lacking the ability to effortlessly link matrices of metalanguage (symbols empty of symbolism) as do the more experienced writers, the youngsters are stuck at the level of trying to articulate, in commonsense prose, the abnormal, the pathological, the perverse, the deviant, the normless ground zero of experience. The elements of decadence—primitivism, minority appeal, impenetrable private experience, the will to weakness, naturalism on steroids, the trivial severed from political context—conveniently cohere in the abnormal personality, hence its recurrent fascination for the MFA-programmed.

Richard Bausch seems to have been guided by a checklist of politically correct agenda items (compassion denatured by technocracy) in his selections: humanitarianism toward animals in Tucker Capps's "Alice" (animals and their caretakers resignedly aging and dying, best friends in the will to weakness, is a repeated motif in the stories); family molestation in Suzanne Rivecca's "Uncle" (like doctors conjuring newfangled illnesses to include every American, our storytellers extend the range of pathologies to leave no mortal behind); exploitation of natives for touristic pleasure in Christopher Stokes's "The Man Who Ate Michael Rockefeller"; the presumed lower emotional intelligence of men in Leslie Jamison's "Quiet Men" (from *The Quiet American*'s global ramifications to the silences in meaningless intimacies, enabling all the characteristics of decadence to meld in one theme); the rapaciousness of Tinseltown mediators in Garth Risk Hallberg's "Early Humans"; the anger-dissolving capacity of exotic locales (here Sri Lanka) for besotted Westerners in Peter Mountford's "Horizon"; early twentieth-century feminist awakening in Lauren Groff's "Surfacing" (Margaret Atwood's resonant exploration of the same title borrowed, cheapened, and airbrushed for a retrospective projection of glamour and fake nostalgia, much in the vein of Munro's story: all progress and no danger, even when people don't connect all the way); school bullying in Dan Pinkerton's "Headlock" (which aims for the effect of

Tom Perrotta's *Election*, the same sacralization of the lowest common denominator, the bottom dregs of petty American education and dating rituals treated like universal truths); the necessary genius of the Attention Deficit Disorder-suffering fifteen-year-old boy in Oriane Gabrielle Delfosse's "Men and Boys" (counterpoint to the morose suffering of the lovelorn female camp counselor); the impossible humanitarian choices to be made in a Thai refugee camp in Sharon May's "The Wizard of Khao-I-Dang" (it is *Sophie's Choice*, the movie version, all over again, the sordidness of the camp administrators preempting any empathy on the reader's part); the devastating consequences for parents assaulted by SIDS (Sudden Infant Death Syndrome) in David James Poissant's "Venn Diagram"; the hazards of Palestinian survival in the occupied West Bank in Adam Stumacher's "The Neon Desert"; and the bane (or is it boon?) of being a Holden Caulfield misfit in bucolic seventies Wyoming for yet another fifteen-year-old in Stefan McKinstray's "No One Here Says What They Mean."

In Tucker Capps's "Alice," the old family dog's demise from cancer is necessary for a cathartic family reconciliation (are we back at the beginning of the age of agriculture?), the symbolism of the dog qua dog (with its domestic solidities, missing in real life) explained in so many words: "I felt there should be some ceremony, but I found nothing to say and began shoveling dirt over her. The truth was that dogs should be dogs, should die like dogs and be buried like dogs. A dog could be in the family, but wasn't family. A dog was a reservoir for whatever venom and hunger and regret pass, or don't pass, between members of a family." The fluid utility of dogs (all-purpose sacrificial animals) opposes the rigid misadaptations of various mindsets: the routinization of therapy fixed in consumer culture, yet masquerading as artistic freedom.

Elsewhere everyone is either dying or dead (the established writers like to be distracted by plots of pure spectacle, acting like displaced screenwriters fighting back the boredom of teaching: no such luck with the trainees, who take grief with the seriousness of morons). Grief is a prop to build up imperialist narcissism. The primitivist gloss means no real character, no evolution toward maturity, typically even regress from it: only an emasculating emotional flatness obtains. We recall the beginnings of this from John Barth's *The End of the Road*, but it is conclusive in stories like Pinkerton's "Headlock," where the shop teacher Mr. Marsh maintains the immobile emotion of the darkest television "character," confounded by his wife fucking the school principal. After a rooftop confrontation with a triumphant adolescent bully, this dialogue ensues:

> "How long have you been married, Mr. Marsh?"
> "Twenty-one years. But I'm probably getting divorced."
> "How come?"
> "My wife was unfaithful."
> "So was Chrystal."
> This surprised Marsh. "Why are you still with her?" he asked.
> Brunk was silent a moment. "I don't know," he said finally.

One might construe some vast neoliberal conspiracy to train us to accept the personal and public travails unloaded on us, but such sophisticated personas behind these experience-less writers wouldn't ring true. Victimization is universal, but nothing metaphysical is to be deduced from this. The quality of obsession with the specifics of American school and childhood culture, in Jordan McMullin's "Mouse" and many other stories, suggests a denial of other cultures and their rituals and symbols of authority that beggars the imagination; it goes beyond arrogance into sheer absence of intention. The political corollary is our treatment of American constitutional contingencies as though they were sacred doctrines, issued from the immortal gods, meant to last until the end of civilization (while the rest of the democratic world wonders at our labyrinthine procedural obstacles to achieving humane progress).

The abstract weight of grief is so great that there are no
real differences between adults and children; certainly this is
true of Delfosse's "Men and Boys," where the ADD genius,
Justin, prompts the twenty-seven-year old camp supervisor,
Jane, to ponder: "Is this my life?... Is this my twenty-seven-
year-old life?" The last sentence, "She lies down beside
him because he is not yet a man," suggests infinite doors of
regression into a vegetable-animal state of preconsciousness,
what Erich Fromm called "escape from freedom." Early
eighties minimalism, as in the work of Bobbie Ann Mason,
was manufactured to constrain revolutionary emotion in the
oppressive age of Reagan. In Poissant's "Venn Diagram,"
grief is the minimalizing bludgeon that crushes intimacy
(and intimacy is the ultimate fear of all totalitarian systems):
"The divorce rate for couples that lose infant children is
almost 90 percent. Most couples split up inside of a year.
Our own one-year mark a week away, I've decided that Lisa
and I are no exception. It's not that we've stopped loving
each other exactly, only that every time I look into my wife's
eyes, all I see is my little girl." The narrator later asks: "Have
you ever been to a baby's funeral?" This, if anything, should
put a stop to incipient anger about government-authorized
torture. Every humanist alternative must be crushed in the
grindstone of grief. In Stumacher's "The Neon Desert," the
narcissism of the American traveler Nathan (escaping grief
at a shattered relationship back home, of course) is almost
conceivable as innocence, begging for instant forgiveness (a
more manipulative, more staged, rendition of our perpetual
innocence, our unchanging childhood state which the rest of
the world misunderstands, is Silber's story—but Stumacher
might yet grow into her shoes).

The summation of these tendencies is McKinstray's
"No One Here Says What They Mean," where the elements
of decadence singularly converge: Joe, the drug-addled
teenager, finds first love with a wispy older girl, whose
aunt is disgustingly dying (what an inconvenience for all
concerned!), but who, try as he will, even in the throes of
love, can't "feel anything" (reminiscent of the feelingless

Mr. Marsh from Pinkerton's story). It's impossible for Joe to care. These are stories where the subjects are not to be seen as altering under the stresses of extreme capitalism, and because their condition must be removed from economic causes, their apathy is correspondingly exaggerated to absurd proportions (this builds toward Haslett and Altschul in the morbid vein, Trevor and Munro in the lachrymose style).

The only exception to the decadence is Razia Sultana Khan's "Alms," about an elderly female beggar in Dhaka one-upping her patrons. Good-humoredly, it does all the traditional story, as we have known it from Maupassant to O'Connor, should do: seamless synthesis of plot and character to suggest a range of transcendent meanings not containable by explicit communication (symbolism constrained by story, not running away with itself), mature thought and action pursuing parallel tracks on visible lines while rumbling over buried earths of valid emotion and insight, and pure invitation to think empathetically about our human condition, without the destroying ironic wink. Khan apparently hasn't had the idealism boiled out of her in academia; a little seasoning and vetting, and she might yet start playing to our buried insecurities (after which she can get a book contract).

Judging by their pure decadence quotient, I predict the greatest publishing success for Silber, Curtis, Krasikov, Haslett, Altschul, and Straight among the elders, and Jamison, Groff (particularly her, of the Krasikov tone), and May from the apprentices. In being so insistent, as Laura Furman, D'Ambrosio, and Bausch are, that they do not wish to judge prevalent tendencies in fiction, the jurors reveal more than they think: that there are no minority cultures actually meant to consume these technical productions; there is only dead form in patent symbols, prejudice against knowledge, self-destructiveness without name—in all, a refusal of (strong) readership.

If the short story is America's quintessential art form, then taking its pulse today suggests a comatose patient. In the novel, perhaps it is a little different. In the last couple of years, the longer form has seen major work from Joseph O'Neill, Aleksander Hemon, Mohsin Hamid, and Claire Messud. However, these are either immigrant writers, or have profound exposure to European culture. An enormous volume of short and long fiction is being churned out, finding little readership at home, and remaining mostly unknown outside America. Its concerns are so insular, to refer to Engdahl again, that it seems to have earned the only fate it deserves. This literature envelops a gory style of decadence that doesn't translate well—unlike the spectacle of Hollywood—to celebration abroad. It is a subset of the dark fascistic tendencies shadowing the nation, much as was the condition of Weimar Germany—intimations of a false strength, when actually there is little but terror at the possibilities of human freedom. The depressing domestic dramas that are the subject of the bulk of American fiction today make little pretense to humanistic growth; the object seems to be to reiterate to readers how weak and pathetic we are as human beings, and how we should taunt ourselves with this defeat. It is a disturbing peephole into the nation's psyche, and it should give pause to distant cultural onlookers wondering whether redemption, after America's recent excesses, might be in the offing.

DON'T BE CRUEL

THE CONFERENCE ON BEAUTIFUL MOMENTS BY RICHARD BURGIN. THE JOHNS HOPKINS UNIVERSITY PRESS, 2008.

To be liberal means to have overcome the urge to cruelty, latent in all of us. In the doctrinal, political sense, this theory was easier to articulate in the early centuries after the Renaissance when tyrannical abusers still roamed the continents, often inflicting barbarism just because they could, with impunity. For the individual, liberality of spirit is an earned practice, built up over time, from earliest awareness to the last days of maturity, much as Buddhists progressively refine concentration. Lapses along the path are often fatal, irrevocable. But what happens in a society so materially advanced that primary physical and psychological needs are easily met, the state never subscribes to overt cruelty, and there is enough time left over to ponder the choice between generosity and cruelty? What is the nature of the pain involved in the choice, and how well may we predict the end result?

This is the territory Burgin explores, in this stunningly effective, tight-woven collection, containing some of the best stories of his accomplished career. Over and over again, we are made to ponder the limits of liberality, in a culture given to stating its explicit beliefs at the loudest rostrums available, as we are put into the shoes of the protagonists and challenged to articulate our humanity in more effective terms, if we dare. Indeed, the whole book is contained by this explosive wager. Burgin is well past the initial shock of the discovery of the rapacious beast lurking beneath our glittering body armors in the civilized gathering places of our metropolitan centers. He has seen the monster, without whose defining presence we might as well not be human. So his characters are forever in search of the space and time of pure beauty, undiluted, unsullied, uninformed by cruelty, the original paradise without whose promise it is difficult to carry on the rituals of ordinary life. But to intensify the contradiction, he mostly operates with characters whose lives are unordinary, who have discarded predictable routines for the most part. Already occupying zones of risk and uncertainty, they confront cruelty magnified many times. This is a more daring narrative task than fixing cruelty within the confines of quotidian life, restricted by material constraints (the "dirty realism" of yesterday). Preexistent hells give way to unforeseen hells, while the ostensible discussion remains centered on forms of finding paradise.

The saturation of cruelty as the provident antithesis of liberalism, its dialectical opponent predicted beforehand, seems to demand inevitable pairs of characters, often reflected in the story titles. "Jonathan and Lillian" describes the infatuation of a somewhat dull journalist, author of a failed novel, with the aging Hollywood actress Lillian Glass, operating in her worshipful milieu in Santa Barbara. Authorized to write Glass's biography, Jonathan is also quickly seduced by Lillian, even as her disgruntled earlier young lover, Kenneth, now working as the butler, hovers in the background, plotting revenge with the theft of a valuable painting. In this story as in several others, Burgin fluidly lapses from the point of view of one character into another's, to reinforce the idea of a pervasively latent ideology of cruelty informing the alleged individual consciousness. The meaning of this opening story is not fully clear until all the stories have been read: the question being posed is, Who is being cruel to whom? Lillian, for exploiting a dullard wannabe writer like Jonathan? But Jonathan is being complicit in his own degraded seduction, so he has evident free choice. Kenneth, in his thievery and resentment, when he knew the deal with the fickle older lover, going in? But we understand the necessity of cruelty from his point of view. Everywhere in this story, characters are afraid to look at their true physical and psychological characteristics, suspending belief in how matters have ended up. It is not so much sympathy or identification or forgiveness toward these flawed beings Burgin is after, not even withholding of moral judgment per se, but recognition that knowledge begins in awareness of inherent evil: a very religious message, if you will, but also a deeply secular one, for these times. We have forgotten how to think of evil. Burgin wants us urgently to get down to this task.

These stories proliferate with characters uncertain of their sexuality, or more accurately, readers being made uncertain of such, in the context of repeated instances of masochism and sadism: our post-liberal culture's superficial barometers of censorable cruelty. "The Second Floor," where Jerome, a middle-aged white man, liberated after coming into possession of his father's fortune, haunts public parks in search of young girls to reduce to submissiveness, plays with all of our culture's standards of sexual propriety (pretty much coextensive with moral propriety, these days): we believe that to be cruel in the sex act is the ultimate moral depravity. With consent, of course, and if it gives equal pleasure to both sides, more lines can be crossed. But in "The Second Floor," we willingly enter a world where Jerome's ultimate secret, whatever dark mystery lies on the second floor (we are allowed to give vent to our wildest imagination), is irrelevant in the end. What matters are the patterns of deceit which are all the more seductive for being laid out in such articulate dialogue between Jerome and his desired Abby (the young girl who fails to show up for the park rendezvous) or the realized Cincy (the desperate girl he does pick up): to contain the contours of pleasure is already to be cruel, contra the politically correct commissars of public morality.

Another ratcheting of the screw is Burgin's creation of the ideal liberal subject of the theorists and pamphleteers down through the centuries, characters like Robert in

"Robert and His Wife," who embody every supposition of the official culture's anti-cruelty manifesto of good behavior and decent forgiveness. One of our culture's preeminent institutionalized forms of the conference on beautiful moments is the writing group, informal or formal, where members gather to deliver the appropriate epiphanies, given the time and circumstances. Robert, we might say, in contrast to the hapless first-person narrator, is what the sixties American male might have evolved into, had rude political forces not intervened, "not only writing more prolifically and better than anyone else but also commenting the most expansively and sensitively about other people's work and thus becoming the most gregarious, popular, and respected person at the meetings." These are qualities all lacking in the narrator, a skittish librarian, who when offered by Robert the chance to date his beautiful blonde ex-wife, Beth, predictably fumbles it, obsessed as he is by the nature of Robert's hypnotic power over his gorgeous women. The deliberate pairing of opposites in the two main male characters serves to dilute their apparent distinction: without the suspicious, resentful, cruel narrator, no magnanimous Robert either, and we are left with an absence of choice as usual. At the end of the story, having finally been invited to Robert's apartment (the contained physical incarnation of sixties ideals), the narrator, having stolen Beth's wedding ring to Robert, contemplates over the object: "I was staring at my shining ring against a field of snow and stars completely immersed in my eternal moment."

Much of late twentieth-century fiction has been obsessed with narrating the worst depredations human beings are capable of, which to our culture seems to mean indifference in the face of reasonable degrees of natural and physical stimuli. Characters are unable to stir up emotions enough to qualify themselves as thinking, feeling humans, always retreating instead into defensive postures. We think of it as cruel to act this way, so we pretend to care. "Cruise" offers another pairing of men, of ambiguous sexuality, where on the cruise ship one of the men, named Anderson (the cruel version of Robert in "Robert and His Wife"), challenges Rider, the other man (a version of the more diffident narrator of "Robert and His Wife"), to tell each other the worst things they've ever done. Anderson's tale involves dominating a submissive, homely if also attractive, blonde, with the predictable backstory of family abuse, desiring to be mastered by Anderson, who dumps her when she becomes inconvenient to him. It takes a certain liberality of spirit to admit to this kind of cruelty, even to celebrate it, as Anderson does, whereas for the less confident Rider, the worst thing he can think of telling about himself is that he is gay. The irony is that Anderson, the supposed liberal, does treat this revelation in an extremely defensive manner, getting almost violent. The paradoxes of this situation, two characters accepting the challenge to relate and act out their worst, are too multifold to be encapsulated here, but suffice it to say that no relationship, even the father-son one, a favorite theme of Burgin's, is exempt from the perpetually shifting equilibrium of cruelty balanced on liberality's head.

The final, title story takes us right into perhaps America's greatest preoccupation in the postindustrial age, convocations that seek to raise self-esteem, convince participants that they are the embodiment of the beautiful, and that they need not find the source of beauty elsewhere: "What had begun twenty years ago as a celebration of beautiful, transformative moments in the arts had in essence become a celebration of beautiful, transformative moments in the members' personal lives about which they were more than eager to testify," observes Dansforth, the reporter tasked with exposing this particular "conference of lunatics" (well might the liberal stars of the cosmopolitan journalistic milieu laugh at such gatherings). Here, in the very first group meeting, Madeline, who turns out to be the conference's co-director, reveals her beautiful moment of finding Heaven's light itself, shafting into her bathroom on an ordinary morning. But those who insist on the impossibility of finding beautiful moments, past a certain threshold are not only strongly censored, but even beaten—

and killed, as happens to Peter Traynor, who never is able to find beauty even in supposedly pristine Vancouver. As Madeline figures out that Dansforth is a spy, she threatens him too with physical destruction, and Dansforth quickly runs away to safety. We understand, keeping the rest of the stories in mind, that while the American heartland is rife with movements of testimony, the same is true also of the putatively skeptical reporter. All testimonial roads lead straight back to cruelty, in a perfect equilibrium of nothing happening.

In Matt Taibbi's *The Great Derangement: A Terrifying True Story of War, Politics, and Religion at the Twilight of the American Empire* (2008), the most resonant recent articulation of the spheres of lunatic illogic inhabited by increasingly large numbers of Americans left behind by the promises of globalized capitalism, conspiratorial churches (religious and secular) assume their own hellish logic, dooming protagonists to the end of choice. Burgin's characters too are in search of the eternal moment, but they operate well above the range of intelligence Taibbi's right-wing and left-wing seekers can claim; while both books seem to have located the essential idea of American derangement, Burgin's task, unlike Taibbi's gonzo reportorial venture, risks more: it is not that cruelty, stemming from external sources like heartless corporations or the government, pushes us into acts our honest, dignified selves would rather not commit, but that the absence of positive input is not necessarily why cruelty rises to the surface. Burgin, at the peak of his considerable powers here, demonstrates the eternal difference between testimony and art, confession and paradox, journalism and fiction, Mencken and Faulkner.

MIDWESTERN PASTORAL AT ITS BEST

DRIFTLESS BY DAVID RHODES. MILKWEED EDITIONS, 2008.

By 1976, young David Rhodes had already published three critically praised novels, the last being *Rock Island Line*, acclaimed by John Gardner in *On Becoming a Novelist*. A motorcycle accident paralyzed him that year, and he fell silent. After thirty years, Rhodes has delivered, in *Driftless*, a version of Midwestern pastoral that shoots him to the highest ranks of American writers. Together, the two books constitute a credible idealization of the American character, free from its political reductions, as worthy of attention as Franklin, Paine, Jefferson, Twain, and Hemingway's characterizations of the ideal American.

July Montgomery is the tying thread between *Rock Island Line* (reissued now by Milkweed) and *Driftless. Rock Island Line*, starting at the beginning of the century in rural Iowa, with July's grandparents, Wilson and Della, moves to his parents at mid-century, John and Sarah. Leo Marx, in the classic *The Machine in the Garden*, focuses on the reconciliation attempted in American pastoral between technology and nature. Rhodes offers a different interpretation of pastoral, vulnerable primarily to death. A series of deaths short-circuits July's happiness. His parents die in a car accident when he is ten. Running away to Philadelphia, he lives underground in a subway station, and comes of age with his rural straightforwardness, even innocence, intact. Paradise is temporarily regained when as an adult he returns to Iowa, only to be lost when his artist wife from Philadelphia is raped and murdered. July wanders for years before settling in Words, Wisconsin, where we pick up in *Driftless*.

For pastoral to work, place must beneficently shape character. Rhodes achieves this, as in describing the solaces of the wintry Wisconsin landscape, without ever romanticizing the Midwestern farmer's hardy virtues.

The ensemble characters of *Driftless* are all splinters of July's original character. Jacob Helm, repairman, has long grieved the loss of his wife Angela. Grahm and Cora Shotwell, with their two young children, struggle to make their dairy farm pay amid discovery of systematic fraud by their milk cooperative. Gail, Grahm's sister, is a talented singer for a local band, able to reach deep melancholy veins. Rusty Smith, a retired farmer, is gradually losing his faculties (evocative of Wilson in *Rock Island Line*). Violet Brasso, active in the church, takes care of her invalid sister Olivia. Winifred Smith, the Friends church pastor, has a transcendental vision of God, which she yearns to verbalize.

Unlike urban protagonists paralyzed by self-consciousness, Rhodes's characters are capable of great leaps of intuition and action. Jacob improbably falls in love with Winifred, moving past the loss of his wife. With July's help, Grahm and Cora's effort to expose the milk cooperative finally gets traction. The young couple's unsullied faith in American values is neither sentimentalized nor patronized. Rusty Smith turns out to be Winifred's uncle, closing that unfortunate gap in his life. Gail remains true to herself by not altering her music to please the successful singer Barbara Jean. Olivia miraculously regains the use of her legs, allowing her feistiness to bloom. While Words seems to be evolving toward integrity and resolution, July dies on his farm, mangled by the tractor, alone. Jacob and Winifred marvel at the "look of death," after one of the most moving descriptions of death in American fiction.

July might have died, but the pastoral ideal is timeless. His independence, freedom from cant, stoicism, skepticism toward any ideology (including theology), and ability to work in the midst of tragedy, live on in the remaining characters.

An urban outsider might imagine today's Midwestern farm economy as threatened by vast economic transformations. From the inside, as Rhodes writes, only the soul's struggle against death matters. If one is rooted enough in a place, is freedom from anonymity—a kind of untainted, simplified immortality—possible? Rhodes's is a heady antidote to the urban solipsism dominant in our fiction.

Much of our greatest fiction has been written in the so-called "regional vein," which, paradoxically, lays the best claim to universality. One wonders what Rhodes might have achieved had he, like Faulkner, been allowed to build a more substantial body of work, engaged with essentially the same character type, immortalizing the ideal moral cadence of the rural Midwest. But perhaps, he already has.

THE DOOZY DECONSTRUCTIVE DELIBERATIONS OF A DOUBLE-EDGED DAME

THE BEST AMERICAN POETRY 2007. HEATHER MCHUGH, EDITOR. SCRIBNER, 2007.

My, what sickening second-hand choices — that is, what others face. I, doyenne of deliberate deliverables (business-borrowed term for poetry, packaged as passion's piss-off, when not inhumorably pale, palefaced and impaled — thank the management consultant and homeland security types, for ratcheting the rigor of language to reposted Robert Frost rostrums), I, mother of (unsurviving) maidens, get to decide who's on first base, who's on second, third and home, who sits too far in the stands to make out the silhouettes of the puppet-players (ninety percent of poetry makes nothing happen, not even soundwaves or heartbeats; the other ten percent is words competing for running-mate roles, like second-tier presidential candidates in Iowa and New Hampshire snowy winters, each with complete résumés and identifiable nondegradable bodies — words are only that, candidates seeking attention). I'd rather not do poetry myself, for the long and short of it, the duration of duration.

Reminds me of domestic war, this acute channeling of fallopian beasts of the faint future, embryonic in status now, but emitting something of the spirit of *Leaves of Grass* every time they sneeze of political allergies. Rustic physicianly Paterson-padding favorite WCW, stuffing crabs in square boxes, or not, is, will be, must be taught to safe aspirants to Byron's unhung dominion. Pulling out these crabs night after night, screening piles of shiny-faced, too-cool-to-becaptured, Guantánamo-denying journals (aka periodical pussycats, pussyfooting around "make it new" with all the whisker-rhymey ruin of metaphysical wits), I wonder, if there's a God in heaven (or in my stove), who knows what it is to count the moments elapsed from one epiphany to another, one statement of the assless lyric "I" to its profound antidotal other, just seconds later (often in the same stanza!). Save us from duplicitous metaphors (which climb the dying elms in my yard like squirrels preening to be themselves), save us from narrative suffixed to the televisions in our heads, screaming, screaming, screaming late at night when suicide is impossible, and save us from beginning, middle, and end, closure, the rhetoric of artifice, that is to say, how to bottle up Sterne's rambunctious energy in one of Thackeray's luminous show-not-tell interludes.

To the work at hand (unlanguage me now, hand-me-down words, unlock the Magna Carta of impossible sequences), apathetic aporia-fed nation loves nothing more than making mush of myth—so we must reproduce in homey mixed-metaphors what otherwise is the stuff of grandiose international cinema productions, bring the gods down to pygmy size. Kazim Ali knows in "The Art of Breathing" what he's up to. These Indian men of the ghazal strains, repetitive in their classical melancholy, yet know how to only connect. "Do you lose yourself / in the cave of endless breath," is of course about the composition of poetry—don't get carried away by form, order, routine. To prevent alienation, as Krishna warns Arjuna, do not try not to know yourself, your limits to verbal disorder. Jeannette Allée, now what she does in "Crimble of Staines" is move by dis(as)sembling prior definition. What do we (we who travel to the past) think of "motherbickered / England dumb with brick / & viper typists"? Don't try to dismantle the "negativity in names"—simply reinscribe it; the fungible distaste of "bodgy bed," "wrunkled skin," and kidney pie tasting "like potty" does it. Above all, seek poems defining definition beyond the backpack-buried thesaurus, which no one carries to college anymore, least of all to poetry workshops: So Rae Armantrout (hi Ray, I love you, if love is how you define one poet admiring another's innocence-defying word-rapes) in "Scumble" being "turned on" by ""scumble," "pinky," or "extrapolate."" Definition defies looseness of the arbitrary citizen, floating on social rules: "What if there were a hidden pleasure / in calling one thing / by another's name?" Thank you, Ray, for summing up my life's (o)mission.

Moving on, next morning while my cats antic-prance, like the "metaphor machine" in Nicky Beer's "Still Life with Half-Turned Woman and Questions"—Savonarola implicating the cognoscente artist in the age of aesthetics, and returning always with answers that are questions: "Q. What's that hanging on the wall, to the left of the table? / A mirror. / A window. / A sliding panel cut in the door of a solitary confinement cell. / A gray eye gone rectangular with its own blindness." No old-school (is there any other?) feminism here, only queries into the alleged components of feminism. Literalness of the seeing eye defi(n)ed, perchance to start off my litany of undefeats. After Christian Bök's "Vowels"—"loveless vessels // we vow / solo love // we see / love solve loss // else we see / love sow woe // selves we woo / we lose" and so on— interrogatory of words resting on no-scaffolds that need to be removed after every uneconomic collapse, lest I be accused of being too obsessed (obsession! a word the bourgeois love to emphatically pronounce, as though to immunize their sad fetishes from observation, from the word-mad scrutiny of Dostoevsky's possessed) with Potemkin behind-the-scenes montages (minus vowels or vow us, as necessary), how about Geoffrey Brock's "Flesh of John Brown's Flesh: Dec. 2, 1859"? *"No blood…and no remission."* This may not have been quite how John Brown, Sr.'s code of discipline appeared to John Brown, Jr., but paternalism is a tactic of the deceased, and America is still alive—yet Brock is on to the wily Freudian narrative, how it prescribes even as it proscribes, how the scenic background to private history (viz. Nabokov at his drunken best) is tame and persuasive, if narrative aims to make it so. So make it so.

Another morning (sweet respite from composing my journal entries, which over the years are more and more resistant to starting at any fixed point on the page and moving smoothly down to the expected end), blissfully Vermontish, enveloping my sky-high ambition with the shadow of the mount of discipline, and I come upon Macgregor Card's "Duties of an English Foreign Secretary." How can you beat this? "My nation bears repeating and adores / the maudit hermit rising without name into gorgeous claimant lumber." From his manuscript of the same name (publisher, I'd ask to see it!), which I read as oriented circa 1952, just past Britain's end-of-empire blues, and written in the style of the derided mid-eighteenth century Spasmodic School (am I spasmodic? My cats might agree) which preceded the Pre-Raphaelites (always the preceding movement anticipates the succession of the immediately following one), although I wouldn't have known it by reading the poem alone. This might be the best of the lot, because of lines like this: "I found myself in a wood of chairs, / the birds were thin as wires, / when information fails, light falls, / the office clock to airy thinness beat." A planet of bureaucracies convulsing to silence. Where no one "reads poesie," and all around them were "trees." Not dissimilar to the absence of noise at the lectures I'm compelled to give at writers' conferences, where people sit like at executions, only to be surprised by my disinclination to associate words with definite meanings when they inquire into my "methods of composition." The earth shifts under them, as it should.

I'm throwing in more traditional fare here, Billy Collins, and young Linh Dinh (I presume he's young, if he can meditate so fresh-facedly, so disorientedly, if I might say so, in "A Super-Clean Country," on the total penetration of shit in our conversation, even as we do everything to hide it in fact—such shortness of poetic breath is difficult after your first sustained period of acclaim), and also Stephen Dunn (I've managed so far to avoid meeting him, imagining him to be a man of many posturing silences, each utterly penetrable to his wives and mistresses and girlfriends, should he have been so prolific in his intimacies), whose "Where He Found Himself" is a quaint little parable afraid to be a parable, very much what one would expect from a humble gray-haired academic of his steady reputation—a poem almost qualified to take on the verities of groupthink, especially when manifested in therapy, but not quite, since he is of the wor(l)ds that make up groupthink, I think. Middle-aged Merrills, Sunday morning quarterbacks, where are the whoresons blessing sanctity on your wide pub(l)ic regions? So! Moving on to more radical stuff...

I do not like to decompose Louise Glück. She is my friend, and I will include her poem, and that is that. Aristotelian convention brought forward naked to the age of therapy, which can't be all that salutary for institutionalized modernism. Nice to see my friend Albert Goldbarth write a small song for once, in "Stopping by Woods on a Snowy Evening." The age of Frost, progressivism for the inarticulate masses, couched in (what else but?) Aristotelian tradition, which was brought to a close by the information-age harbinger known as Lee Harvey Oswald, and here we contemplate, in the year 2007, with shock and wonder, how image has replaced reality. A little too cute, with "the inward flying" of the night, is Albert, but I make concessions for his relapse into the short form. How can I resist Mark Halliday's (another dear friend) "Best Am Po" even as I enact (or is it all true, like bad breath and unclean shit?) the rituals of selecting (I, who have not yet selected my bridal dress, refuse to make that choice, even if I were to reread my vows in the blessed South of France, that fecund territory of the marriage-minded bourgeois) the best of the blessed?: "In this shtupfdin I feel I have lowered the stress index / in order to permit a valorizing of perforation / which I feel is the only platform for revisioning culture / not already under erasure from Microsoft." I feel we have come centuries from the canon-making of E. D. Hirsch and Allan (Ravelstein) Bloom of the early eighties, don't you? Back then, literature departments talked to creative writing departments, expecting productive discourse, yielding common meanings. Hah! As for Halliday's "the rhizome of all that I have suffered / to be caramelized into a non-narrative narrative, an anti-story / that laughs bitterly in the teeth of story," let me tell ya, pardner, so have I (suffered caramelized narrative from nonexistent husbands and deans).

A week has gone by, wherein I have been depressed after watching the news. Imagine the satisfaction then of encountering Matthea Harvey's "From 'The Future of Terror/Terror of the Future' Series." She says, "We'd killed all the inventors and all / the jesters just when we most needed humor / and invention." We're all "flying solo," end of the dream of collectivity, as bad in Stalin's Russia as Bush's America, no two ways about it, and only the old-at-heart from twenty on can see it, among whom I must definitely count Harvey. "O there's no way to nectarize this moment— / it's entirely without sweetness." This is stasis without statists, and I (y)earn it, like nectar off my nose. I'm afraid not to include "Bush's War" by Robert Hass; it would be questioned by friend and foe alike, the exclusion of this politically correct war against the war of words, taking us back to a safe past. The safest way to deaden the terrifying present: include the whole past, indiscriminately, entice a pacific rage. I include this to see which of my astute readers will pick up on the anomaly. Jane Hirshfield's "Critique of Pure Reason" is another politically correct past-is-present-is-past poem, though I must include it too, if I've fallen for Hass's trick. A safe list poem, Milton Kessler's "Comma of God." Damn, there should be a ban on listmaking, when the bourgeois, since Defoe's time, do nothing but. Still, I must include, to be safe rather than sorry. Why is the business end of poetry so much sorry-making, so little ecstasy? My young friend Linh Dinh, of the shit-eating eye, is right, it's everywhere. Wonder of wonders, here's Brad Leithauser with "A Good List." Is he modernist, is he formalist, is he neotraditonalist, God in Heavens, what is he? But he's good here, since he will "draw up a list, / Of everything I've never done wrong." One can't get enough of poets without conscience, since the bourgeois world cannot function without. In opposition is supposition (of victory by default, since no one else has taken the stance). Guns melting into butter. "It's the good who do not sleep," concludes Brad. I do not sleep. I never slept as a baby.

Mad perception of historical-geological-anthropological slant sums up our gnawing knowing of the embryo social lust from which we all burst, and so Joanie Mackowski's (how come we haven't met yet?) "When I was a dinosaur." We've all been there, my dear, and we are returning there, just as soon as peak oil and the housing collapse (no Wal-Marts, yeah, yeah, yeah) become reality (what, you think, I'm like a Deadhead, roaming the writers' conferences in search of acolytes of the self-I-never-was, don't pay attention to climate change and other headbanging shit? Shit is everywhere.). And then what happens to the death of the author? The conjoining of wor(l)d etymologies, the body politic realized in the forced juxtaposition of disciplines, per Foucault, per his succeeding genealogists of archeology, leads to Campbell McGrath's "Ode to the Plantar Fascia," and there is nothing about the fascist underfooting of bourgeois culture, only an address to that part of the foot, and that, my friends, is the radicalness of this (im)posture, to dare to be a poet who addresses objects by their name, ignoring the universal bureaucrat's forced adjoining of impaled forces. Everywhere, in Leslie Adrienne Miller's "On Leonardo's Drawings," in Ed Ochester's "Voltaire at Cirey, 1736," there is less than meets the eye, history is not present even if titular indications are that it will be, and as I read, the poem dissolves before my eyes. Nothing more radical is imaginable in this age of surfeit of words. It's been a long evening, my cats are snoozing, the fireplace is sparking, and the telephone hasn't rung for hours.

I wake up to a drizzling morning, bleak as only spring in Vermont can be, and resolve to ignore history for the rest of my life. Marilyn Nelson's "Etymology," Danielle Pafunda's "Dear Pearce & Pearce, Inc.," and so many others, take a clear snapshot from a part of history completely understood, and fog it over with how the present may process it, thus demystifying the already demystified. Another radical gesture of the utmost silencing capacity (the empire makers, canon builders, and tub thumpers thrive on making us accept history as fact). Isn't Nelson mocking her own politically correct stance (working for the civil rights movement, all that jazz, in the King era) by cowriting sonnet sequences with Elizabeth Alexander on the boarding school for colored girls in Connecticut in the 1830s? Minorities can take these sharp pictures from the past (oh, so many, so many of them, enough to last poetry workshops for millennia) and reconstruct how a person of today's sensibility might well have experienced those moments in history, and what have you? A deconstruction beyond the norms of deconstruction, hence its fatal success. The peak of this meretricious service to the literary arts today is Robert Pinsky, who in "Louie Louie" (the safest best to include in this anthology) says, "I had heard of Yale but I never / Heard of George W. Bush." I tell you, Pinsky would have sat down Emma Goldman and Rosa Luxemburg for a lecture, and they would have been eating out of his hands in no time (while Stein sputtered her sputtering etymologies of American-born disgust), turned into settlement workers. To make it inconceivable to mobilize the bourgeois fascists, remove the poet from the scene, so at least he is not affected. Any higher ambition and the poet gets swallowed up in the fire first (do we need Akhmatovas in this country?). I cannot but also include Pinsky's "Stupid Meditation on Peace" (I know, two poems each from two poets so blasted by the scatological kitsch-product of the poetry Wal-Marts), which concludes: "The teaching says Peace is a positive energy. // Still something in me resists that sweet milk, / My mind resembles my restless, inferior cousin / Who fires his shit in handfuls from his cage."

Another week, another sentence in spring purgatory, when I yearn to be free of words tying me down, enslaving me to history, which cannot be crushed quickly enough, should you (t)ask my cats, Cowper-toned. I include

Frederick Seidel's "The Death of the Shah" (despite never having liked him, because he seems to enjoy writing poetry, and expects his audience to enjoy reading it, both of which seem to me anomalies history cannot tolerate at this stage of the Hardt and Negri empire-busting multitude) because there is no Shah in this poem, only psychoanalysis's various approaches to him, which is to say not even heat and dust, not even trail and vapor. Perhaps Seidel will vaporize himself during a reading and reappear as a monkish cat. I'd pay to see. Alan Shapiro is a good, good man, who I feel convinced cares about injustice to minorities, who seems like he treats his wife right, so I will include him. Balzac would throw fits at Carmine Starnino's "Money." Money is not currency of exchange, never was, never will be. Words are! I wonder, if I include Brian Turner's "What Every Soldier Should Know," if readers will pick up on this soldier's self-pity, as he talks only about *his* fear of being attacked— "*I will kell you, American.* // Men wearing vests rigged with explosives / walk up, raise their arms and say *Inshallah*" (after defining and redefining *Inshallah and Sabah el khair* and their other cultural standbys)—and never about the people the Americans are killing. I suspect not. No twenty-first century regular American poetry reader is that evolved. This is why I love them, when they cozy up to the harmless dame they think they hear at readings. I'm not up to the task of screening the rest. Arthur Vogelsang defines "The Family." He's in. Charles Harper Webb defines "Big." He's in. Joe Wenderoth defines "The Home of the Brave." He's in. Richard Wilbur defines a bunch of opposites, in "From 'Opposites' and 'More Opposites,'" like those of baby and kite and down and earth and heaven, so he's in. Would one of my graduate students have done as good a job of selection? You bet! I am useless—the highest aspiration, the sweet-smelling old-as-curiosity-shop friend Stein never buttered.

All my neighbors are dead. The workshops are fallen quiet. Somewhere in the deep turn of the valley, Wordsworth's lyre suffuses the spirits of the cut-off trees with words' worth, which is to say, if in a blind forest the tree falls, there is always the semblance of a poet to oversee it, administering last funeral rites. So with this caveat, not to take poetry too seriously (for it just might make things happen that ought not to happen), boys and girls, it's off to dinner at the neighbors', to regale them with the persona of mine they've gotten used to appreciating, mad old poetess of the association-free definitions, implanted perhaps with the mind of Sylvia Plath had she gone on to be lobotomized of her rage, persiflage. It comforts my neighbors and friends, this pose. May all your poetry-making days be so free.

THE NEW BIOGRAPHY OF PATHOLOGY

CHEEVER: A LIFE BY BLAKE BAILEY. KNOPF, 2009.

HIDING MAN: A BIOGRAPHY OF DONALD BARTHELME BY
TRACY DAUGHERTY. ST. MARTIN'S PRESS, 2009.

John Cheever (1912-1982) came from a Boston South
Shore family of good name fallen on hard times, was expelled
from high school (and published a story about it in *The New
Republic* at eighteen), remained married to the same woman
for forty years while struggling with his homosexual urges,
wrote dark stories about suburban life while physically
embodying its spirit, and conquered alcoholism late in
life, going out in a blaze of recognition. Donald Barthelme
(1931-1989) came from a privileged Texan background
(his father was an influential architect in Houston), made
the most of his hometown journalism stints to launch his
mature art, married four times while personifying the über-
heterosexual, exemplified vitality as he helped found the
University of Houston's creative writing program, and yet
never overcame alcoholism, dying of cancer at fifty-eight
with his critical reputation at a low point. Cheever was always
running from his origins, inventing an aristocratic self early
on, and never feeling comfortable with his father, mother,
and older brother. Barthelme had little trouble replenishing
from his origins, despite his greatest productivity coinciding
with his New York sojourn. Cheever obsessively kept a
journal, amounting to several million words, the source of
information about his homosexual impulses. Barthelme,
despite being a diligent literary activist, comes across as
inscrutable, leaving a permanent mystery about why his

marriages dissolved, what he felt about countercultural New York, or how he assessed his own writing. Each, now, has earned the biographer he would most have enjoyed sparring with. Both biographers have sharpened the unique aspects of their subjects' personalities to the point of unavoidable centrality.

Whoever takes the first shot at an author's biography establishes the pattern for others to follow. In Cheever's case, it is his daughter, and in Barthelme's case, his second wife. Shortly after Cheever's death, Susan Cheever published *Home After Dark* (1984), which admitted Cheever's alcoholism and his struggles with homosexuality, without making them the sum of his character. Her memoir proliferates in flat, almost graceful, statements. On Cheever's homosexuality: "My father was a man with intense and polymorphous appetites that caused him tremendous guilt and self-loathing." On Cheever feeling betrayed by *The New Yorker*: "The New Yorker has always been an eccentric institution." On Cheever's fantasies: "My father knew that [actress] Hope [Lange] was not really available, but that didn't keep him from daydreaming." On the distance between her parents: "My parents' arguments became worse." On Cheever's alcoholism: "It became clearer and clearer that my father was the worst kind of alcoholic." On his late homosexual relationship with Max Zimmer: "Rip [Zimmer]'s attitude from the beginning was one of humorous irreverence that was just my father's style." Susan divides her father's life in two neat phases: the struggle to establish his career took up the first forty-five years, and the escape from self-imposed upper-middle-class norms occupied the remainder. Scott Donaldson's *John Cheever: A Biography* (1988) avoided building on the sensational aspects of Susan's revelations. Instead, Donaldson's reverence subdues Susan's explosive charges. Donaldson skates over Cheever possibly having had an incestuous relationship with his brother Fred, the Cheever household's discord as the father lost his job as a shoe salesman and the brash British-born mother started a gift shop, Cheever's financial and social distress in New York during the Depression, and the nadir of Cheever's life, when he taught at Boston University in 1974-1975 and almost drank himself to death, leading to his rehab at Smithers Center and dedication to Alcoholics Anonymous. Cheever never wanted his correspondents to keep his letters and saved his revelations for his 4,300 page journals, so his son Benjamin's publication of *The Letters of John Cheever* (1988) didn't add much. The same is not true of Robert Gottlieb's selection of *The Journals of John Cheever* (1991), where Cheever's inability to gain the daily affection of his wife is a central issue. Lyrical and self-questioning, *The Journals* allow Cheever's charm to seductively come through.

Bailey's tack has been to revert to each of the flat openings in Susan Cheever's biography, vastly magnify their emotional scale (relying on the unpublished portions of the journals), and construct alcoholism and suppressed homosexuality (each inflaming the other) as the primary engines of Cheever's life. He follows rather a neat schema, with a redemptive end more pronounced than the turnaround Susan Cheever posits. Bailey's Cheever is suspiciously reminiscent of the Richard Yates in Bailey's biography of the other tortured, alcoholic chronicler of suburbia, *A Tragic Honesty: The Life and Work of Richard Yates* (2003). As with Yates, Cheever's critical estimation, especially among writers, was at its peak when Bailey took him on. The complete collapse due to alcoholism while teaching in Boston is a particularly striking similarity. From a publishing point of view, moving from Yates to Cheever makes sense. Bailey would not lack for sensational material. He could tell a redeeming story, bonded to the larger political arc: Cheever being terrified of his sexual impulses during the dark McCarthy years, then feeling liberated after the early stirrings of the gay rights movement in the seventies, reaching an equilibrium toward the end of his life. Bailey's voluminous biography does provide an in-depth account of the publication of Cheever's fiction, wondering why he had such a hard time moving from stories to novels. But as is common with literary biographies, the connections between the author's life and writing are often spurious, and don't necessarily illuminate either. Cheever fantasizing about fratricide in his fiction may not tell us anything important about how he felt toward his brother. The great artist's ability to transcend the raw material of his autobiography to create new worlds of imagination is typically underestimated in the average biography's cause and effect linkage between life and art. Similarly, Bailey's inquiry into characterizations of the fallen aristocrats in the Wapshot books being the result of Cheever's desire to purge his system of the anguish of his own ruined family doesn't seem particularly illuminating.

A biography more interested in purely literary matters might have assigned a different ranking to Cheever's personal turmoil. Cheever's negotiations with his *New Yorker* editors, particularly William Maxwell, are some of the more interesting parts of the book (as are Barthelme's dealings with his *New Yorker* editor, Roger Angell, in the Daugherty biography). Cheever kept pushing against the limits of what was publishable in the magazine. In this most professional of relationships, Cheever didn't mix business with pleasure. The intellectual atmosphere at Yaddo in the thirties and forties, under Elizabeth Ames's supervision, is nearly drowned out by accounts of Cheever's unsatisfied homosexual lusts. For Bailey, Cheever's lifelong demonstrations of manliness— swimming, scything, biking—were excessive reactions to the fear of effeminacy imposed by his father. Cheever wanted gay sex without the gay lifestyle. In thinking of Virginia Woolf and other androgynous female writers, we focus more on the expansive possibilities than the psychic inconsistencies. The evidence from Gottlieb's *Journals* is that Cheever understood himself better than all three biographers credit him. Some measure of writerly competitiveness is unavoidable. Bailey makes much of Cheever's competitiveness toward John Updike, yet the two apparently had an overall supportive relationship, and Cheever's warmth toward Saul Bellow, in particular, suggests that his ability to form professional male relationships was if anything strengthened by his voracious sexuality. Two late relationships, during the course of his teaching, with Allan Gurganus and Max Zimmer, bear out the point. Gurganus refused Cheever's overtures, while Zimmer gave in, yet Cheever's affection for either seems not to have been particularly related to his responsiveness. Like Barthelme, Cheever was apt to put literary judgment above personal like or dislike. Many of the apparent paradoxes of Cheever's life—his content suburban existence in the midst of dark fictions about it—can be explained by resort to the author's literary self transcending contingent circumstances.

With Donald Barthelme, Tracy Daugherty didn't have the luxury of responding to points of view taken in previous full-fledged biographies, or relying on extensive journals such as Cheever assiduously maintained. Barthelme was an innovator in writing self-distancing fictions of the most ironic kind, and the natural tendency on the part of superficial acquaintances, or mere readers, would be to ascribe a similar persona to the author himself. Daugherty is a former student of Barthelme's, an exceptionally involved teacher who went beyond the call of duty to help establish his students' careers. Daugherty has gone about his project by incorporating all of the content of Helen Moore Barthelme's *Donald Barthelme: The Genesis of a Cool Sound* (2001), without questioning any aspect of Barthelme's second wife's recollections. Helen's memoir encompasses the early fifties, when she met him at the University of Houston, through the mid-sixties, when they divorced. She presents Barthelme as a forceful editor of *Forum*, a cross-disciplinary journal at the University of Houston, and a cutting-edge director of Houston's Contemporary Arts Museum. In the early sixties, Harold Rosenberg invited Barthelme to come to New York and edit a new journal of art and literature called *Location*, extending the eclecticism Barthelme had established in *Forum*. Helen fondly recollects Barthelme's early successes with *The New Yorker* (having rejected Cheever's more experimental ventures, the magazine now promoted Barthelme's radical experimentation as a mainstay), and the publication of his well-received first collection, *Come Back, Dr. Caligari*. Helen locates Barthelme as a visionary who saw Houston's cultural coming-of-age, and pinpoints the philosophic influences which shaped his breakthroughs. As editor of *Forum*, Barthelme solicited work from Walker Percy, and was interested in all manner of existentialist writing, later evidenced in his own stories, such as the exemplary "Kierkegaard Unfair to Schlegel." Barthelme moved to New York without hesitation. His stories of urban alienation wouldn't have had the same flavor had he stayed in Houston. The Houstonian had willed himself to become a New York writer par excellence.

In all this, Daugherty faithfully follows Helen's rendition. What Daugherty has essentially done is to add an extensive prologue (Barthelme's childhood and adolescence in the thirties and forties) and epilogue (Barthelme's continued publishing in the seventies and his early lead at the University of Houston's writing program in the eighties), without probing into Barthelme's personal anxieties, such as his motivation to end three different marriages, or even his lifelong addiction to alcohol. Where Helen accepts, and Barthelme gives the appearance of accepting, so does Daugherty. This strategy, so different from Bailey's, perhaps accomplishes a similar final outcome. How much of the final impression was within the biographer's control? Whereas Cheever recorded every unsolvable emotional conflict and perhaps meant his journals for publication (late in life he allowed Benjamin to read some of them), Barthelme's image accords with how we imagine the author of such erudite, hyperconscious, postmodern fables to have been. Did Barthelme possess the charisma to stamp the impression of controlled emotion on his wives and friends, his students and colleagues, the persona which has dutifully come down to posterity?

Daugherty imparts a certain inevitability (also the bane of biographies) to how Barthelme evolved from the seemingly infertile grounds of Houston in the first part of the century. Donald Barthelme, Sr., was a prominent modernist architect who designed some of the city's most innovative landmarks. His home in the West Oaks suburb was a modernist spectacle, which attracted onlookers. Lively discussions of art and culture occurred in the Barthelme home. The son might have disappointed the father with his choice to study locally, but he made the most of it. Apprenticeship at the university newspaper, where he tried to inject black humor, and later at the *Houston Post*, which taught him economy and discipline, provided him a good launching pad for his later fiction. He was stationed as a public information officer in Korea, and like Cheever's involvement with the Army Signal Corps, this taught him just enough about the military to sharpen but not deaden his consciousness. Barthelme's sense of the avant-garde exceeded that of the staid University of Houston administrators overseeing *Forum*. He divorced his first wife, Marilyn Marrs, upon returning from Korea, because she now seemed too much of a cold intellectual to him. Barthelme set a wedding date with Helen even before his divorce from Marilyn, and Helen's from her first husband, was final. Daugherty has fleshed out these details with help from Barthelme's early Houston friends, so that Barthelme's intellect, destined as he was to become the avant-garde writer, remains front and center. The pupil's loyalty asserts itself, and anything disagreeable about the master is quickly passed over.

Daugherty's biography comes closest in flavor to Donaldson's version of Cheever. Emotional flags are raised, then lowered without second thought. Why Barthelme ended the marriage with Helen isn't quite clear. Helen returned to her advertising business in Houston, and though the two eventually resumed a friendship, Barthelme enjoyed the freedoms of New York too much to be bound to Helen. Or is that true? He desired to be tied down shortly thereafter to Birgit Egelund-Peterson, a Dane with serious mental problems, with whom he had a daughter named Anne. The nature of Barthelme's attraction to Birgit is not clear, Daugherty's tentative psychological speculations notwithstanding. The breakup with Birgit remains obscure as well. As for Barthelme's fourth wife, Marion Knox, again the passion seems under control, the conflicts well buried. Has

Barthelme the writer won, as our collective understanding of his all-embracing irony precludes engagement with him as a man?

Barthelme's most productive period probably ended shortly after his newfound domesticity. *Snow White* (1967), his best novel, and two of his better story collections, *Unspeakable Practices, Unnatural Acts* (1968) and *City Life* (1970), arguably were produced while the fumes from his early New York years still ran strong. His work after that—the novels *The Dead Father* (1975) and *Paradise* (1986), and the story collections *Sadness* (1972) and *Amateurs* (1976)—received equivocal critical reception. The final return to Houston in 1981 seems to have severed him from the source of his inspiration altogether. On Barthelme's decline, Daugherty is reticent. He finds much to praise about Barthelme's weakest work of the eighties, as he took to teaching with a passion. Barthelme was eclipsed by a new type of minimalism, in tune with cultural conservatism. Ann Beattie and Raymond Carver, the newly favored *New Yorker* writers, could do no wrong, while Barthelme's flamboyant self-detachment became passé and a critical backlash set in. Uniformity of praise for Barthelme's work restrains Daugherty from exploring the fall-off in Barthelme's prowess. Susan Cheever was able to end her father's life on a high note, in the wake of critical acclaim for his 1977 prison novel, *Falconer*, where he dealt with overt homosexual themes for the first time, and the 1979 Pulitzer Prize for *The Stories of John Cheever*. Barthelme probably couldn't have revived his career in similar fashion had he lived past fifty-eight. The best of his writing dates to the end of the sixties. It was perhaps to fill the vacuum of relevance that he plunged himself so ferociously into teaching in his later years, but Daugherty's venerating conception of Barthelme as always having been a conscientious literary citizen, active in organizations like PEN and making things move behind the scenes on behalf of his favorite writers, preempts investigation of teaching not so much as fulfillment but as compensation. Daugherty consistently refrains from the sharp edge, while giving us an author whose project of becoming the supreme ironist of his age seems improbable even in the retelling. We come away from the Cheever biography humbled by his sincerity; we come away from the Barthelme biography awed by his detachment.

Some preternatural force of will led both men to create themselves as major authors, when early circumstances would have predicted little of the sort. In that sense, the books are authentic chronicles of Cheever and Barthelme's lives, even in the sentimental meaning of inspiring would-be writers. Both Cheever and Barthelme early perceived the contours of greatness, as the literary culture of their times had mythologized it, yet chose to reshape it to their own needs. They both succeeded in large measure, for instance in bending the *New Yorker* story to unprecedented curves. Cheever in the forties, fifties, and sixties, and Barthelme in the sixties and seventies, pushed the American short story in directions it had not gone before. They were both authors of immense influence—Cheever personally, Barthelme institutionally—whose joint legacies constitute a large part of what we think of as creative writing in America today. Taking advantage of commercial outlets to reach a broad audience, they retained admirable distance toward literary institutions. The vital genius of neither man was harmed by personal angst. The best estimate we can gain of each author is ultimately from close study of his fiction, which these two biographies, having given us a glimpse of the essential man, fervently prompt us to do all over again.

LICENSE TO KILL: THE BIOGRAPHER'S DEADLY ART

THE CARDBOARD UNIVERSE: A GUIDE TO THE WORLD OF PHOEBUS K. DANK BY CHRISTOPHER MILLER. HARPER PERENNIAL, 2009.

Christopher Miller has pulled off the impossible. He has written the funniest book of the year—perhaps of the decade—which also happens to be the most profound metaphysical inquiry into the status of the writer in relation to his readers, his critics, his market, his personality, his limits, his phobias, and his innocence that I have ever read, leaving Martin Amis and Philip Roth's speculations in the dust. This is the faux-biography to test all "real" biographies against, as our vampiric urge to "know" any great writer exceeds our present capacity to let his imagination affect us.

The novel is told in the form of a collaborative encyclopedia written in 2007 by Dank's biggest fan, William Boswell (professor at Hemlock College in Hemlock, California, founder of the Dank Studies program there, and Dank's housemate from 1994 to 2006) and Owen Hirt, supposedly Dank's harsh critic, whose literary opinion Dank nonetheless appreciated all his life. Boswell's entries about Dank's fiction and life are fawning, while Hirt's are rudely dismissive. Dank has recently been found bludgeoned to death in his house, and Hirt, the leading suspect, is emailing Boswell from some presumably idyllic spot as together they compose the encyclopedia. Or so we are led to believe...

Phoebus K. Dank is based loosely on the life of Philip K. Dick, also neglected until almost the end of his life, but canonized since. Like Dick, Dank's prolific output barely fits into the SF category, the settings often near-future dystopic worlds roughly like ours, except for a few key variables changed. Dick's oeuvre was somewhat more concerned with altering political variables, while Dank often alters the individual's senses. In "Abruptophobia," a cameraman "develops a morbid sensitivity to everything *sudden*." In "The Toe," a yogi tunes out all bodily sensations, other than the toe.

Dank's premises are so fecund that all of Kafka or Calvino's productions are dwarfed by a few entries of the encyclopedia. Yet he would be considered a hack writer, because of his sloppy prose (which Hirt constantly mocks), and his astounding copiousness. Wanting to go "legit," he once follows a guide called *Get Some Respect: The Disgruntled Scribbler's Guide to Writing Serious Fiction*, with chapters like "Pumping Irony" and "The Six Big Themes No Book Reviewer Can Resist." Dank's lack of self-consciousness—academia's bane—is the secret to his market-worthy productivity.

Dank is set up as a caricature of everything the modern reader fears of authors' paranoias (Dick broke down in 1974, leading to his "religious" novels, while Dank undergoes lesser breakdowns every day). Dank is obese, married only briefly to unsuitable women, and endures personality disorders ranging from agoraphobia to fear of fatal insomnia. Yet, as biographers ought to know, the greatness of the writing is usually obversely related to the writer's "normality." Dank is lovable because of his innocence toward objects and senses. Dank is a modern saint not despite, but because of, his "faults."

The "shocking" revelation at the end, of who really killed Dank, destroys our established view of the carping Hirt and the fanatically sincere Boswell, while reiterating the equations relating the published to the unpublished. Boswell keeps dwelling on the seven unpublished novels, according to him Dank's greatest, which Dank's agent has rejected. While the concepts of these novels, such as *Planet Food* (where a man's life story is told through the memories the various groceries evoke), are more striking than Dank's published work, the end makes us realize that a literary hand would be unable to tackle such wildly inventive stuff, and so the novels must remain unpublished.

Miller's novel is ultimately about the hierarchies assigned to art. Can honest hack work be superior to labored "literary" work? This is an encyclopedia not of an obscure Northern California SF writer, but of every one of our culture's deficiencies toward the power of imagination. A Yoda figure in a Dank novel says, in inimitable hack fashion: *"The warp drive of imagination will outstrip the ramjets of mere craftsmanship."* The near-future dystopia, the police state of consciousness, that Dank (and Dick) so prolifically invented, is already upon us. Head to the nearest academic "Studies" program, not to mention writing workshop, to smell its obese morbidity.

ANNOUNCING THE DEATH
OF THE POST-9/11 NOVEL

It was fun while it lasted.

Novelists didn't have to think much in the way of plot. 9/11 happened before, during, or after, to change everything (as Bush and Ashcroft had it, the world changed, nothing was the same after 9/11).

"Before" was the easiest scenario. Take any family or personal situation, let 9/11 strike, and see how everyone scrambles. It would expose rifts in psychology the protagonists weren't aware of before. In this case 9/11 becomes a terroristic psychiatrist par excellence, bombarding the subconscious to yield the hidden (untruths).

"During," as in Claire Messud's *The Emperor's Children*, really gave the novelist a lot of rope to hang herself with (not that Messud did, hers was one of the best productions in the genre). Still, there was the predictable climax, so that we could compare the before and the after, and decide that yes, indeed, in the pre-9/11 period we were shallow, materialistic, greedy, superficial, Gary Condit/Chandra Levy-obsessed, shark-scared morons who didn't fathom that—gasp, people die! Yes, they suddenly die, even in America. Oh my God! That was easy.

"After" was the easiest of all. Simply let the narrative build to the predictable climax of 9/11, with people falling from the top of the towers, the image to end all images. The rhythm here was the easiest to calculate. 9/11 happens, the book ends, end of story.

By now every variation of the 9/11 novel has been exploited.

Immigrants carrying along with their cute patois and bashful ways, in love and in hate with America—then 9/11 happens and they became targets of racism, profiling, persecution, whatever. In the worst cases, they end up being tortured, taken to Guantánamo, or at least choosing voluntary deportation. Every variety of immigrant was described this way, from Latin Americans and Africans, to East Asians and Europeans. The 9/11 immigrant persecution complex knew no racial, religious, or ethnic boundaries. It was the gift that kept giving and giving.

On the surface, the exploration of persecution looks cool. Didn't 9/11 help us explore the hypocrisies of that aging whore America, who showers her benefactions on selective groups of people, but not all? Yes, that is a whore we can all love to hate. America, kick out your raggedy and poor, send them off to torturing shores, so that you may be purified. That whole immigrant-comes-to-America-and-makes-it-on-sheer-merit deal? It was a phony shtick. Now we know.

The most exploited variation was this. Dysfunctional family, grieving over all sorts of superficial things, split up over non-issues, maybe with children and parents inhabiting opposite coasts. Somehow 9/11 brings them all together. *Of course* it brings them all together. It is the event to end all interfamily disputes. The image of people falling off towers, flying to their death, somehow puts petty family grievances in their true perspective. A lot of novelists tried their hands at this genre, and no doubt will continue to do so until at least 2020. Or maybe until environmental collapse finally makes it into the novelist's imagination (it hasn't obstructed environmental apocalyptics from offering all but ready-made novels, so real novelists, take note!).

A lot of novelists, unwilling or afraid to take on Islamic terrorism directly, dusted off the Weather Underground and other terrorist groups of the 1960s and 1970s. The Baader-Meinhof gang, the Panthers, you name it, it was a field day for research in the late great days of the counterculture, the post-1968 unraveling. Nixon was an overwhelming brooding presence over the last decade's fiction. Nixon seems like a pussycat compared to the monsters who have followed him one after another, and we can never get enough of the polyester/disco 1970s, so this became really fertile.

The goofiness really took off in the last few years. Intrepid journalists. Underground missions. Stuff happening in the White House we would never have imagined. The attempt to present everyone—even the fucking war criminals who ought to be hanged by the noose—in sympathetic terms. Hey, it's the war on terror (like the Cold War, you know), so we can be forgiven if we merely carry out orders, it's bigger than us, this whole thing transcends any individual, it's the way our society has gone, and we're all just trying to do our job.

Exactly a decade ago, American fiction seemed in pretty dire straits. It was so bad that Jonathan Franzen's *The Corrections*—an okay book, if padded by 250 pages, monstrously self-obsessed, and in love with its own production values—was the greatest thing we were capable of. He dissed Oprah and we loved him all the more for it.

Dave Eggers had just published his memoir to end all memoirs, and we thought he was our best friend, because he told us that it was okay to be ironic, all-ironic-all-the-time, even if he was saying that with a touch (or more) of irony. He was the voice of our generation, and that generation, X or Y or Z or whatever—Bang! What was that? The sound of the falling towers! No more irony, Dave, you've gotta reinvent yourself in that serious, earnest, journalistic vein, you've gotta learn to tell us how we can get better, save this lost generation from its worst sins of affluence and iPod-mania and soon the Facebook scam. We liked that very much. We wanted to hear about genocide refugees and African and Latin American civil wars and brutal dictators in Central Asia and the heartlessness of American tourists in Southeast Asia. We got a lot of that after 9/11. See, 9/11 changed everything!

It seems like *no* fiction got written between 2001 and 2003. Absolute silence. Or so it seems now. Publishers were taking a break. Writers were taking a break. We had to let it all soak in, we were portentously warned (and if you were a fledgling writer pursuing editors in that dark, dark era of early Ashcroft, you'd know exactly what I mean). It was too early, oh yes, it was too early to decipher the meaning of 9/11, novelists who rushed to the event made a big mistake in judgment, the public wasn't ready for it, we had to let the event ripen, or very bad, undigested fiction would result.

And indeed we got very, very bad fiction from circa 2003 to circa 2007. Don DeLillo fell flat on his face. He had been writing about an undertone of terrorism all his life, but when the real thing (or whatever!) happened, his novels became compressed, pancaked, like the dust of the towers, unable to rise up and assert their concrete and steel narrative volume. John Updike tried very, very hard, and we were grateful to him at the time, but now his earnestness on the topic wears ill. Jonathan Safran Foer wrote an Extremely Bad and Incredibly Stupid novel, but anything else from him would have shocked me into permanent critical paralysis. They were all just flailing and failing, and we were making excuses for them, Oh well, the event is still too close.

Then came the good stuff, the really good stuff. Ken Kalfus, Mohsin Hamid, Claire Messud, Laila Halaby, Joseph O'Neill, and to up the ante, in 2009, Torsten Krol's *Callisto*, and now, finally, Teddy Wayne's *Kapitoil*. To change the tone here, I speak in awe of Krol and Wayne, two of the great writers of our time, whose books will far outlast the moment. As a fiction writer I am flabbergasted by what they've both accomplished. *Callisto* and *Kapitoil* are immense and unrepeatable, all credit to the editors who made these books a reality. It is almost worth it to live in this too-earnest, humorless, politically correct, terrified-of-our-own-shadows era if we can once in a while read books like *Callisto* and *Kapitoil*. Really, I have no words with which to go on.

But here we come to the end, because these two books—especially *Kapitoil*—are so good, so unimaginably good, that one fails to see what more can be done with the genre. Like James Joyce with the bildungsroman, they've killed off the fucking genre. There's nothing left of it. They've owned it, transcended it, made some sort of powerful fictional advance that I'm still trying to come to terms with, and done it all without breaking stride. I mean, speaking of immortals...

But the point again is that we have moved from 9/11 as a specific event to a generalized state of dread (its extreme form of generalization, so that it's both consummate myth and consummate reality, can be seen in James Hynes's *Next*, another very advanced form of the genre, one that predicts its decline and end).

So we've come full circle. We cannot possibly go back to where we were in 2000/2001 (remember, 9/11 changed everything), but we have exploited—as we Americans always will, we won't just dig out a few barrels, we'll take over the goddamn country that has the oil, yes we will!—the grief and terror and error of the day for all it's worth.

Meanwhile, life has gone on and novelists have ignored most of what's really interesting about the world.

Not that no one is writing about these things, but just as a reminder:

The American middle-class has all but ended, and it's not coming back.

We are in some sort of depression, but we don't quite know how it started and how it will end.

We have inaugurated a liberal regime which is more repressive on every measure than Nixon ever was—or at least dared to be, in good company.

The rise of China is inevitable (as inevitable as the rise of the seas by 200 feet in Al Gore's imagination—but I kid).

Immigrants are being deported in greater numbers than ever; immigrants are choosing not to come to our shores, they're voting with their feet (or stranded boats or camels or what-have-you), and so no more Google and eBay and California agriculture and whatever else they gave us.

There is a raging fascism gaining ground in all parts of the country; if the economy doesn't improve, or if we can't massage the numbers enough to prove that it has improved (more or less the same thing), then these movements are going to take center stage.

Somehow the quality of life in this country feels immeasurably impoverished. Everyone feels that. We don't know how that's happened.

To the extent that novelists participate in the myth of 9/11—that it was the most important event in the world since at least Pearl Harbor—they evade the trenchant reality around us. They empower the fantasists, they debase language, they prevent comprehension.

Why was it so easy to exploit 9/11? It was *grief* written large, and it totally fit into our sense of victimization at the beginning of the millennium. That millennial anxiety—manifested in the absurd hunt for the Y2K bug which never showed up—didn't exempt novelists, and they moved in pretty quickly to seize the day.

9/11 has become filler, agitprop candy, drama's rape, the magician's cap (and cape) we all put on when we don't know what to do. It's default mode run amok, secondary input masquerading as primary insight. Enough with it.

It is time to move on. Don't nobody else try to compete with Teddy Wayne, he's done it already, he's finished the genre, okay? Now go home and read some Dostoevsky and Proust and clear your heads. There's gold in them there hills, fictional gold all around you, so go be wildcat prospectors again.

AMERICA'S MOST PROMINENT EMERGING POETS RESPOND TO THE OBAMA ADMINISTRATION

STARTING TODAY: 100 POEMS FOR OBAMA'S FIRST 100 DAYS. RACHEL ZUCKER AND ARIELLE GREENBERG, EDITORS. UNIVERSITY OF IOWA PRESS, 2010.

Rachel Zucker and Arielle Greenberg asked one hundred of the best-known, mostly emerging, American poets to respond with a poem for each of Obama's first 100 days. *Starting Today: 100 Poems for Obama's First 100 Days* is the result, and the anthology is very revealing. Typically, American poets avoid going anywhere near politics, but when they do occasionally feel compelled to venture into that arena, the efforts are strained and a bit desperate, as though they were quite out of their element. So did the onset of the Obama administration, after the dark Bush years, let loose some new vein of creativity among our poets? Did they break through the existing molds, or does the excitement of politics in the end fail to compete with the usual stuff our poets tend to write about?

The first thing to note is the overwhelming uniformity of the political ideology behind these poems. Among these 100 stars, there is not a single poet who reveals himself/herself to adhere to anything other than a strict middle-of-the-road Democratic politics — the mildest of liberal correctionism in response to the Bush agonies. There's not a Republican, not a conservative, not a libertarian, not a radical of any sort here, as far as I can tell; there isn't a socialist, an anarchist, a revolutionary, any sort of agitator in evidence here, apart from what you might expect from a bunch of Democratic party functionaries solemnly penning the party platform. There's not even a Ralph Nader lover among the bunch, let alone a Rosa Luxemburg or Emma Goldman devotee.

One doesn't need to be a socialist to have street cred as a political poet; but one needs a fighting spirit, a disrespect for authority, an abiding skepticism that presumes all officialspeak as bullshit from the word go. So there is a variety of styles here, from the slightly experimental to the fashionably experimental, but there isn't anything like true diversity of political beliefs and aesthetics. The Age of Auden or Ginsberg, this isn't.

The editors hope in their introduction to have avoided 100 Elizabeth Alexander-type inaugural poems, but in essence that's what they got. True, as the 100 days go by, the unalloyed hope of the poets suffers slight erosion—but even by the end it's a very hopeful response, one very much in tune with majority feeling in the country by Day 100. There isn't a strong voice, relishing minority status, that really sticks out. The voters behaved like a herd in responding to the empty message of hope and change—substituting for any coherent political philosophy—and like kindergarten children soaking up such fables, so did the poets.

Rita Dove gushes in her Foreword: "The first one hundred days of a new era: one hundred breaths of fresh air after nearly three thousand days of staleness. One hundred days and counting. And though a hundred days are nothing like a decade and nowhere near a century, the world can change in a few months, in a few days, in an instant. Suddenly, there's a frisson in the air—risible [*sic*], catching—and to our amazement turning into a new reality. Since November 2008, passersby do their passing with eyes sparkling, a smile tugging at the cautionary mask. Can you see it? A twitch. A twinkle. Clustered strangers and spontaneous smiles, short bursts of laughter. Spirits lifted even as the markets crash." Rachel Zucker and Arielle Greenberg echo this spirit: "If we were to pick out a common thread [in this book],…it would echo our president's message of personal responsibility, of loving this country enough to expect a great deal of it, and of having the courage to be hopeful." A more complete negation of political philosophy was rarely uttered.

Elizabeth Alexander's "Praise Song for the Day," the inaugural poem, presumes as fait accompli a political destiny which hasn't even come close to being realized: "Say it plain: that many have died for this day." And what exactly did they die for? That a black man should become president? But what if that black man were a tyrant in the vein of George W. Bush, with little respect for the rule of law or constitutional protocols? Just supposing... Would it still be the day so many have died for? The New Agey stuff piles on: "What if the mightiest word is love?" The poem concludes as a "praise song for walking forward in that light." The mightiest problem of politics is power. Love has little to do with it. To interpret politics as a problem of love is to be in a very infantile position indeed. Later, Cornelius Eady, in "Praise for the Inaugural Poet, January, 2009," on Day 14, praises the one who praises: "A black woman is here. / All the black women in her are here to sing." Or yodel? As BJ Soloy says in "Last Migration, a Dead, Common Yellow-," on Day 17, "Still, / on election night, // I felt an urge to yodel. I livened up."

Matthew Rohrer on Day 2, in "Poem," exclaims: "I know / it's hard to believe but / the new president said science." That's a pretty low bar for a president to meet, isn't it? An even lower bar is for the president to just smile. Diane Wald writes in "Nonromantic Obama Valentine for America, February 14, 2009," on Day 27: "for our president / is smiling. // just a man. / openly smiling." He hasn't been smiling much lately, has he? Wald concludes: "we can smile again in america and now at least we have / a person in the white house who knows honestly how to do it." Similarly, Martha Silano echoes, in "His Springboard Resolve" on Day 3: "From this day forward, a little less fetus, a lot more science." Yvette Thomas, in "Missing Metaphor for Time," on Day 6, concludes the poem with "Change is." And I say, exactly: the sentence is unfinished; change is what? It's anything and nothing. Lyn Lifshin's "Michelle's Citrine

Dress" on Day 8 is more of the same, responding to the media persona built up for Michelle (who cares what she wears or doesn't wear?): "I think of / tulips when I think of / that dress." I think of intellectual bankruptcy.

The urge for identification—as with all stars—is overwhelming. On Day 11, Leslea Newman in "Prayer for a President" says: "And just for a moment / she was just a woman / in a fancy white dress / dancing with her husband / and just for a moment / he was just a man / in a crisp black tuxedo / dancing with his wife." No, they're not just husband and wife, he's the leader of the free world, as they like to say on the talk shows. Newman prays: *"keep them safe / keep them safe / keep them safe"* (thrice will do it?). Rebecca Wolff asks, in "The Most Famous Man in the World," on Day 12: "Are you like me / jug ears / of purpose / defined positively / by your positive / action and the clear vision / toward a common // sense?" And later, "I / feel you. You feel / me." Cole Swensen, in "Taking Cover under the Sun" on Day 18 wonders "what it feels like to know / that approximately half the world has a crush on your husband." Jeanne Marie Beaumont remarks, in "Rite (to Forge Amor for an Orphan)," on Day 78: "Let all that thrives in air conspire to keep you safe, / and character be wrought six-fold."

Well, if we insist hard enough, maybe Obama will become true. That's John Paul O'Connor's wish in "New Time Old Time" on Day 10: "O, Obama, be not the chosen, but the unchosen / of the unchosen revolution, not around the corner / but here on St. Nicholas Avenue where the swollen tribes / of unchosen are chanting, *Africa come home*, and raising / their sunbroad arms to demand you be what they believe / you are." On Day 9, Sasha Steensen is talking about emotions unfreezing, in "Wintry Weather and Job Slaughter": "hope / isn't eight times hotter / this time of year / just eight times / over / and melting / what? / fear?"

Children are taught in shades of black-and-white— at least by tyrannous parents. So Republicans (Bush) bad, Democrats (Obama) good; that's the reigning formulation. Shift the blame (it's fantastic that the politically correct academy has no problems tainting everyone except those of the Democratic persuasion as being the "other"). Marvin Bell, in "The Book of the Dead Man (Day 51)," establishes this binary division: "The dead man has been newly roused by a president of many colors. / There has been a worldwide lifting of downcast eyes for good reason. / The fog has lifted that hid the systemic violations of law, and the dead man feels the ground shifting. / Now the indigent can hope for more than weeping. / For America was ambushed by the vile and the wicked. / Quickly, it was midnight in America, and the chuckle-heads were in charge." What David Axelrod told us from the pulpit, about Obama being the new uniter, is swallowed whole and repeated by Patricia Carlin, in "Thinking My Way Out of a Paper Bag," on Day 79: "No more With or / Against, Black or / White."

The American workshop poem tends to follow a certain pattern. Some narration, some private feelings, ending with a slight epiphany. It's striking that the Obama poems have fallen so neatly into this established schematic. Just as the workshop poem typically ends in a glimmer of hope, so does the Obama poem. Cin Salach's "The First Easter, 2009," on Day 84, concludes: "That is how I feel when I walk / in the world now. My palms are up. Open. / This is what I want to tell you." In a way, the American workshop poem has become generally a form of religious expression, in the structure it follows (every crucifixion-confession must have a resurrection-redemption). Politics under Obama is also a form of religion—although an exceptionally childish one, even as religions go.

It would be unfair to discuss this book without the bright spots—of restrained hope, subdued excitement, and guarded skepticism. Michael Dumanis, in "Occasionally, I Write a Poem," on Day 21, concludes warily: "I have nothing to say about the president." Bravo! Perhaps more of these poets should have had nothing to say about the new president. One of the strongest poems, Major Jackson's "A General Theory of Interest & Money or Getting the Country in Bed," on Day 22, has just the right tone;

Jackson is not taken in by the hoopla at all. He concludes the poem: "You must strong pitch the rich on Capitol Hill / to support the applause of your Senate Bill." There's a bit of Ezra Pound's ornery materialism here. Money is where the game begins and starts, not love—not when it comes to presidential politics.

Brian Teare's "Citizen Strophes (Oakland)," on Day 29 is very good too: "All I know is // he's so depressed he's / me: lovelorn, jobless, a lot of uninsured trouble // with teeth and vision, as in: / sidewalks seem longer // under construction in midday sun," and later, "he's thinking there's no way / the city's going to beget tenderness / anytime today." Katy Lederer strikes a more moderate skeptical note, in "I Think You Are a Good Manager," on Day 30, asking: "Are you willing to be / more political, to learn how // to influence? / Have you thought about // confronting M.?" This is a variation of hope, however; the issue is not having a forceful personality, but the power interests the office of the president serves—and that has nothing do with lacking or not lacking a spine.

Another excellent poem is Joyelle McSweeney's "Poem for Comrade Duch," on Day 31: "In the box is the fetid dictator / Going south in his agebox / Going south in his box of hair / The body of judgment has been assembled / And has been disabled by the war on terror / And is a disabled box / In the box the choices are limitless / In the box the choices are meaningless." This is an appropriate commentary on the vacuity of postmodern politics, where everything fits into everything else, where ideology has given way to infinite promise and perpetual satisfaction. I like Elizabeth Scanlon's mockery of "choice" in a similar vein, in "What People Say" on Day 33: "The commander-in-chief has, in his first act as such, / authorized 17,000 more troops to Afghanistan / and Karzai's spokesman says 'We have opened a new page.' / We have paged a new open we have known an open page."

Deconstructing the language of politics works really well for Jen Hofer too, in her poem written on Day 85, with the impossibly disassembled title. Political language is utterly debased; to construct narratives of hope (or of any emotion whatsoever) from the ruined language is foolishness. Hofer's collection of words shows how anything belongs next to each other, which is to say that nothing belongs next to each other; a sample: "summit leaders relations government the case the president / momentum change policies decision a departure / administrations tightrope wages allies pay help governor / mayor speech a challenge the tenure a gap the budget."

Brenda Hillman comes excellently through the Obama hope morass. In "Guilt Armada," on Day 98, she says: "Do presidents get stoned on power or what. Give him time, say my friends. Even the people crouching in the Shadow Banks & changing their shadows in shadowy corners say Give him time." Toward the end, she says: "Look behind or you might back up over the neighbor's cat. I don't feel like looking forward. I want my heart not to stop again. I want to look back at the women crouching in their houses." Hillman addresses a constant refrain among Obama's defenders. Time? Why should we give him more time? Why should we look forward (past the crimes)?

If there's anything more fun than taking apart a workshop poem, it's to read the blurbs poets are sometimes expected to extemporize, to justify/apologize for/self-deprecatingly praise/preemptively neuter their own poetry. So the explanations by each poet at the end of the book are completely consistent with the poems themselves; again, even in the blurbs there's not a threatening radical among them, not a glimmer of revolutionary angst, or even simple anger.

Very typical of the blurbs is Becca Klaver's note, which conveys well the self-righteous unaccountability of her generation, a very American sort of entitlement, as though nasty, terrible things were being done in the dark political realm, but hey, they were young then, and we can't really expect too much now either, because those bastards left an ugly mess: "People my age graduated from high school the spring of the Columbine Massacre, were in college on September 11, 2001, have seen the war in Iraq drag on and on, and now are starting careers (or exiting them due to layoffs) in the midst of a recession. After growing up in the seemingly carefree 90s, we're trying to grapple with the world in which we've become adults. If not for Obama and his rousing calls for hope, my generation might not feel motivated to help clean up; on the other hand, that hope coexists with indignation over the mess we've been handed. Like the words 'earnest' and 'pissed' in the poem, these feelings sit side by side, almost rhyming but ultimately irreconcilable."

Oh, what terrible sufferings this generation has gone through! This classroom boilerplate pep talk to self (minus any sense of historical responsibility) is okay for consumption by a dull visiting dignitary, but a poet addressing fellow poets and poetically-inclined readers? Dear younger poetry generation, perhaps your father or uncle worked in the defense industry these last ten warmaking years; perhaps you got a relatively free higher education because empire has built up excess capital by making wars, and you're the direct beneficiary; dear poet, where do you think your cozy suburban privileges and urban fun come from?

Perhaps if the same poets had been asked to respond to Obama after the end of the first year, they would have been more skeptical. But I don't think so. Let me throw out a radical thought: perhaps these prayers for safety, these thrills at Obama's articulation, these hosannas to his smile and his beautiful, normal wife are a sanctioned, politically correct form of racism. He's our child prince, our dark savior, and we are benevolently, patiently watching over him, hoping for his success, because to criticize him would be so awful... Nah, it doesn't even get that complicated. This is just how American poets write political poetry.

REFLECTIONS ON THE CONVERSANT BUDDHA SOUL

THE CAVEAT ONUS: MEDITATIONS BY DAVE BRINKS.
BLACK WIDOW PRESS, 2009.

Dave Brinks started writing these poems in December 2004, less than a year before Hurricane Katrina drowned New Orleans, yet the arrival and aftermath of the flood are utterly absorbed in his cycle, his form vast enough to comprehend that great calamity. We have been waiting for something like this since John Berryman's *Dream Songs*. The persona in these meditations—thirteen poems of thirteen lines each in thirteen sections, adding up to 169 poems in all— is of a citizen of a lost republic neither blowing his agonies out of proportion, nor falsely deprecating himself. It is as symmetrical a being as we imagine our most sensible poets to be. Madness, if that was the preoccupation in Berryman, has here become transmuted to anti-prophecy—prophecy never having been the summa of fluid identity.

To meditate means to exercise the mind in contemplation. The difficulty with American poetry of the last four decades has been that the mind has refused to take in a whole picture of things. It is susceptible to fragmentation, one-sidedness, single-mindedness, obsession, compulsion, unreliable subjectivity, disconnection. Much of language poetry can be read as the mind's admission of inability to meditate, since language and its materials are not in synchronicity.

Brinks opens up (or closes down?) a different kind of gap. He explains that "each meditation should function loosely as a hexagram, actually two hexagrams (the first six lines and the last six lines); thus leaving the middle line (the seventh line) to serve as a kind of spine, or as ...an axis mundi, the center of a sphere, with a line moving through that point in space, in both directions." Additionally, he conceives his thirteen-line "sonnegrams" as moving in this direction: "first line—last line; second line—second to last line; third line—third to last line; and so on, moving inward, until one reaches the final line, which is the seventh line." Whereas the sonnet is a form of argument, with thesis, antithesis, and perhaps synthesis, Brinks's meditations move in circles, yearning to seek the center, which we can see shifting before our eyes, but which we know for certain is there.

We don't need to know Brinks's design to appreciate the poems, but scrutiny of any of the poems bears out the clarity of his intentions. Take poem forty-six:

> the cave at onus
> is actually a place
> I've been there many times
> it's kind of like the poor man's
> oracle at Delphi
> a voice speaks to you
> from oblivion
> whose mouths are zero-shaped
> and all in the key of blue
> before entering you'll be asked to drink
> from the headwaters of that loneliness
> where silence becomes a song
> ending with the mind of an owl

"From oblivion," the seventh line, would be the spine, above and below which two hexagrammatic spheres rotate inwardly, aiming for the core. The caveat onus (the warning against blame?) becomes concrete, centralized, as opposed to escaping insight. If one tries Brinks's first line-last line etc. operation on this poem, and then reads the poem straight through, the difference is undetectable. This is a different metaphysics of the self than in John Ashbery's breakthrough early work. Brinks addresses himself to Ted Berrigan, Anselm

Hollo, Jerome Rothenberg, David Shapiro, Bernadette
Mayer, and John Cage, but his rococo symbolism calls upon
the sanity of an Epicurus or Montaigne. If some of the poets
Brinks is influenced by seem caught in a perpetual mental
asylum, Brinks's city (New Orleans) is the asylum extending
outward to the far reaches, without ever fully succeeding in
colonizing the human core.

To illuminate this further, consider poem fifty-three:

I am the aesthetic mirror of bad taste
my mind is made up of birdseed & sorghum
I have a penitent anger
which is well-manicured and egged on
in the frying pan I become
my rococo self
I prefer embolisms to metaphor
at the cosmic bazaar I exchange trinkets
with symbolists for self-pity
I have luxurious uses for anything
    taken at random
this question rarely depends
on the definition of love
today the paper writes the tree

Brinks's surrealism has a rationality about it that lets
us distance ourselves from the traps of language. It is a
significant move, distancing him from, say, Charles Simic,
whom we think of as a poet gloomily in love with terror.
Brinks's meditations consider whether there is a way out of
the morass of absurdist self-consciousness (which language
poetry makes a fetish of) without descending to triviality
(such as domestic narrative represents).

The flood poses a huge challenge to the last man, as in
poem ninety-six:

it's been eight months since we evacuated
the purpose of meaning is useless
if you consider it in reverse

as one does with dreams
we're making up the words as we go along
the trees are newly painted
spouting branches over uninhabited playgrounds
dear sacred members of the bla bla church
I've traveled across impossible waters
it's not late August
Megan's adding mulch to the flowerbed
my mind is made up of birdseed & sorghum
I never know which way the day is blessed

The first and last lines point to a dichotomy that has been so fully established, in twenty-first-century American man, that the mild term "irony" no longer applies. The meditation refuses the comfort of dreams, and doesn't make of quotidian activity a remarkable quotient of meaning. Note the repetition of the second-last line, an operation which proliferates in the later poems, reinforcing the idea of circularity, inwardness, a closing down of something we don't quite understand (and are perhaps not meant to).

After the flood, the reckoning, the resumption of meditation as an act of communal insight; hence poem one hundred and forty-two:

O litterateurs O immortelles
O emporiums of dissected nirvanas
is there something left over from your walking
your moon is cold
and packed for travel like a souvenir
even your stomach digests itself
I should wear sunglasses & plastic gloves
as I lay out your tongue & entrails
and bury them certain fathoms in the sky
let it form a new constellation
I'll even pretend this moment
    doesn't have a name
the acedia of the scribe is a sad trope

O American poesy you disappoint me

Meditation always requires self-containment; literary engagement, so-called, feeds on its own corpse, though Brinks points to something beyond self-cannibalism. This poem knowingly flirts with the risk of being no more than the sum of its parts, and it is here that Brinks's long cycle, by connecting each of the poem's lines to what has gone before and what is yet to come, makes of it a phase, rather than a stoppage, compelling us to demand less of it in emotional punch than in an isolated poem. Brinks makes brilliant use of the emotional overflow of the cyclical form; each poem simultaneously compresses and decompresses upon reading, standing as an eternal question mark.

Roundedness accelerates toward the end as line repetitions multiply: "what's your neighborhood look like"; "O emporiums of dissected nirvanas / as ghosted as I am"; "there are no medium-sized emotions"; "my mind feels like a piece of furniture"; "I sing the colostrum the body epileptic"; "everything happens once many times"; "infinity x 1 = ZZZzzzz"; "the evening Buddha flickers and reappears'; "my vocabulary did this to me" (a reference to Jack Spicer). In the twelfth, rabbit, section, entire poems speak to each other like strangers acting as neighbors (or vice versa) in the aftermath of the storm (which deceptively appears as a one-time event). The effect is not so much epiphany toward language's arbitrariness, as the language poets strive for, but toward the situatedness of the embodied self. It can't get away from itself; and why would we want it to? It remains the one worthwhile subject for poetry.

Not coincidentally, poem one hundred and sixty-two, the single outright poem of prophecy—a Jeremiad in the old-fashioned meaning of the word—occurs in the coda, and as an afterthought. Yeats, Eliot, and Pound formulated their personal myths to anchor their poetry, giving it allusive substance. Brinks's resort to the I Ching and Mayan mythology, which he seems to have made his own, similarly challenges us to seek the basis of origins, to rely on intuition and light, not the dark walls that have been sold as windows to the outside. This is a prime candidate to be one of the more durable long poems of our time.

RECKONING GLOBALIZATION'S DISCONTENTS

RISING FALLING HOVERING BY C. D. WRIGHT. COPPER CANYON PRESS, 2008.

American poets today have the nearly impossible task of feeling sorry about assorted global misdeeds, ranging from baseless war to willful torture, without falling into the trap of objectification. Collapsing the distance between the poet's own safety and the dangers of the zone of embattlement is subject to the charge of phony gesturing. The poet, after making such a thankless attempt, is likely to come away a loser. But even the most hypersensitive reader will refuse to skimp on credit owed to Wright for her bottomless leap.

Wright truly came into her own with 1991's *String Light*, when her sympathies exploded into her unique voice of wry rapprochement, a sense of tragic well-being, if you will, in poems like "Remarks on Color," "Utopia," "Living," and "The Ozark Odes." The new poems, though unprecedentedly open for her, are direct descendents of the initial groundbreaking efforts, steeped in familiar repetitions of the poet's recognition of being seen for what she is: a privileged observer of crimes committed at a far distance, yet feeling the pain of her obligation. Wright has always seemed to want to compress the poetic ego to its smallest dimensions, so contrary to the Pound-Eliot-Auden patriarchal trio's inflation of ego, sometimes to monstrous proportions, in the service of empathy. *Rising, Falling, Hovering* is a very feminine, even feminist, collection, without wearing its politics on its sleeves; a warmth fiercely at odds with the coldness dominating the warmongers of the day penetrates each line, providing the reader a place of repose amid the condemnations of turbulence.

From the first three poems onward, "Re: Happiness in pursuit thereof," "Like Having a Light at Your Back You Can't See but You Can Still Feel (1)," and "Like Hearing Your Name Called in a Language You Don't Understand," we accept a rhythm of abrupt awakenings, guided by the poet's loneliness as she contemplates sorrows ultimately too great for art to render. The last mentioned poem contains these lines:

> I saw the white trousers of the vendor flapping in the dust
>
> his body engulfed in balloons,
>
> the children selling Chiclets dispersed;
>
> the shoeshine boy putting away his brushes, the sum
> of his inheritance…
>
> I have stood small and borracha and been glad
> of not being thrown down the barranca alongside the
> pariah consul
> in the celebrated book

The lyric sense is rooted in something firmer than the rubric of the protean self. A kind of inviolate collective tragedy, which will play out into eternity, is really the source of the knowing voice. It is immeasurably confident precisely because of its untenable position, as mere tourist of misery. Its statements all fold into themselves, erasing the unsaid parts, before they have become dust and memory. The voice is remote like a dead director's, or a partisan god's, who has been newly objectified by scholarship.

The title poem, constituting almost half the book, is a major contribution to contemporary poetics, bearing favorable comparison to Yusef Komunyakaa's "Autobiography of My Alter Ego" in his *Warhorses* (2008).

It is, quite possibly, the most complete poetic account yet of how our sensibilities have been warped through the last several years of untold crimes against humanity, the abrupt return of barbarisms we thought had been put behind for good. Under these circumstances, to be able to write poetry is itself an exception that takes some explaining. Why not remain mute? Yet speak she must:

It devolved on her to speak through the shadows of events themselves:

Animals or men passing through the night
al otro lado

Without documents, blankets, contacts,
without water, without *with*

Freeze, dehydrate, burn

A knot of ummoving human forms
waiting for a bell to quicken them

from pueblo without medicine maize or milk

from colonia of cardboard without fuel or flour

Mira: you will never see faces like this again

All of globalization's current torrents and torments, from illegal Mexican border crossings to the bureaucratic authorization of depravities in Iraq, merge and swell and crest in a rolling river of rhythm, words subject to reconsideration from the very moment they are uttered. We contemplate the poet contemplating her smallness, the only endearing gesture possible in her position of privilege.

The immensity of the barbarisms on view has elevated Wright's voice to a music that never falters, issuing from an Olympian distance where all, however, are invited. That the fall of civilization might call forth such beautiful lyricism, of its time but far beyond it, is perhaps the only hope we may dare to harbor in these times. "Rising, Falling, Hovering" is a poem that should last, from a poet who has finally put it all together.

THE NEW ECOPOETRY

READING NOVALIS IN MONTANA **BY MELISSA KWASNY.
MILKWEED EDITIONS, 2009.**

"The true philosophical act is the slaying of one's self,"
the title poem quotes the German Romantic poet Novalis—
an apt motto for ecopoetry. To infuse nature with feelings,
to question the separation of man and nature, defines
Romanticism. Twentieth-century ecopoetry by Robinson
Jeffers, Gary Snyder, and Wendell Berry goes farther
in breaking such artificial barriers. Kwasny is a worthy
successor to these spirits.

In the first section, elements of nature—redpolls,
mule deer, pond ice, brook trout, black geese, butterflies,
bee balm—invite meditation, yet civilization's turmoil
intervenes. The poet worries in "Redpolls": "I was there
when the hundred redpolls decided / to leave my life, scarlet
tag / on their foreheads, pink wash on their breasts." The
consolation of nature is fleeting: "I read of Artaud who was
tortured by his own mind, / how he felt his own mind wasn't
his." Eliot's *Wasteland* haunts contemplation of Montana's
natural beauties. It is a beautiful corruption, but corruption
nonetheless.

Even at her most ecstatic, as in "Mountains," the
tranquility is provisional: "I split wood to last the month,
stack the larder / with wet aspen, which smells dirty when
it burns— / blackened herbs, the dust of mountains. / I am
too busy to be happy, studded with the snow." Do we stop
being happy when we think about it? In "Pond Ice," after
disturbing "its sleep with rocks," the poet reads "about the
surrealists, / their goal to infuse reality with the divine."

Yet contemporary surrealism might be considered pure narcissism. The poet edges up against the limits of language. To stop thinking of the environment as inert, exploitable, endless, and feelingless requires syntactical breakthroughs beyond surrealism.

The anxiety increases, as intellectuality sharpens. In "My Heart Like an Upside-Down Flame," the poet grieves: "The heart has been looted of its small valuables." "Is it Oblivion or Absorption When Things Pass from Our Minds?" is the title of another poem, borrowed from Emily Dickinson. The undecidability of the question brings the ecopoet to the brink of a new language. "Lepidoptera" asks: "Why do Dark Wood Nymphs visit flowers more than others? / Would you trade your eighty years / for their two weeks of bliss, blue gentian, a chance / to mate in air?" The ecstasy of identification is tenuous.

The book later takes a darker turn toward ruin. While Wordsworth wrote at the beginning of the Industrial Revolution, today's ecopoet writes at the end of two centuries of rape and pillage. In "Waterfall," about the massacre of Cree near Helena the poet writes that "when the women saw the soldiers coming, / their spirits fled into these rocks." Not only are rocks alive, but they are alive with the sins of men: "Who believes enough to have a vision now?" A Thoreauvian instinct informs "When I am alone, I am godly," but the hope is forlorn that "If we can close / our eyes, the shade of trees will find a home in us, / brown butterflies of the fallen cones." Whither Thoreau, when "How huge this country is and / how we've filled it"?

The final two sections sharpen the anxiety toward insufficient language. In the long poem "The Directions," "Creator" ponders: "We call god deaf and dumb / We call vegetation *it* because we don't know its gender / We serve raspberries and the room fills with their perfume / It is difficult to imagine beyond anything." The misplacement of the overthinking cosmopolite is complete in "The Ceremonial": "Moonbeam coreopsis next to green beans in the garden, / cosmos, Icelandic poppies, bachelor buttons of all hues— / constant growth that makes me feel that I am shrinking." How to please the gods when we don't have the language for it? The Romantics' faith in beauty is long gone. In "Herbs," the poet wonders, "Can beauty be compensation for grief?"

Profound humility is the distinguishing mark of contemporary ecopoetry. "The Under World," the sequence of prose poems, concludes: "If I am sea, I am anaphora. Casting a calm above the undertow. Speak to me, work, or I will be forever lonely. Help me to remember who I am." The business of nature's education is forever half-undone.

Two Poets of Southwestern Alienation

The Book of What Remains by Benjamim Alire Sáenz. Copper Canyon Press, 2010.

Burn Lake by Carrie Fountain. Penguin Books, 2010.

Sáenz, who has published five previous books of poetry, was born in Las Cruces, New Mexico, was once a Catholic priest, and now teaches at the University of Texas at El Paso; *The Book of What Remains* puts him in the front ranks of major American poets. Fountain, author of the National Poetry Series-winning *Burn Lake*, is younger; she was born and raised in Mesilla, New Mexico, studied writing at the University of Texas, and now teaches at St. Edward's University. But despite their differences in age, gender, and race, Sáenz and Fountain's books are dominated by similar themes: schizophrenic identity, rage at various forms of exploitation, and loneliness in the midst of postmodern barrenness.

Sáenz confronts history head-on. His raw dialectic explores a peculiar American schizophrenia, internalized as a form of well-being. The Southwest is a particularly apt location to explore the split identity. It promises openness, freedom, and liberation from the burdens of history, but the other side is continuing repression. Sáenz's poetics expose this schism at every turn.

Sáenz challenges monologue masquerading as conversation popular among poets these days. David Kirby and Albert Goldbarth have mastered a form of logorrhea, embodied in poems that run on endlessly, in breathless lines that meaninglessly skip from topic to topic. Sáenz's longer poems accumulate by logic, despite their apparent laxity; they are a severe rebuke to the surfaceless skittering hither and thither of Kirby and other pseudo-conversationalists.

The way Sáenz both presents and overcomes schizophrenia is by interposing long, discursive, free-flowing, open-form, even exhibitionistic poems with very short "Meditations on Living in the Desert" which transcend the concerns—often racial paranoia and cultural denial of mortality—of the preceding longer poem.

These lines from "Translating the Universe or Morning of the Lunar Eclipse" are typical:

> I know an older woman who hates Mexicans
> Because they don't know English. (And she doesn't believe
> They know how to take baths.) She still mourns the death
> Of the Latin Mass even though she thinks it's okay to
>   shoot
> Mexicans in the back if they're trying to get here
>   illegally.
> There are senators and congressmen who agree with her.
> I wonder how many of our immigrant relatives simply
>   overstayed
> Their visas? Remember this: you may be the child of
>   an illegal.
> Relax. Smoke some marijuana. Sometimes I think
>   Catholicism
> Is more a mental illness than it is a religion. Me, I think
> We should show more discernment when we apply
> The death penalty. Latin. Some languages refuse to die.
> Even languages that are dead.

It sounds random, but the flow is logically connected. Repetition, from the rest of the poem, and the rest of the book, creates a kind of protesting rhythm—people angry at "illegals," people using the cover of religion, and in this poem, worshiping a dead language while acquiescing in the misery of live human beings, add up to a stifling repression.

Yet consider the short succeeding riposte in "Meditation" 14:

Jesus spent his entire life living in the desert.
This is why he is not bothered by the impure language
and the impure thoughts and the impure people
that inhabit the border.

He knows what it has cost us to survive.

Compression—folk wisdom, prophecy, literary epigram—provides spiritual freedom, though the landscape is hedged by rabid border politics and rabid border people. Each short meditation highlights the speaker of the preceding lament as someone worthy of compassion.

Similarly, "What I Have to Sing About" is a long lament about divorce, and like many poems, enters into the schizophrenia caused by extreme shame. "Soliloquies and syllogisms have never, *not once*, / Helped me solve one fucking problem concerning my relationships with / The people I've loved." The speaker is in a confessional rut. Yet the succeeding "Meditation" optimistically concludes: "Living in the desert has taught me to conspire with lizards."

Sáenz keeps running back and forth between corrupt public places and the (empty) desert. For Fountain, the schizophrenia is realized by her juxtaposition of standard-issue confessional poems—mostly about growing up, but with markedly small-time concerns—with the public depredations of repeating poems entitled "Burn Lake," "El Camino Real," and "Oñate."

"Ordinary Sadness" is one of her mother-daughter, father-daughter recollections, but the extraordinary sadness of the history of the Rio Grande is the harder reckoning. "Starting Small" (she and her little brother watching a fire), "The Change" (the mother's menopause), "Restaurant Fire, Truth or Consequences," "Rio Grande" (two brothers drowning), and "Mother and Daughter at the Mesilla

Valley Mall" almost parody the predictable epiphany of confessional poems.

"Burn Lake" describes the accidental creation of a "lake" while the Burn Construction Company built the I-10 bypass: "When nothing else worked [to fill the pit], you called it / a lake and opened it to the public. / And we were the public."

Contrasted to her privileged American childhood are constant reminders of what it took to settle the desert—going back to the Spanish governor Juan de Oñate, who reached the Rio Grande at El Paso del Norte in 1598. In "El Camino Real" Fountain says: "This is how they made the New World: / every once in a while they stopped, / they tied two yucca stalks together / to make the sign of the cross, they prayed." And concludes: "And they went on, bearing those / absurd yellow silks up through the valley / and on into the desert."

More than the desert, it is the road that suggests to Fountain stasis in apparent movement. In "Progress," Fountain writes about the streets of Mesilla being paved: "A road is the crudest faith in things to come." In "Oñate 2" we're reminded of an earlier journey in the service of colonization: "Praise God, we've found / the river again, we're back / tonight at the lip of wanting." The desert is a mirage, but so is the road, or water. In "El Camino Real 2," Fountain describes Oñate's expedition being saved from starvation in the nick of time, as the colonizer feverishly imagines good tidings to report to the king: *"Dear Sirs, / We're here. / The coast is very much / as I'd imagined it: / water indefinitely, empty / and ours."*

In the last poem, "El Camino Real 3," the young speaker is retracing the colonizer's path, this time in search of a liquor store with her girlfriend: "Beyond the store, / the road gets thin / but doesn't disappear. As far as we know, / it goes on forever." The trivial-confessional private, and the repressive-historical public, have for now merged, like the effect Sáenz gets with his short meditations.

Confessionalism remains our dominant poetic mode,

but it is utterly exhausted, and it plays on narcissism for its own sake. Sáenz and Fountain are reaching out for the next language beyond confessionalism's petty whininess and small disorders. There are plenty of glimpses in both books as to what that next language could be.

WHY THE *NEW BEST AMERICAN POETRY* SUCKS EVEN MORE THAN ITS TWENTY-ONE PREDECESSORS

THE BEST AMERICAN POETRY 2009. DAVID WAGONER, EDITOR. SCRIBNER, 2009.

For years, the *Best American Poetry* series, edited by David Lehman, has been on a downward slope (using slope in the most generous sense of the word). For its 2009 edition, it seems to have reached a final resting point—its funeral home, with Lehman's past and future ghosts reading out the last rites. The *BAP* is supposed to be the Holy Grail for American poets, with bountiful material rewards for the chosen; but one cannot escape the feeling, twenty-plus years after the inception of the series, that it has absolutely run out of steam, having become a coterie affair where one goes not so much to seek the most exciting in poetry, but to admire, with horror, the quaint artifacts and robust machinations of the Old Masters—often their least effects (much as *The New Yorker* culls gorgeous little unwanted turds from otherwise admirable poets like W. S. Merwin and Richard Wilbur) jostling for their fifteen seconds of infamy.

Compile Lehman's increasingly desperate forewords in defense of his precious anthology year to year, and you have the record of the poetry establishment's grotesque self-justification. *We do not need to be relevant or exciting or new or accomplished or anything, damn you!* It's the reductio ad absurdum of an aesthetic that builds from banal diversity and ends in democratic piffle. As if anticipating exactly this harsh review, Lehman objects: "Poetry criticism at its worst today is mean in spirit and spiteful in intent, as if determined to inflict the wound that will spur the artist to new heights if it does not cripple him or her." Get ready, Professor Lehman, for a "mean" and "spiteful" review of the low-hanging fruit you've offered me yet again. You preemptively advise critics like me (unwanted thorns from your point of view): "If you have too good a time writing hostile reviews, you'll injure not only your sensibility but your soul." Thank you for your concern about my soul, but let me assure you that I'm *not* having a good time writing this review.

It's a pretty lengthy foreword; it defends the existence of poetry against hostile readers, reviewers, and indeed non-readers, as the out-of-work salesman for a Rolls Royce establishment might defend his companies' alleged masterpieces in a time of Toyotas—or bicycles. It's best for the soul to skip it altogether, and ditto for David Wagoner's desperate defense of his choice of the year's best of the best.

What I'd like to focus on is the aesthetic that seems strewn all over this particular anthology: poetry as a mechanical art. Walter Benjamin talked about the lost aura of the work of art in an age of mechanical reproduction. What we have here is poetry that is so seeped in the mechanics of mechanical reproduction that it seems to be looking beyond its status as a work of art, and reaching toward something of populist gnosis. It is poetry as facsimile, poetry as self-imitation, poetry as garbage in, garbage out. If there's one impulse defining this grab-bag of remainders and leftovers, it's that poetry is a robotic enterprise turned in on itself, self-sufficiently generating new items from within its own production sphere. Poetry is presented as working best when it shows least reliance on looking outside itself to be shocked, surprised, horrified at what it finds. *Everything* in this anthology is self-contained, sealed off, hermetically profuse.

Let me select a few stitched-together products from the factory floor to illustrate my point. Here's the beginning of Mark Bibbins's "Concerning the Land to the South of Our Neighbors to the North":

How does it feel, Hawaii, to be first, for a change?

The state bird of Delaware flies too fast to be identified —
see, it's already over Nebraska, booming a sonic boom.

Comprised of two ovals, Michigan is known as The
    Infinity State.

Illinois has some imposing adult stores along the
    railway.

West Virginia was made overseas and brought to us, chunk
    by chunk, aboard container ships.

During his final days, Hiram Warren Johnson, governor of
    California
From 1911 to 1917, subsisted on scorpions and grapes.

No one could have foreseen what a handful Utah
    would become, influenced
as it is by the contrarian zephyrs of New Hampshire,
    three states away.

Scientists predict that Colorado will soon be an
    archipelago,
though not in our lifetime, and Florida shall turn dusty
as the Necco Wafers scattered nightly across
    Massachusetts.

It is the custom in Maryland to honor the stegosaurus
on Stegosaurus Day.

This is gibberish pretending to be poetry. What on
earth does any of it signify? This is what I mean by poetry
generating itself from itself, without relevance to the
empirical world or any sense of reality. *All right, I'll say weird
stuff about the fifty states, just meaningless stuff, and string it
all together*, thinks Bibbins's clogged brain one fall morning

at the New School. How hard can it be? Which is precisely
the point, because everything in this anthology screams:
Poetry is not hard at all! Anyone can do it! You don't need
to know any actual art or music or politics or philosophy
or history or geography or biology or physics or even other
poetry to do it. The subjects and predicates in the above
poem are completely interchangeable. It could have been
"Colorado" rather than "West Virginia" that was brought
over "chunk by chunk." And what does it mean anyway?
In his explanation, Bibbins remarks, "I realized after writing
the poem that it's a sort of gawky distant cousin of John
Ashbery's 'Into the Dusk-Charged Air,' to which the former
tips its star-spattered hat." May I suggest, Professor Bibbins,
that it's more like inbreeding first cousins, incest's ravishing
deformity?

Catherine Carter's "The Book of Steve," where God
makes not Adam and Eve, but Adam and Steve, signals a
familiar outpost in the American poetry landscape: poetry as
jokery, poetry starting from a weird/ironic/crazy premise to
generate its own flabby middle and end. More and more, the
poet in America is forced to assume the guise of comedian,
pressing the entertainment function to its limits. It's the
Billy Collins brand of poetry, where once you establish the
basic alteration among a set of existing variables, absolutely
nothing unpredictable follows.

Here's some of "The Book of Steve":

So he was scratching and chatting, naming away,
when up came Adam (Yahweh had been practicing men).
"Hey, dude." "Hey, Adam. You think this looks
like a crocodile?" "I dunno. More like a fox?"
They had a few beers (Yahweh's work of the day),
Named five kinds of ants: Steve got carpenter,
Leaf-cutter, sugar; Adam took fire and soldier."

All I can say is, I'm glad God made Adam and Eve,
not Adam and Steve, because the human race would have
died of sheer boredom with Adam and Steve in charge

from Day One. The most irritating thing about this poem is its earnest political correctness—a political constituency pleased, some kudos earned, all at no cost to the poet's soul. Pretty "lighthearted" (and lightweight!) as Carter explains in her note.

Here's another "list poem" (can I also call it the rant poem, the invocation poem, the chant poem, the mechanical fart poem?): Rob Cook's "The Song of America," part of which reads:

> I'm raising my child to follow the scatter of flesh across the sky,
>   birds and their wingprint trails to Alaska.
> I'm raising my child to predict the sicknesses left of summer
>   by the number of shadows he sweats.
> I'm raising my child to plant pennies where he'll find rest
>   and good fingerpaint for one night.
> I'm raising my child to chop down the televisions of peasants
>   and their machine that picks thunderstorms from a leaf.
> I'm raising my child to write a treaty for his own smells,
>   the ones that hurt the self and the ones that hurt others,
>   and a treaty for the poison sumac whose only emotion is hunger.
> I'm raising my child to conquer the fickle magnitude of clouds,
>   the raw cover that inhabits unwanted dreams, and the signal
>   from the meadow permitting him to bow down in lust.

The last three lines are mine. It's a line-machine, try it for yourself. And again, I have no idea what any of this means. Is the poet raising his child to be a surrealist-in-diapers? A baby Breton? Is it an argument for childlessness? I don't know, and that's the point of this kind of poetry: its denseness masks any honest emotion, but does it with a smile on its face. A smile of complicity. A smile of unearned honor at the widespread dishonor tainting everyone else. It is a poetry of mockery, because it denies the brute facts of life and death. Yes, poets must imagine alternative, superior worlds, but they cannot deny the present world—even if they're tenured.

One of the stanzas of James Cummins's "Freud" reads:

They co-opt Jesus into their hired gun—
that rabble-rousing Jewish kid, with head lice—
then claim he cut this strange deal with *his* Mom?
And he'll return—to give the "sons" a beating?
No wonder we're devouring poor old Freud!
We'll swallow any tale "revealed" by "Dad."

Somehow this feels like a huge letdown after Nietzsche, whom I read in my teenage years, along with Freud, the two-headed deity of adolescent angst. I'm not sure what Cummins is trying to bring into disrepute in this poem. It's a pretty light spanking Christianity is getting at the hands of Cummins, one that leaves me wanting to kiss and play at the feet of a true-believing Christian, instead of wanting to see him written out of history. I think this comes from letting the ornate bubble of the premise be determinative, enclosing, complete, instead of a wild ride into the nowhere. I return via this poem to a familiar America, which leaves me unimpressed.

Here's another Freud poem, "First Time Reading Freud," by Douglas Goetsch:

I don't know how I got into her room
or how Freud's language crept into my head—
superego, pleasure principle,
displacement, latent and manifest,
and all that ugly Oedipus business—
babies with sex and murder on the brain,
little Viennese girls hard-wired
to admire their first glimpse of *zomething egstra,*
yet why hadn't I touched mine till I was 16,
and why did our professor have to tell us
about the woman he saw at Woodstock
lifting her naked baby to manipulate
his penis in her mouth, both mother
and son cooing, he said, with pleasure?

It's interesting that this is someone discovering Freud for the first time in a classroom, taught by a professor, a sort of antisex education between the covers. As with every personage touched by this kind of poetry, Freud ends up becoming a lighthearted joke.

If modernist poetry was the enlightenment on steroids, and postmodern poetry its even snarkier cousin, refusing to accept the veracity of any observation/belief/dogma, then the bulk of the academic poetry written today is from a stance of moderate, earnest, entirely boring emotion; there is nothing at all subversive about it. It is almost a return to premodern feelings, where one expresses wonder at things the human being is supposed to have dominion/authority over—I imagine a Bangladeshi or Zimbabwean poet, completely removed from the crushing history of the last 250 years, writing like Debora Greger, in "Eve in the Fall":

I heard a rustling, insistent,
a tree trying to shake off the past
or a river feeling its way past a wall

toward some vast body of tears
it hadn't known existed. Down the street,
trucks trundled their dark goods

into eternity, one red light after another.
Though it was morning,
street lamps trudged down the sidewalk

like husbands yawning on the way to work.
On puddles, on rags of cloud,
they spilled their weak, human light.

With shadow my cup overflowed.

This sort of stuff is easy to write as parody, though for the life of me I have never been able to write seriously in this vein of earnest simplicity, and it seems astonishing to me that early twenty-first-century poets can possibly write like this, without a trace of irony and self-consciousness. This sort of poem demands to be imitated, and it is extremely easy to do. "A tree trying to shake off the past" and "a river feeling its way past a wall?" It's like talking about nightingales and summer rain and fleshy shoulders with the seriousness of the premodern.

I'm tempted to like Jim Harrison's "Sunday Discordancies." The plaintive fear of mortality that creeps in seems incongruous in this anthology: "I heard on the radio / that we creatures have about a billion and a half / heartbeats to use. Voles and birds use theirs fast / as do meth heads and stockbrokers, while whales / and elephants are slower. This morning I'm thinking / of recounting mine to see exactly where I am." Yet if there's one thing American poets can't do, it's mortality. It always comes off as preening denial of it, especially when it seems to be acknowledging its inevitability. Harrison's poem is almost an exception, yet it proceeds by constructing parallels, comparison after comparison, in the muddle of which the human being is lost or misplaced. The poem doesn't have a philosophical base—we might say that it takes off from an observation, and doesn't know where or when to stop.

There is the poem of nonsensical sophistication, which is so filled with private code words and diffuse references that one can't possibly find a steady toehold. This sort of poem is slippery as an eel, and again very easy to imitate, because the second one is pinned down by a thought one can slide over to another. An example is Terrance Hayes's "A House Is Not a Home," part of which reads:

> I decided then, even as my ears fattened,
> to seek employment at the African-American
> Acoustic and Audiological Accident Insurance Institute,
> where probably there is a whole file devoted
> to Luther Vandross. And probably it contains
> the phone call he made once to ask a niece
> the whereabouts of his very first piano.

I already know there is a difference
between hearing and listening,
but to get the job, I bet I will have to learn
how to transcribe church fires or how to categorize
the dozen or so variations of gasping, one of which
likely includes Ron and me in the eighth grade
the time a neighbor flashed her breasts at us.

What? What is the "African-American Acoustic and Audiological Accident Insurance Institute"? You'll find lots of this made-up capitalized stuff in current American poetry—an easy way to import portentousness when the material is flimsy to the point of nonexistence. Luther Vandross, transcribing church fires, eighth grade breast flashing—what the hell is going on? Also the pseudo-profundity: "There is a difference between hearing and listening." Because it is an African-American writing this poem, we must impute jazziness to it—its saving grace, its code of honor, its point of entry.

In his ode to Walt Whitman, "A Democratic Vista," Daniel Hoffman imitates "The Poet" thus:

We turn the page to see his
Democratic Vista—"Never was there more
Hollowness of heart...the underlying principles
Of the States are not honestly believed in
Nor is humanity itself believed in," he told us before
A century and a half brought us to the future
He believed in, saying, "I know nothing grander,
More positive proof of the past, the triumphant
Result of faith in human-kind than a well-contested
American national election," a sentiment we
Perhaps had better leave Open-
                                                    ended—

Hoffman explains: "How reassuring that a plurality of Americans have validated Walt Whitman's idealism and mine." If idealism has been reduced to what happened during and after the 2008 election, then idealism is a puny toy indeed. I suspect this poem to have leeched everything of protest and remonstrance from Whitman—it's a calm symposium of self-satisfied poets indeed from which such a content communiqué could have issued. In a way, all American poets imitate Whitman—still, it's nasty to see it done so casually.

There is a lot of God-revisionism going on in this anthology; God is always ready to be reinterpreted, he's the last entity these days you're going to hear a pipsqueak from. So Tina Kelley, in "To Yahweh," defines God (I suspect this is not the first such attempt in three thousand years):

> God is weequashing: The spearing of eels or fish from
>   a canoe by torchlight.
> God is the inventing of words like *weequashing*.
>
> She is not the fire darkening down.
> She is the goldfinch singing the whisper song.
>
> And the birthing of a second child, to feel your body
>   blooming.
> To feel head, then shoulders, thighs then cord tumbling.
>   To live. To life!

All right, God as weequashing is rather innocuous, and sedative. Perhaps the most common technique in American poetry is to simply take a concept and define it, loading it down with descriptions that explicitly acknowledge their disconnectedness from the thing being defined. It's a rather easy trick, once you get the hang of it. Kelley explains the poem: "The epigraph came from a selection of my book club, *weequashing* surfaced during some quality time with the *Oxford English Dictionary*, and the fire darkening down is how firefighters talk, overheard on my late-night rewrite shift at the *Times*. The whisper song came from the Audubon bird encyclopedia, curing mice in a cello was a delightful bit found online while researching the cello I was learning to play, and the acrid or burned quality of space from an article in the *Atlantic* by William Langeweische." But what do these serendipities add up to? And again, it could have been any five or ten things put together, and the result would have been the same non-definition of God (or Bach, or Einstein, or Heaven, or Peace). Because to define God is not the problem at all; in this trick poem the idea is to put together glamorous-sounding fragments to lend glamour to the poet.

And poets in America today are defining nothing as much as they are defining poetry itself. Almost every other poem Billy Collins writes seems to be some sort of definition of poetry. Lance Larsen, in "Why do you keep putting animals in your poems?" says:

> ...A poem is grave
> and nursery; the more creatures you bury in one place,
> the more hunger bursts forth somewhere else,
> like bats at Carlsbad when the brightest day turns dark.

He could have defined poetry by putting not animals but airplanes in the poem. Or antiques. Or architecture. Of course a poem is like all kinds of animals. Or all kinds of architecture. There's nothing to it.

There are lists and there are crazy lists, and Thomas Lux's "The Happy Majority" is of the latter variety:

> Before I join the happy majority (though I doubt one
>   member happy
> or unhappy) I have some plans: to discover several
>   new species
> of beetle; to jump from a 100-foot platform
> into a pile—big enough
> to break my fall—of multicolored lingerie;
> to build a little heater
> *(oh not to join the happy ones,*
> *until some tasks are done)*
> beside each tulip bulb to speed its bloom;

to read 42,007 books (list available
on request); to learn to read and/or write
Chinese, CAT scans, Sanskrit, petroglyphs,
and English.

And blah-blah-blah. I think this is the ridiculously easy
kind of thing they must teach at MFA programs all over the
country. Like, what are the things I would do if I met Moses
in a laundry room in a twenty-fifth century spaceship? The
list doesn't have to make any sense at all. It just has to sound
good.

I conclude with Sharon Olds's self-described
"descriptive frenzy" in "Self-Exam." She explains that she's
"pretty amazed to see that there are no similes here, it's
all metaphor—whereas often…[her] poems seem anxious
about the extent of the 'transformative claim' in metaphor,
seeming more comfortable with the more literal-minded
'like.'"" Olds's anxiety about metaphors versus similes
aside—it's rather an earth-shattering worry, isn't it?—the
content of the poem is easily reproducible, once one accepts
Olds's basic metaphysic of human being as the sum of the
body:

…And the matter feels primordial,
unimaginable—dense,
cystic, phthistic, each breast like the innards
of a cell, its contents shifting and changing,
streambed gravel under walking feet, it
seems almost unpicturable, not
immemorial, but nearly un-
memorizable, but one marches,
slowly, through grave or fatal danger,
or no danger, one feels around in the
two tack-room drawers, ribs and
knots like leather bridles and plaited
harnesses and bits and reins,
one runs one's hands through the mortal tackle
in a jumble, in the dark, indoors.

Is this a self-exam, or the Siege of Stalingard or the Fall of Berlin? This is very, very easy to duplicate. Take an ordinary corporeal act (especially if it's something redundant and politically correct) and turn it into a massive act of war or metaphysical breakthrough. We all in the end have our irreducible bodies to turn to. Look at your body, look at it hard—there's enough stuff there to make a Best American Poet out of you, if you take care not to say anything that means anything.

So there you have it. Workshop students, take notes, sharpen your pencils, get to it. If you follow these simple rules of poetry-making—follow the code that's been laid open for you—one day you just might end up in the rarefied place David Lehman has created for you, where you can go and die. No mortals will intrude on your peace, only a machine's steady hum, lulling you to deny that you ever existed on earth.

BOULEVARD SYMPOSIUM: "IS POSTMODERNISM IN DECLINE? WHAT, IF ANYTHING, IS REPLACING IT?"

Postmodernism in the narrow sense, such as fiction aware of its fictional status—that particular movement in literature known variously as Black Humor, metafiction, or surfiction, which arose in the 1960s and 1970s—is dead. There was a time for that movement, but it passed long ago. The same is true of poetry, where the various avant-garde movements, whose central point is self-consciousness, have become irrelevant. This is particularly true of language poetry, in its present moribund state. The same applies to postmodernism in music, art, and architecture, which long ago peaked—with John Cage, Andy Warhol, and Robert Venturi.

If one compares metafiction today with the early efforts of the 1960s, the imitative Barthelmes and Coovers pale by comparison; Raymond Federman may have wanted surfiction to replace naïve realism, and that desire is still valid, but the form for that desire is not yet fully choate for the new global/Internet era.

But movements do not pass into extinction; like children carrying genes, they inherit and perpetuate legacies, they pass on their essence to the next generation. All fiction is more like literary criticism than it was before postmodernism; this is wonderful, and this trend will continue and accelerate. Some of the most durable recent books—Orhan Pamuk's *The Museum of Innocence*, J. M. Coetzee's *Boyhood, Youth,* and *Summertime* trilogy, and Kenzaburo Oe's *The Changeling*—are fully postmodernistic, being always aware of their status as fiction, yet they're not ironic in the narrow postmodernistic sense. Naïve realism doesn't stand a chance against this combination. There must be respective analogies for the standouts in music, art, and architecture.

Postmodernism's most enduring legacy is a cultural/political pessimism, because it privileges aesthetics over logic and action (this principle accords very closely with fascism's definition as the aestheticizing of politics). Postmodernism has been the handmaiden of various forms of anti-enlightenment unreason, complying with late capitalism to impose degrees of illiberality around the world (in sites ranging from the academy to the workplace). With belief in reason, truth, and beauty passé concepts, there is no way for a political mobilization against the new illiberalism. There were two sides to postmodernism's ascendance—it had a liberationary aspect to it, precisely because it privileged play (irrationality), but it also had a nihilistic aspect to it, for exactly the same reason. In the political sphere, the second, nihilistic aspect has clearly won out over any impulse toward liberty.

As to what comes next, no one knows. We're suffering in different ways from the huge wave of appropriation, mixing, and flattening that carried all of us along with it. We know what won't replace postmodernism. Generation X's vaunted "irony" (as typified by the McSweeney's crowd) was dead on arrival. There was much hope for this generation (among whom? The successors of Leslie Fiedler, who thought there was a way to reconcile low and high?) but their reverence for junk is too great; they haven't known anything else but video culture, and they can't think past it, let alone ironize time and space, restructure it in new narrative, as a postmodernist of the first generation, Kurt Vonnegut, did in *Slaughterhouse-Five*.

We might go so far as to say that the problem of postmodernism is the problem of irony; as hard as postmodernism tries to be ironic, its opposite tendency, sincerity, defeats its thrust. The craze for memoir is nothing but a craving for authenticity (viz. David Shields's *Reality*

Hunger, which absurdly and very sincerely posits the death of imaginative fiction); it is the exact counterweight to narcissistic/ironic Generation X fiction. Who will find a way out of this conundrum? Jonathan Franzen in his new novel *Freedom*? He's not a Coetzee or Oe or Pamuk. He's working in the realist tradition, and if there's anything worse than cute postmodernism past its sell-by date, it's cute realism.

When establishment commentators said on 9/11 that "irony is dead," they really meant the death of postmodernism (Eco equates postmodernism with irony). Postmodernism's moral relativism had weakened us, left us defenseless against unironic Islamofascist ideology, is what these neoconservative commentators meant. Clearly, in that sense (of a vacuum of moral/political legitimacy), irony is more alive than ever—meaning that postmodernism is more alive than ever, even as it is deader than ever as a life-giving force.

Conservative suspicion of postmodernism as amoral is not misplaced. It *is* amoral. Derrida, Foucault, Lyotard et al. presented it as a great skeptical renaissance (the American academy too easily succumbed, which suggests the horrible void of morality that must have preexisted in the Cold War-era academy), but it quickly devolved into lack of agency for the human being. If all takes place at the level of text and language, then we can only fight language wars, which is a perfect way to escape the hurly-burly of politics and economics. Hence we get our postmodern fascist ruling elite, who can't be confronted with any grand narrative about theft and corruption, since postmodernism has already destroyed any inherited political doctrine (certainly old labor politics) as patriarchal/colonial/logocentric constructs.

Everything is text. Text is everything. What about the human context? Postmodernism soon became antihumanist, and moreover reveled in this description. Smart writers like Pamuk, Oe, and Coetzee understand the freedom suggested by the postmodern movement, borrow from Beckett, Calvino, and Borges—postmodernism's first giants—and move on to a new insurrection on behalf of humanism. We cannot behave as if postmodernism never happened. Yet we cannot give in to its escapist impulses either.

George Saunders has spawned a whole industry in American short story writing. Hapless, agency-less, dehumanized characters, barely breathing alive, played upon and crushed by the various enterprises of simulacra (playlands and malls, highways and suburbs) offered by late capitalism. It's fun, and appropriately nihilistic, but it is conducive to fascist suggestiveness. The new fascism thrives on fear, insecurity, relativity, and loss of reason. How to find a way past this, accept the existence of mass culture and mass psychology, and yet create an art that is neither escapist nor obscure? How to look past parody, pastiche, and fragmentation for something approaching a morally acceptable whole (no pun intended)? Again, no one knows yet.

Truth, reality, and beauty must be the summum bonum of all art—even when irony is the ruling principle. The founders of postmodern art and literature started a legacy which its later adherents couldn't live up to. Now we have to live with not only the horrible political consequences, but we have to do so with full knowledge of the new tragedy.

Let us return to modernism's main task: to find a way out of the impasse of the abuse of language. Late postmodernism misunderstood that language is all. Language is nothing without the human.

The MFA/Creative Writing System is a Closed, Undemocratic Medieval Guild System that Represses Good Writing

The comparisons to the medieval guild system are obvious, ominous, ubiquitous, irrefutable, and illuminating. Apprentices, journeymen, and masters join together in solidarity to impose control over quantity and quality of production, and enforce rigid rules to exclude outsiders. The oligarchical system sustains itself with well-told myths of internal solidarity and well-timed rituals to enhance fellow-feeling. The "craft" learned in the "workshop" is a thing of mystery, passed on from master to apprentice, a hands-on learning so precious that rules of monopoly must be imposed to prevent its dilution. They have their own religion, their annual banquet, their festival spirit. Modern creative writing program, meet your origin and fate in the medieval guild system!

Just as the guild structure was socially conservative—and hence easily superseded when the more progressive market system, flourishing along with the industrial economy, came along—so is the present MFA credentialing system. Any guild system cannot but be conservative by nature. The limitations on entry, the exaction of high entrance fees, and the social distinctions inherent in the master-journeyman-apprentice division alone dictate so. All this wouldn't matter so much—we might dismiss the system as a mere method of organization—were it not for the fact that conservativeness in organization usually results in conservativeness of product as well.

Let us try to understand how the finely-tuned guild

system came about in writing, explore how it operates in practice, and try to imagine conditions under which it might break up.

Just as the medieval guilds came into being as a reaction of craftsmen against the encroachments of feudal lords, to carve out a space of relative freedom for themselves, similarly modern creative writing (though early parallels such as the Iowa Writers' Workshop already existed) really took off in the 1960s, and then went into overdrive in the 1980s and 1990s. Before the 1950s, the majority of literary writers were not part of the academy; writers might sometimes teach as well, but this was not an essential condition of their identity; it was still a minority affair. The ideal was to be free of the restraint the academy, or really any institution, imposes. In 2010, literary writers not attached to the academy are so rare as to be almost nonexistent.

Why the 1960s? Why would integration of writing into academia begin to occur at the same time as the counterculture? Why not accelerated emphasis on doing it yourself? We need to think of the other side of liberalism, the mythologizing of experts and professionals, which very much went hand-in-hand with social libertarianism. The professionalization of human, spiritual, and psychic needs was very much part of the sixties scene. The AWP (Association of Writers and Writing Programs) was founded in the late 1960s, as writers clearly saw the stresses associated with being on one's own in a culture dedicated to hyperconsumerism. The late 1970s and early 1980s became really telling—with the arrival of Ronald Reagan's cowboy militarism, writers were pushed into a corner. Nobody was safe. The culture had lost its senses. The choice was made to retreat behind the barricades as protection from the masses, and to create MFA programs all over the country, where those who were scared of the easy talk of nuclear Armageddon could take permanent refuge.

As with all other institutional developments, it is easy to tell a retrospective tale of origins and growth that makes complete sense, but this has some truth to it. In brief, writers no longer wanted to be part of the market economy. If they could create a self-sufficient guild, they would be removed from its vicissitudes. The inherently conservative nature of this impulse should be more evident now. There is glory in uniting against the abusive capitalist system. Medieval guilds were endowed with the right to combine and make their own regulations—precisely this impetus is behind the MFA system's retreat from the world of unabashed capitalism (also known as "reality" in the industrialized world).

Organizationally, the parallels to the medieval guild system are everywhere. It is the rare freelancer who can shun the creative writing guild, because he would then lack social distinction. The character of the master (the creative writing teacher), as in the medieval guild, is an indispensable element. Here we notice the emphasis on "mentorship," a different tone than the prevalent attitude towards the masters (professors) in the rest of the academy, the overarching guild that accommodates the writing guild. The character of the master should be such that he brings along the apprentice (the MFA student) and even the journeyman (the writing teacher) into the rules of social solidarity upon which the system thrives.

It is not enough to learn the "craft" (the techniques of creative writing, such as "show don't tell," "write what you know," "find your own voice," "kill all your darlings," etc.) but to learn how to put yourself in the shoes of the master should the need arise. What are the ethics of the master when he is approached by an apprentice? How does he evaluate his potential to be a contributing member of the guild? If the master were indisposed, can the journeyman fill his shoes without a noticeable difference in ethical standards?

Let's get more into these standards—what exactly are they? Good conduct for medieval guild masters was extremely important for the maintenance of reputation vis-à-vis the outside world, and without this credibility the guilds would have fallen apart in no time. Freelance craftsmen would have found it easy to identify individual buyers, and the whole system would have collapsed. With the guild product, you had the guarantee of a certain quality. In terms of the character of the master/journeyman/ apprentice, what you get—as a cost of removing writing from the hurly-burly world of rude market principles—is a certain tame, politically correct liberalism (universally in effect throughout the American creative writing guild now), which makes appropriate, but extremely subdued, noises about political depredations. Actually, it does not accommodate a political worldview of any consistency and significance, and so the protests are diffuse, vague, honorable, and inarticulate to the point of utter irrelevance. That is very much part of the social bargain whereby writers are "left alone" to implement their craft, as opposed to being harassed or hounded out of existence; they get their NEA and Guggenheim fellowships, and everyone is happy since the power equations in society remain undisturbed.

So we have the profession of faith, the participation in fraternity, and the declaration of oath to the principles of social conduct in the MFA guild. Along with the watered-down politically correct liberalism, the master, journeyman, and apprentice alike should express in public their modesty, their lack of divine inspiration (otherwise the system couldn't sell itself as being able to teach craft), and the predominance of sheer luck and fortuitousness in any success they've had. They should always say that their writing career just happened; it certainly wasn't planned from the very beginning. Such an attitude might scare away potential apprentices (MFA applicants) for implying very high levels of awareness, which they may not possess. The system is utterly undemocratic, once one is a member of the guild, toward the outside world, but for it to survive in today's politically correct world, it must always present itself as the quintessence of democracy (everyone can learn writing, given enough application and discipline—at least we can make you competent, we can teach you the rules of the game, we can save you years of heartache from going it alone and making avoidable mistakes).

But it is an undemocratic system from the inside, just as the medieval guild system was, despite expressions of social solidarity among the chosen fraternity. Certain über-masters (Antonya Nelson, Heather McHugh, Jorie Graham, Sharon Olds, Lan Samantha Chang, Philip Levine, Charles Baxter, Donald Hall, Marilynne Robinson, Galway Kinnell, Mark Strand, Robert Pinsky, Robert Olen Butler, Jane Hirshfield, Tim O'Brien, Tobias Wolff, etc.) exercise disproportionate control over the distribution of rewards and honors. Woe betide any journeyman, let alone an apprentice, who crosses one of them! It is easy to displease an über-master by getting too big for one's britches—by wishing to undertake political writing, for instance, or violating the narcissistic confessionalism of fiction writing or the pseudo-liberalism of the "poetry of witness" we hear so much about these days. Actually, the whole point of early workshop humiliation (masquerading as instructive peer commentary) is to weed out any such troublemakers from finishing their period of apprenticeship, so in reality outright challenges to the authority of the masters must be rare indeed. The system measures its success by the frequency of non-events.

Social distinction, like with any guild system, is rife. There are MFA programs and then there are MFA programs—the elite on the one hand, the mere go-getters and wannabes on the other hand. Iowa, Michigan, Columbia, NYU, Brown, Hopkins, Texas, Cornell, Irvine, Houston, etc. rule the roost. There was a great brouhaha recently about a journeyman's attempt to rank MFA programs in *Poets & Writers* magazine according to input from potential apprentices as opposed to evaluations by journeymen and masters themselves; obviously such prospective evaluation couldn't be allowed. There are those star apprentices who get recruited by agents early on, thanks to the support of concerned masters, and there are those who, no matter how hard they try, can never get such attention. There are those to whom the multicultural veneer—and this mode of expression proliferates into many social niches—comes more easily than to others, and such apprentices and journeymen find rapid and early success, toward becoming potential masters one day.

There are the MFA graduates, and then there are the MFA/PhDs—the latter a growing subset, a sure way to social distinction, and having your poetry manuscript plucked from one out of a thousand entered in a "contest." Apprentices must undergo plenty of hardship (or what substitutes for it in the unreal world of the guild) by teaching a lot of classes, and putting up with a lot of stupidity from sub-apprentices (undergraduates with an interest in writing who may one day want to be full-fledged apprentices) to prove their mettle to the masters. The guild is self-governing, and masters theoretically have equal rights. Masters may be fiercely, resentfully, insanely competitive with one another, but this may never be expressed publicly; yet it is clear to the members of the guild which masters are on the rise and which are going down. It is better to anticipate the waves of the future, to be on the good side of the ascendant masters.

The system is profoundly undemocratic when it comes to the quality of the product it engenders, and its relentless crushing of any incipient freelance competition. There is an undeclared boycott in place with the famous residencies, conferences, and awards, and non-guild members need not apply (unless they want to waste their fifty or hundred dollars in application fees). Yaddo, MacDowell, Bread Loaf, etc. among the residencies/conferences, and the well-known awards/fellowships/grants committees do not welcome outsiders. There is a de facto ban, though probably, with the minute number of writers outside the guild these days, it is something they have to worry about less and less. The same is true of the Stanford Stegner fellowship, and the Provincetown Fine Arts Work Center fellowship, which absolutely exclude those not already privileged enough to be members of the guild. You may pay a few thousand dollars to attend Bread Loaf as a "paying contributor" and soak in the mystery surrounding the über-masters, but you may never become a scholar/fellow/waiter unless you are a certified member of the guild. Yaddo and MacDowell simply will not admit you, even if you have published well, because you will not have the necessary recommendations from über-masters to get you into such places. There is the phenomenon of the roving and repeated fellowship recipient—the few people who seem to go from Provincetown to Stanford to Ucross to Wisconsin to Virginia to everywhere else—as though to hold up to apprentices a model of the hyper-diligent medal recipient. Rather than spreading the wealth around, to concentrate so many awards in a few chosen people year after year holds up these apprentices for imitation of how to work the masters' favor.

This is all in defense of the economic aims of the guild, whose articulation can be found in *Poets & Writers*, which is a perfect chronicle of the economic principles at work. First, the quotation of first lines of recently published books (along with names of agents, editors, and publicists) by favored journeymen, then valorization of small presses and little magazines and independent bookstores as though they were the drivers of the engine rather than mere appurtenances, the inspirational stories (often from utterly marginal apprentices) to emphasize the democracy of talent, the workshop-style interpretation of a modern master by a journeyman to locate it in the tradition of craft, the interview with the editor or agent which further elaborates the "mystery" (can one learn it in workshop?) inherent in acquisition decisions, and then on to the relentless business of how to get from modest apprentice to having your book's first line be quoted at the beginning of some future issue of the magazine, i.e., the listing of contests and awards and how to send your twenty or thirty or fifty dollars to entitle yours to be one among a thousand manuscripts to be screened by journeymen and finally picked by some über-master for publication.

It might be called "restraint of trade" in modern terms, due to the monopoly of craft exercised by the guild. We are talking about a house style, a uniform product literary magazines (generally affiliated with writing programs) and so-called "independent presses" can buy without hesitation.

All this churning activity is predicated on the continuous generation of the MFA house style. In fiction it means generally apolitical, domesticated narrative that remains willfully ignorant of modernism (the highbrow style doesn't work with the guild's self-presentation), leaning strongly toward the confessional, memoiristic, autobiographical, narcissistic, and plainly understood. The same qualities apply in poetry—the standard workshop poem is a narrative or associative slight effort, taking off from the quotidian, to rest in an uneasy or understated epiphany. There is also a language poetry subcomponent, but this has its own utterly predictable rules (the language poets think the lyric and narrative poets are closet fascists, yet they are blind to their own brand of conservatism).

One outcome of the craft monopoly is the extreme specialization among writers. Almost nobody writes in multiple genres—you do lyrical poetry based in a particular place, or creative nonfiction dealing with illness, or surrealistic short-shorts, or hillbilly novellas, or whatever. You do not cross boundaries as a poet into fiction or vice-versa, or, horror of horrors, from poetry into criticism or fiction into criticism. "Literary" writing (choked with metaphors, abstracted from political reality, and overwritten in that peculiarly self-conscious writerly style) is set in opposition to genre writing, merely commercial writing, since part of the mystery of the guild is that it is not aiming for commercial success. Lately, however, the MFA system has started to adopt genre writing, giving it a literary twist, as an accommodation to apprentices soaked in the principles of genre writing; it had to happen sooner or later.

It is in the interest of the mystery of the guild to banish criticism altogether, and they have pretty much succeeded, reducing criticism to glowing, one hundred percent positive 700-1,200-word blurbs masquerading as reviews in the back pages of literary quarterlies, when they are allowed in at all. A new genre of "criticism" has arisen—one hesitates to call it that, since it doesn't meet the definition of criticism, but is rather hollow hagiographic appreciation (something like what criticism used to be in the pre-scientific days, before New Criticism), often written by one master in praise of another. This can be found in journals like *American Poetry Review*, and is fairly close in language and style to the "craft workshops" taught at conferences like Bread Loaf and Sewanee, getting into the nuts and bolts of fiction or poetry by popular contemporary masters without imposing any rigorous discipline of literary knowledge upon the learner.

The MFA house style is integrally connected with the conditions of production under the guild system; uniformity of product, and severe control over its amount, is essential for the guild to maintain mystery about itself, and without mystery there can be no exclusion of gate-crashers. Not only is the product uniform, but its quantity must be small. Writers cannot be allowed to be prolific—Joyce Carol Oates and T. C. Boyle mess up this paradigm for everyone. Hence the MFA fetish of constant revision—as undergraduates in my day used to talk about how many all-nighters they'd pulled, apprentices, journeymen, and masters these days exaggerate the number of drafts they wrote before daring to publish the book (Twenty! Fifty! A hundred!). This is cause for bragging rights; the more drafts, the more committed the writer declares himself to execution of craft.

In the May/June 2010 *Poets & Writers*, Ben Percy talks about hearing from Fiona McCrae of Graywolf Press after submitting a novel; the editor wanted him to radically revise the novel, including changing the point of view and adding six different subplots. Happy to oblige, Percy accomplished the task, and then started all over again, when the editor requested further fundamental changes. The writer must never, ever complain about revision; he must only express unqualified gratitude for it. It is the one thing that guarantees democracy of membership: genius is inspirational, it strikes when we don't expect it, it is limited to the rare elect; but revision is accessible to everyone. The guild can keep forever expanding, as long as revision keeps the upper hand. Percy begins and ends his article by talking about buying an ugly house with good bones and rebuilding it to his satisfaction;

the whole piece perfectly illustrates the extended metaphor of meticulous craft practiced in workshop conditions.

But the economic aims of the MFA guild would be unrealizable without its social aims, which perpetuate solidarity. All the rituals of medieval guilds can be found in their modern versions here. There is the annual bacchanal, the AWP gathering (with almost 10,000 assembled craft practitioners), which celebrates pedagogy and publication and prestige. Here the social distinctions are manifest, among über-masters, ordinary masters, preferred journeymen, struggling journeymen, and apprentices with widely divergent pedigrees of popularity. The apprentices, of course, constitute the overwhelming number of attendees, so the ritual gathering becomes a celebration above all of the potential of apprentices to aspire to higher levels. There is the vast bookfair at the AWP, the huge exhibition a tangible expression of production—despite harsh controls over quantity of output, the overall output is large enough to shun market forces. These days there is an explicit recognition that only poets buy other poets' work (except for Mary Oliver and Billy Collins), and if a small number of books is sold that way, that is enough to go on. Journeymen conduct panels where they are duly modest, democratic, politically correct, and multiculturally astute. Readings accommodate every apprentice, of however modest talent—this is one of the inborn rights of apprenticeship, to be able to read to an appreciative audience.

The modern reading was initiated by Dylan Thomas and Allen Ginsberg's high performative art. To listen to a recording of Ginsberg reading "America" in 1956 is to hear the echoes of a dream that has died; gone is the revolutionary, or even anti-establishment, potential of the reading; it functions these days not to stir or provoke or enlighten or anger or frustrate or cajole, but as an endorsement of the democracy of talent, and that alone. Writers as stand-up comedians, seeking desperately to hold the audience's attention, to get its love and approval, are not a pretty sight. But the ritual purpose is well-served, and it is an extension of the ultimate justification of MFA programs: this too is a space for apprentices to develop themselves without criticism of their essential identities in the company of peers, that is, removed from the tribulations of the marketplace. No major foreign writers are invited at AWP, and they're typically not part of what we think of as the national reading circuit, stopping at bookstores, universities, and auditoriums across the country. I haven't seen Gabriel Garcia Marquez or Kenzaburo Oe or Chinua Achebe as keynote speakers at AWP, have you? No, it is typically some über-master (2011: Jhumpa Lahiri) who must at all times, in front of apprentices, declaim modesty and commitment to the common religion. Note too that most of the durable writing in this country is by writers either only peripherally or not at all associated with MFA programs— Tom Perrotta, Dana Spiotta, Mohsin Hamid, Laila Halaby, Joseph O'Neill, for example—but these are not who we think of as über-masters presiding over the AWP banquet. In any event, after some success, incorporation into the guild and employment as journeyman is all but inevitable for almost everyone who has had even modest success in the marketplace; the guild is eager to remove such authentic literary writers from the marketplace as soon as possible, to eliminate the competition.

The medieval guild was deeply rooted in its local community (the rise of industrial capitalism was a nationalist movement, and precisely the locality of the guild was merchants' bete noir); it is part of its prestige, its aura, its mystery, its honorable secrecy. MFA programs follow the local orientation. They are diligent about performing readings in the local community. Creative writers perform a number of "community" functions: teaching at local schools and prisons, organizing local festivals at a small level, and instructing adults or school children, that is, those without aspirations to becoming full-fledged apprentices, as a mark of honor. It is a necessary act of philanthropy, as is the peculiarly local flavor each major MFA program acquires over time, so that the flow of writers in and out of the program is supposed to be a boon to the community, which may come and join in appreciation of the invited masters and be a part of the ongoing celebrations from time to time.

Are there natural limits to the creative writing guild system? What are its prospects for the future, and is there any chance that the guild might collapse of its own weight? The answer seems to be that given present political and social conditions, there appear to be few natural limits to how far it can expand. The writing guild's opposition to literature departments comes in very handy—in recent years, the guild has been preferred by many who would previously have gone into the study or teaching of literature or other humanities, since the intellectual requirements (to write a memoir of illness or dysfunction, or a story, which these days is more or less indistinguishable from memoir) are minimal, compared to, say, writing a dissertation on Chaucer or Wittgenstein. So the writing guild is rapidly eating into the rest of the humanities, and at the MFA level, it is very profitable too. It somehow humanizes the whole university.

A really depressing fact is that in the last few years the MFA house style has been finding increasing acceptance among the major New York publishing houses. It is one thing to talk about a renaissance in the American short story (is there really?) confronted with stacks of unread literary journals, and another thing for major houses to put out books by journeymen who have mastered competency but lack any trace of genius; it seems another way to kill the American short story. Yet some journeymen have ascended to truly great heights recently—Wells Tower would be a good example of someone in complete mastery of the house style, who works commercially as well, because of the minimal demands he places on the reader's attention. Reading him is like taking in a horror movie of relentless brutality that leaves one feeling rather complacent because at least one possesses basic human emotions. In poetry, the talentless journeymen Michael and Matthew Dickman might be apt examples of favored stars, whom the masters—and their friends in the

New York publishing and reviewing communities—have decided must ascend to the top. The inauguration of such stars comes with the grandiose gestures familiar from the old Hollywood studio system (the Dickman brothers received a *New Yorker* profile). Three or four of these stars-in-the-making are necessary every year to keep hope alive among the legions of apprentices and journeymen that fame and fortune can be theirs too. The major publishers have become part of the grand bargain by accepting that so-called literary fiction has a minimal audience anyway, so they might as well go with the chosen stars (getting into the *Best New American Voices*, a celebration of workshops, pretty much guarantees a contract by a significant publisher), so that their commitment to *literature* may remain unquestioned, and the book in question at least generate some minimal level of sales (all those famished apprentices), awards, recognition, reviews, buzz, etc.

The medieval guild system collapsed in the end because its exclusivity, control, and mystery didn't accord well with the rise of the industrial system. It was a transitional phase between feudalism and capitalism, allowing relatively pleasant, even sometimes leisurely, space for creativity. It was a retreat from barbarism into a predetermined aesthetic zone. When a greater system, with all-embracing aspirations, came to the fore, the guild system died—although it survived in some forms, primarily the university guild, and its vestiges can be seen in labor unions. Yet recall that the MFA guild system was carved out of an already existing fully omnivorous postmodern capitalist system, so it has already, in a sense, confronted its own worst enemy (the Kennedy/Johnson/Nixon militarist/capitalist/liberal state with extreme emphasis on professionalization of all aspects of life, and its predictable even worse successors) and dealt with it. So collapse on those terms is unforeseeable. In fact, all the present trends in publishing—certainly the rise of digital publishing—herald continued strength for the MFA guild.

Again, the most important thing about this discussion

is the socially conservative writing that results from the socially conservative organization of the literary writing guild. In thinking of an analogy for the medieval guildmen as they related to the Counter-Reformation, we might think of the rise of the creative writing programs at precisely the time of the Reagan ascendancy, when liberalism with a commitment to even the mildest redistributionist philosophy went into permanent retreat. A new kind of conservative writing—Raymond Carver, Ann Beattie, Jay McInerney, Bret Easton Ellis, Amy Hempel, Mary Robison—became ascendant at the time. A continuous Inquisition has been in place in American cultural life, and certainly in the writing guild, ever since then, and the writing product is shaped by that. In essence, the writing guild makes it possible for apprentices to internalize the principles of the Inquisition. One is made to feel guilty and ashamed if writing compels one to move toward areas forbidden by the Inquisition. Workshop humiliation is very much part of this enforcement of Inquisition rules; it is astonishing to notice—even at the undergraduate, non-guild level—how quickly students acquire these principles of writerly conduct, and rake their fellows over the coals for the minutest transgressions ("You switched point of view in the story, you're not allowed to do that!"). One quickly becomes invested in the Inquisition; the advice manuals written by the masters convey these gently, in the guise of techniques of writing, but the social principle behind them is manifest.

Talent, in the modern writing guild, has been discounted; it is craft that counts. When the writing guild was in its infancy, thirty, forty, fifty years ago, one heard of arbitrary, cruel, even violent masters, legendary for their drinking, womanizing, and sheer idiosyncrasy. These have been snuffed out. Now the code of conduct proscribes any such flouting of the rules for even the most accomplished master. The system is in a very fine state of consolidation. All writing produced under the guild system has the dual purpose of not only functioning as writing but also as social manifesto for the guild system which produced such writing; this is the dual aspect in which we must read today's acclaimed master fiction writers and poets. The apprentice produces a "masterpiece" —*a chief d'oevre*—to pass muster and receive the license to teach—the *ius docendi*—upon conclusion of his period of training in the workshop. This signifies adherence to standards of production, and forever after, as a journeyman and perhaps as a master himself, he must not deviate from these standards. The master always retains the right of correction—the *ius corrigendi* of the medieval guilds—to guarantee quality; there is an infinitely intricate system of withholding rewards and recognition from deviants.